THE ECONOMIC PRINCIPLES OF CONFUCIUS AND HIS SCHOOL

Volume 1

Introduced by
Morgen Witzel

THOEMMES

Printed in England by Antony Rowe Ltd, Chippenham

THE ECONOMIC PRINCIPLES OF CONFUCIUS AND HIS SCHOOL

I

Chen Huan-Chang

With an Introduction by
Morgen Witzel

THOEMMES PRESS

This edition published by Thoemmes Press, 2002

Thoemmes Press
11 Great George Street
Bristol BS1 5RR, England

http://www.thoemmes.com

The Economic Principles of Confucius and His School
2 Volumes : ISBN 1 85506 994 6

Reprinted from the 1911 edition

British Library Cataloguing-in-Publication Data
A CIP record of this title is available from the British Library

Publisher's Note

The Publisher has gone to great lengths to ensure the quality of this reprint but points out that some imperfections in the original book may be apparent.

This book is printed on acid-free paper, sewn, and cased in a durable buckram cloth.

INTRODUCTION

In 1800, China was *the* global economic superpower. Its economy accounted for over a third of world gross domestic product, and its export trade with the Western world was generating huge cash surpluses. The impact of China was felt around the world, in economic as well as political terms. Chinese trade with Britain had made the British East India Company the largest global corporation the world had yet seen; in 1773, Chinese tea thrown into Boston harbour by anti-tax protestors helped spark the American Revolution two years later. In many Western countries, tea, silk, porcelain and spices from China were making the transition from costly luxuries to ordinary commodities.

A century later, a vastly different situation prevailed. China's share of the world economy had shrunk to under five per cent. In part this was due to the very rapid economic growth of Western Europe, Japan and, especially, the United States; in part it was due to the decay and decline of Chinese government, economy and society, exacerbated by imported opium, but primarily due to a Chinese government and governing system which refuse to modernize. In the 1790s, the Chinese emperor famously told a British ambassador that China had no need of or interest in British goods, being able to produce all that it needed at home. During the Opium War of 1840–42 the same myopia prevailed, and even after China's crushing defeat by the British, little attempt was made to modernize in terms of either government or technology.

As a result, the Taiping Rebellion of the 1850s and 1860s came very close to bringing down the ruling Manchu dynasty, devastating central China and killing upwards of 20 million people. The Taipings were motivated at least in part by religion; their faith was a kind of fusion of Christian and Confucian ideals, based on some poor-quality Chinese translations of the Bible, and their leader was a prophet who claimed to be the younger brother of Jesus Christ. The eventual suppression of the Taiping required foreign assistance from the Western powers, but it left the ruling classes in China even more suspicious of foreign ideas and technology, especially Christianity.

Wiser heads among the elite recognised, however, that without some measure of reform, the dynasty and probably China itself were doomed. The Western powers were already nibbling at the frontiers, snapping up treaty ports and concessions. In the 1880s the ancient enemy, Japan, began an astonishing process of reform which saw her leap from being a backward, feudalized state to a modern industrial economy in a mere two decades. Reformers like Li Hung-chang (Li Hongzhang), the talented general and mandarin who had put down the Taiping rebellion, sought to imitate the Japanese example.[1] Li was able to modernize the Chinese army and also to establish a number of Western-style business ventures, most notably the China Steam Navigation Company, to compete with foreign companies trading on Chinese soil. Even these modest efforts at reform, however, were blocked by the powerful dowager empress T'su-hsi, an arch-conservative who believed that the ancient virtues of China would eventually prove stronger than the powers of the foreigners.

The irony, and the tragedy, of the situation was that the reformers too believed that Chinese culture was stronger than that of the West, and that the modernization of China could not be achieved without due deference to the ancient virtues. Appeals to Confucian ideals were used by both sides in support of their positions. In the 1890s, the brilliant Confucian scholar Kang Yu-wei proposed his own scheme of reform based on adopting many of the *forms* of Western government and economy – universities and a reformed education system, industrial modernization, streamlining of government and the civil service – based not on the principles of Western liberal economics, but rather on the philosophical core of Chinese civilisation, Confucianism.

Born in 1847 in the southern province of Kwangtung, Kang had made a name for himself as a scholar at a young age, and had easily passed his civil service entrance examinations. Through the 1870s and 1880s he developed his own interpretation of

[1] In *The Economic Principles of Confucius and His School*, Chinese names and terms are presented using Wade-Giles romanisation. Although today in China this has been superseded by the more modern pinyin system, to avoid confusion I will henceforth give names only in Wade-Giles. For more information on Li Hung-chang/Hongzhang, see M. Witzel (ed.), *Biographical Dictionary of Management*, Bristol: Thoemmes Press, 2001, pp. 583–7.

Confucianism, by which Confucius was seen not as a conservative guardian of the unchanging ideals of society, but as a reformer, determined to root out inequality and promote an eternal brotherhood of mankind based on the principle of the Golden Mean. A number of other scholars were attracted to him, and formed a circle of like-minded thinkers. One of those who studied under Kang during this period was Chen Huan-chang, the later author of *The Economic Principles of Confucius and His School.*

In 1898, Kang and a fellow reformer, Liang Chi-chao, gained the ear of the young emperor Kuang Hsu, who agreed to implement a reform programme. What followed became known as the 'Hundred Days', during which Kang, Liang and the reformers struggled for control of the emperor and the government against the reactionaries led by the Dowager Empress. In the end the reactionaries triumphed again. There was a palace coup, in which the Dowager Empress seized control and the emperor was imprisoned in the Forbidden City and effectively stripped of all power. Kang and Liang fled into exile; other leading reformers were executed, and a conservative backlash began which would culminate in the Boxer Rebellion just over a year later. The door to reform had been slammed shut, and the fate of the Manchu dynasty had been determined; thirteen years later, in 1911, it fell, to be replaced by the short-lived Republic of China.

* * *

The year of the fall of the Manchu dynasty also saw the publication of *The Economic Principles of Confucius and His School.* As noted, the author, Chen Huan-chang, was a student and later a friend of Kang Yu-wei. Very little is known about his own background. In dedicating the book to his father, he notes that the latter 'suffered poverty, adversity and many bitter disappointments in order that his son might lead a scholar's life'. This could indicate a humble background; poor families would often devote virtually all their resources to putting a son who showed promise through school, so he could sit the entrance examinations for the Imperial civil service and thus raise the fortunes of the family as a whole. On the other hand, this statement could be simply a conventional statement of filial piety.

This is the only indication Chang gives about his own background. His date and place of birth are unknown; it is probable that, like Kang, he was a southerner. After passing his examinations and joining the civil service, he seems to have showed promise and was appointed to the Grand Secretariat in Peking, the highest civil service body which reported directly to the emperor and his chief ministers. Whether he was one of the 1,300 scholars who signed Kang's memorial to the emperor in 1895, calling openly for reform, is not known, but is certainly possible. His subsequent movements after the Hundred Days are likewise a mystery, but it seems a reasonable conjecture that he was at least dismissed and very possibly forced into exile. Shortly after 1900 he appears in New York City, where he enrolled as a student at Columbia University and made the acquaintance of some of the leading economists and political scientists of the day, including Edwin Seligman, John Bates Clark and Henry Seager, as well as the eminent sinologist Friedrich Hirst. *The Economic Principles of Confucius and His School* is the publication of Chen's doctoral thesis at Columbia.

The events given above thus form the backdrop to Chen's work, and are an essential pre-requisite to understanding both the work itself and his motives in producing it. Uniquely, Chen had a foot in both worlds. A classically trained Chinese mandarin, coming from one of the last generations to go through the millennia-old imperial examination process, he was deeply imbued with the principles of Confucianism and had studied intensely the entire canon of Confucian literature from the sage himself down to later interpreters and synthesisers such as Chu Hsi in the thirteenth century and Wang Fu-chih in the eighteenth century. He was also familiar with the Legalist school of Han Fei Tzu, and knew the works of competing schools of thought such as the Taoists, Mohists and Buddhists, if only for the purposes of critiquing them. Over a hundred works, spanning a period of almost 2,500 years, are mentioned in *The Economic Principles* at various points.

At the same time, thanks to Kang, he was a modernist and reformer, and his time at Columbia had given him a strong grounding in Western political economy. It is important to understand Chen's perspective when considering this work. He was not a Western observer looking at the Chinese system and comparing it to his own; rather, he was a traditionally educated Chinese, albeit one with a strong agenda, seeking a reinterpretation of Chinese thinking in light of his new knowledge. In setting out the book, he conciously adopts the framework of political economy: there are sections on consumption, factors of production, distribution, public finance and so on. This could lead to an attempt to shoehorn Chinese philosophy into a Western economic mould, but Chen is well alive to danger: 'I have been very careful not to read into the writings of the ancient Chinese ideas drawn from modern Western economists' (p. xi). Indeed, apart from occasional references to Adam Smith or Malthus, there is little overt comparison with Western thought. Instead, what we have is a careful dissection of Chinese classical philosophy and a teasing out of those elements which can be considered economic; only then does Chen 'classify' these elements according to a Western system.

* * *

Ancient Chinese contained no word for 'economics'; the modern term, *ching chi*, is a Japanese loanword and does not appear until the end of the nineteenth century. There is, however, a very ancient term, 'administering wealth', which appears in the *Book of Changes* (ascribed by Chen to Confucius but in fact pre-dating him) and which Chen argues is for all practical purposes the same as 'economics'. The term itself is an important one. In Confucian thinking as interpreted by Chen, human agency is an essential feature of economics. No invisible hand here: in the Confucian scheme there are three factors of production, land, capital and the virtuous man, and of these three it is the latter that is by far the most important.

Moreover, the administering of wealth is not an end in itself; it is done for a purpose. In Confucian thought, wealth is inseparable from ethical and social considerations. The modern Confucian scholar A.S. Cua has referred to Confucianism as being at heart a system of ethics, and in Chen's work we see emerging what might appropriately be called an 'economics of virtue'. Chen sums this approach with a quote from the *Great Learning* (p. 293):

> The superior man must be careful about his virtue first. Having virtue, there will be the man. Having the man, there will be the

> land. Having the land, there will be the wealth. Having the wealth, there will be its use. Virtue is the root, and wealth is only its outcome.

At an individual level, profit leads to pleasure; we seek economic goals in order to derive pleasure for ourselves. Like Malthus, Confucius saw the two overriding human needs as being for food and for sex; others, notably Mencius and Hsun Tzu, argued for a progressive scale of wants including personal honour and dignity, and the end result looks rather like Maslow's hierarchy of needs. Whatever our needs may be, however, we seek to fulfill them, and the means we most commonly use is economic activity.

This looks at first like an argument for the free market, but Confucius and his followers take the opposite tack. In order to remain virtuous, economic activity must be managed and controlled. Doing this is the task of sages and kings, whom Confucius advises to remain above or outside the economic system and act as external agents; hence his often repeated call for those in positions of power to avoid personal enrichment. Most notably, whereas Western economic theory often focuses on increasing supply in order to match demand, Confucius favours curbing demand so as to meet supply. He proposes not only economic controls (such as sumptuary laws to inhibit demand for luxuries) but also the curbing of human wants through moral and social education. Himself a government minister in a North Chinese kingdom of the pre-Empire period, Confucius was once asked what should be done for the betterment of the people. His answer was twofold: educate them, and make them wealthy. Education bred an understanding of the uses of wealth; wealth made possible the benefits of education, and both led to self-development.

At the highest ethical level, economics is linked to religious belief. Referring again to the concept of graduated needs, Confucius says that when people have enough to eat (and also, presumably, enough sex), their minds can then begin to dwell on higher, spiritual things. Noting this, Chen comments that 'economic satisfaction is the condition necessary for the development of religion' (p. 57).

The rejection of *laissez-faire* and of competition is, in some of the writings, absolute. Of Confucius's followers, Mencius is perhaps most emphatic in rejecting both. Chen sums up the position (p. 169):

> If we should follow closely the *laissez-faire* policy, and should let competition be absolutely free, the world would be left to the few strongest only. Although we cannot do very much against nature, how can we bear to see the sufferings of the weak, who constitute the greatest part of mankind? Therefore, no great religious teachers, nor great moralists, nor great statesmen, let nature alone without some sort of regulation. Since natural selection is good, not for the weak, but for the strong only, artificial adjustment for society as a whole is necessary.

There is an irony here, of course, one of which Chen seems to be aware: *laissez-faire* is itself almost certainly Chinese in origin. The term derives from the Taoist concept of *wu-wei*, literally 'non-action', and refers to the view that the most efficacious way of achieving a desired result is through stillness, causing things to happen without intervening. In economic terms, this means letting natural economic laws run their course. During the eighteenth-century Enlightenment, Chinese and especially Taoist ideas were studied, and *wu-wei* came to the attention of the physiocratic school, who adopted it as *laissez-faire*. Although Adam Smith never uses the term, it is clearly behind his concept of the invisible hand.

Chen considers *laissez-faire* and disapproves of it. The concept has its origins, he says, with the Taoists and the Mohists, competing schools of thought. These two schools, as well as Buddhism which in its Chinese form took on a number of Daoist influences, favoured a rejection of worldly things. The highest attainment of mankind was not virtue, but rather enlightenment, and this was only to be achieved through the sublimation, even the annihilation, of the self. The most famous Taoist tract, the *Tao Te Ching*, argues that the best ruler is the one who interferes as little as possible in the affairs of his subjects and leaves them to live their own lives and seek enlightenment in their own ways. Thus, by rejecting the world and its works, the Taoists ironically open up a justification for unrestricted competition. Chen, like many Confucians, believed the Taoists were abdicating responsibility. The Confucian social system, by contrast, impressed upon everyone their reponsibility to their fellows and the notion that virtue lay in behaving well towards others.

At the same time as rejecting competition, however, the Confucians also rejected monopoly. Chen argues that everyone who wishes to engage in economic activity has a right to do so, and there should be no barriers to entry. The task of the market regulator (the state) is to prevent any one player from gaining advantage over the others. The means by which this is done is the matching of supply and demand, principally (as noted) by restraining demand. When supply and demand are perfectly balanced, then goods will be brought to market at a price which is fair to all buyers and to all sellers. Everyone will fulfill their economic aim of enhancing pleasure. Needless to say, this Confucian version of the 'perfect market' proved impossible to realise, and Chen himself lists a number of unsuccessful attempts in the past. Like most Confucian scholars, he blames these failures on the execution of the projects themselves, and argues that their proponents did not follow Confucian doctrines closely enough.

For Chen, as for Kang and the other late-nineteenth-century reformers, Confucianism was a progressive doctrine. While Max Weber and other contemporary Western observers saw Confucianism as rigid and opposed to progress, responsible for the ossified bureaucracy that had governed China for the last two thousand years, Chen argued that this ossification had occurred because China's rulers had abandoned the true principles of Confucianism. For example, he attacked the education system which siphoned off the country's intellectual talent into the civil service, leaving agriculture and industry to make do with leavings and thus inhibiting innovation and creativity in those areas. The aim of Confucianism, he insists, is to build the perfect society. The ultimate aim of society is the Great Similarity, or Extreme Peace, a utopian vision in which all of mankind will be equal and conflict and poverty will not exist. Achieving the Great Similarity requires not only the cultivation of virtue, but also the cultivation of wealth.

The Great Similiarity, when it is achieved, will include not only China but the whole world. An overlooked aspect of Confucian thought, says Chen, is that it applies not only to China but to all of mankind. In Confucian economic thinking, the smallest economic unit is the family, while the largest unit is the world. All people in the world are interdependent economically, and all behave economically for the same reasons. Thus, two and a half millennia before Wallerstein proposed the concept, Confucius and his followers were groping towards the idea of an economic world-system.

* * *

The Economic Principles of Confucius and His School has its flaws, and the reader should be aware of these. First, as will be quickly apparent, some of Chen's scholarship has been overtaken by later work by Chinese and Western researchers. As was common in his day, he ascribes authorship of a large number of works to Confucius, whereas we now know that some had no Confucian authorship and others are palimpsests with contributions by many hands over a period of centuries. Unravelling what is the work of Confucius and his immediate circle and what is of later (or earlier) date is a task which will occupy scholars for a long time to come. In Chen's time as for many preceding centuries, it was customary to attribute important works and ideas to the Master in order to cloak them in greater authority, in the same way that Confucius himself consciously 'borrowed authority' by attributing his ideas to semi-mythical sage-kings of the past such as King Wen. This is probably not as important as it seems. The ideas and texts studied here form the core of the Confucian belief system, regardless of whether they are by the hand of Confucius himself.

More critical is the position from which Chen wrote, including the background events described in the opening section of this introduction. Chen's agenda is first, that China must modernize, but second, that it must do so by reference to its own culture and its own inner strengths, not by adopting Western ideologies and belief systems. He is strongly against importing Christianity into China, and launches a vigorous attack on Christian missionaries; he promotes Confucian beliefs to the status of a religion, and frequently describes the Confucian canon of work as a 'bible', insisting that this is a superior religion to Christianity, or at least, a faith more suitable to China. Not all would agree that describing Confucianism as a religion is accurate. Chen's urgent need to prove the validity of Chinese thought and its relevance to the needs of modern China occasionally causes him to overreach himself.

Further, despite by and large avoiding the trap of false analogy when comparing Confucian and Western economic ideas, he cannot resist comparing Confucianism with socialism. The phrase

'Confucian socialism' even appears, uncomfortably, on several occasions. One is left wondering how familiar Chen really was with socialism. True, the emphasis on economic regulation and on achieving an economic system which promotes equality is common to both; but the happy acceptance of, even emphasis upon, personal wealth as a social good was definitely not a part of mainstream socialism by 1911. The chapter on socialistic policies is, at best, confused.

Setting these complaints to one side, how important is this book? Firstly, of course, it is unique. Chen is one of the few people ever to have trained as both an Imperial mandarin and a political economist, and this is the only major attempt to describe Confucian principles in economic terms to have appeared in English. Reading the work, and discounting for the biases described above, one can see the framework of an economic system which evolved over a long period and which owes little, if anything, to Western influence. And, it is important to realise that this system did not end with the fall of the Manchu empire.

After 1911, the Republic of China quickly fragmented into territories governed by feuding warlords. A brief period of enforced unity under Chiang Kai-shek ended with the Japanese invasion and the communist rebellion under Mao. From 1949, China was governed under a very centralized command economy system, which lasted until the economic reforms instituted by Deng Xiaopeng from 1979 onward. It has been customary to see the three decades under Mao as one of 'pure socialism', or alternatively as a left-wing dictatorship derived from the model of Stalinist Russia; while the reform period under Deng and his successors is seen as a slow but inexorable slide towards Western-style democracy and free markets.

There are those who call this view into question, of course, and it has been argued that Mao's style of rule was closer to that of the early emperors of China and that Maoism had strong Confucian roots, with loyalty to the Communist Party, for example, slotting into the place of loyalty to the family. Similarly, it is argued that the reforms of Deng and his successors are heading not towards an adoption of the Western model of capitalism, but towards a new model which will owe much to the successful ideas of the West but which will be founded on a hard core of traditional Chinese values and philosophy. To both these views, Chen's interpretation lends much support. The ethic of the command economy and of state regulation of markets can be seen, not as a Maoist interpolation, but as something fundamental to Chinese economic thinking. Similarly, the Deng and post-Deng reforms do not, on close inspection, appear to rule out state involvement in the economy. Such involvement has been scaled back, of course, notably through widespread privatizations, but state interference continues in many areas and it is remarkable to note just how many instances of interference are in fact attempts to restrict demand, rather than control supply.

The struggle in China today is not so much between conservatives and reformers, as it is often portrayed in the Western media, as it is between reformers who favour adopting Western models and Western values, and those who favour returning to old-style Chinese values. This debate is as intense in the economic sphere as in any other walk of life in China today, possibly even more so. In Chen, we see a distant echo of the latter school, a call for China to grow strong and modernize, but to do so by referring back to its ancient roots. At first glance, it is a typical Chinese paradox: look backward to go forward. But there is no doubt that many Chinese find this logic compelling. In *The Economic Principles of Confucius and His School*, we have not only a strong statement of Chinese-based economic theory, but a fascinating indication of how Chinese economics may progress in the future.

Morgen Witzel, *2002*

STUDIES IN HISTORY, ECONOMICS AND PUBLIC LAW

EDITED BY THE FACULTY OF POLITICAL SCIENCE
OF COLUMBIA UNIVERSITY

Volume XLIV Whole Number 112

THE ECONOMIC PRINCIPLES OF CONFUCIUS AND HIS SCHOOL

VOLUME I

BY

CHEN HUAN-CHANG, Ph.D.,

Chin Shih of 2455 A. K. (1904 A. D.)
Former Secretary of the Grand Secretariat,
Peking, China

New York
COLUMBIA UNIVERSITY
LONGMANS, GREEN & CO., AGENTS
LONDON: P. S. KING & SON
1911

THIS BOOK

AS A TOKEN OF GRATITUDE AND AFFECTION

I DEDICATE TO THE MEMORY OF MY FATHER

CHEN CHIN-CH'ÜAN

陳 錦 泉

WHO SUFFERED POVERTY, ADVERSITY AND

MANY BITTER DISAPPOINTMENTS

IN ORDER THAT HIS SON

MIGHT LEAD THE SCHOLAR'S LIFE

FOREWORD

Dr. Chen Huan-chang, the author of *The Economic Principles of Confucius and His School,* has seen some service as a mandarin in one of the metropolitan offices in Peking; he is deeply versed in his native literature, of which the so-called Confucian classics have occupied him for many years; he is a personal friend and has been a pupil of Kang Yu-wei, one of the originators of the modern Chinese reform movement and himself a profound connoisseur of Chinese literature. Thus armed, he came to New York about five years ago to study English and take courses in political economy at Columbia University. Kang Yu-wei's moral success among the masses of China was largely due to the fact that, while being thoroughly convinced of the necessity of reform in social and political life, he continued to be an eager adherent of Confucian principles. Dr. Chen proves a disciple worthy of his great teacher. His enthusiasm for the great sage and his doctrine could not be surpassed; western readers will find in his book the representation of Confucianism from the purely Confucianist point of view by an author who is a Confucianist himself and has had the advantage of sifting his ideas through the methods of western science.

Friedrich Hirth,
Professor of Chinese, Columbia University.

New York, October 15, 1911.

PREFACE

In presenting the economic teachings of Confucianism, Dr. Chen has adopted the same order of arrangement that has become usual in English treatises on political economy. The danger which this plan involved of creating the impression of a more systematic exposition of economic principles than is to be found in the sacred writings, is much more than outweighed by the large number of clear anticipations of the accepted economic teachings of to-day which it reveals. Incidentally it enables the author, with his wide acquaintance with the best English economic literature, to bring out many interesting contrasts between Chinese civilization and the civilization of the Occident. His discussions of such institutions as the family, marriage, private property and the position of woman have an interest and value quite apart from their relation to the main purpose of his study.

No one can read these pages without becoming convinced that Confucianism is a great economic, as well as a great moral and religious, system and that it contains most, if not all, of the elements necessary to the solution of the serious problems that confront China to-day. That these problems may be speedily and happily solved and that Dr. Chen may take the prominent and distinguished part in the reformation of his country for which his high character and unusual attainments so well fit him is the earnest hope of his American friends.

Henry R. Seager,
Professor of Political Economy.

Columbia University, October 15, 1911.

AUTHOR'S PREFACE

THE following treatise includes a discussion of the economic principles of the chief disciples of Confucius in successive dynasties, as well as of the teachings of the Master himself, and, briefly for purposes of comparison, of the leaders of other schools, *e. g.*, those of Kuan Tzŭ, Lao Tzŭ, Mo Tzŭ, Shang Yang, and Hsü Hsing. It was deemed best to combine with the discussion of economic theory some consideration of economic history. Consequently the conditions out of which the theories arose and to which they were to be applied have usually been described. The canonical writings were taken as primary sources, and the historical writings as secondary. In connection with every theory and institution considered, the attempt has been made to throw light upon its origin and earliest development. Because of the wealth of material, only the most important or most interesting historical facts since the Han dynasty have received attention. Although some information in regard to conditions in China to-day is given, it was not thought desirable to go very much into detail, because these conditions are in process of revolutionary change and many questions are still unsettled.

The treatise is, therefore, essentially a study of the old régime in China. It is a survey of the Chinese thought and Chinese institutions which developed independently of the Occident. Although my arrangement of the material follows that which has become conventional among western writers and my understanding of the old texts was greatly helped by western thinkers, I have been very careful not to read into the writings of the ancient Chinese ideas drawn from modern western economists. All my statements are based upon the words or the spirit of the words of the original texts, and are in harmony with the whole system of Confucius as revealed by a comparative study of the various sources. In support of my interpretation numerous quotations and references are given. The Confucian writings may be compared to a great mountain containing rich mineral resources. I am in the position of a miner, extracting a particular ore and contributing it to the world's production. As the miner does not create the ore itself, but through his labor in exploring, digging and refining makes it available for human use, so I have tried to add something to human knowledge. My task has been so great that I have doubtless made some mistakes, but I have earnestly tried to be accurate in all my statements. This is the first attempt to present the economic principles of Confucius and his school in a systematic form in any language. At some future time I intend to translate this book into Chinese.

I am under heavy obligations to many persons. My greatest indebtedness is to Kang Yu-wei, my former teacher, from whom I obtained a general view of Confucianism. From my American friends, especially among the professors and students of Columbia University—*e. g.*, Professors John Bates Clark, Edwin R. A. Seligman, Friedrich Hirth and Warren B. Catlin—I received many ideas and secured assistance in various ways. My greatest obligations, however, are to Dr. and Mrs. B. M. Anderson, Jr., who corrected the greater part of my manuscript; to Professor Henry Rogers Seager, who made numerous suggestions and corrections throughout the whole book; and to Professor Henry Raymond Mussey, who read all the proof sheets.

CHEN HUAN-CHANG.

COLUMBIA UNIVERSITY, NEW YORK, *the seventh day of the seventh month, two thousand four hundred and sixty-two years after Confucius, (August 30, 1911 A. D.).*

CONTENTS

VOLUME I

FOREWORD. By Professor Friedrich Hirth vii
PREFACE. By Professor Henry R. Seager ix
AUTHOR'S PREFACE xi

PART I

INTRODUCTION

BOOK I. CONFUCIUS AND HIS SCHOOL

CHAPTER PAGE
I. Life of Confucius 3
II. The Fundamental Concepts of Confucius 15
III. Writings of Confucius and His Disciples 23
IV. Historical Movements of Confucianism 39

BOOK II. RELATION OF ECONOMICS TO OTHER SCIENCES

V. Economics and Other Sciences in General 48
VI. Economics and Sociology 52
VII. Economics and Politics 73
VIII. Economics and Ethics 94

BOOK III. GENERAL ECONOMIC PRINCIPLES

IX. Economic Development as the Chief Cause of Progress 119
X. Economic Organization 139
XI. Economic Policies and the Divisions of Economics 168

PART II

CONSUMPTION

BOOK IV. CONSUMPTION

CHAPTER		PAGE
XII.	General Principles of Consumption	185
XIII.	Happiness for Both Rich and Poor	207
XIV.	Different Ways of Getting Pleasure	216
XV.	General Standard of Expenditure	242
XVI.	Particular Expenditures	269

PART III

PRODUCTION

BOOK V. FACTORS OF PRODUCTION

XVII.	Three Factors of Production	293
XVIII.	Labor—Population	297
XIX.	Nature and Capital	340

VOLUME II

PART III

PRODUCTION

BOOK VI. BRANCHES OF PRODUCTION

XX.	Branches of Production in General	367
XXI.	Agriculture	380
XXII.	Industry	398
XXIII.	Commerce	411

BOOK VII. DISTRIBUTION

XXIV.	General Principles of Distribution: Rent, Interest and Profits	460
XXV.	Wages	480

BOOK VIII. SOCIALISTIC POLICIES

CHAPTER PAGE
XXVI. The Tsing Tien System 497
XXVII. Monopoly 534
XXVIII. Exclusion of the Ruling Class from the Economic Field 543
XXIX. Government Control of Demand and Supply 552
XXX. Government Control of Grain 568
XXXI. Government Loans and Public Relief 586

PART IV

PUBLIC FINANCE

BOOK IX. PUBLIC FINANCE

XXXII. Public Expenditures 605
XXXIII. Taxation in General 621
XXXIV. Direct Taxes 638
XXXV. Indirect Taxes 683

PART V

CONCLUSION

XXXVI. Conclusion 717

APPENDIX I Table of Chinese Chronology 731
APPENDIX II List of Authorities in English and Chinese 733
INDEX 737

PART I

INTRODUCTION

BOOK I. CONFUCIUS AND HIS SCHOOL

CHAPTER I

Life of Confucius

An objective attitude toward the ideals and sages of one's own country is not easily to be attained. There is a corresponding difficulty in gaining a sufficiently sympathetic attitude toward the ideals and sages of a strange people. For these reasons it has seemed best to the writer to undertake a general estimate of the worth of Confucius and of Confucianism at the end, rather than at the beginning, of this study. The reader who has gone with him to the conclusion can better judge how far the estimate is objective, after seeing the evidence on which it is based; and he will also be better enabled to view the problem sympathetically. The words of a western writer shall, therefore, serve as our introduction.

Von der Gabelentz says:

Quite unique is the position occupied by him who, as no other man, was a teacher of his people, who, I venture to say, has become and continued to be a ruler of his people, the Sage of the family K'ung in the State of Lu, whom we know by the name of Confucius. Unique is his position, not only in the history of philosophy, but also in the history of mankind. For there is hardly any other man who, like Confucius, incorporated in his own person all the constituent elements of the Chinese type and all that is eternal in his people's being. If we are to measure the greatness of an historic personage, I can see only one standard applicable for the purpose: the effectiveness of that person's influence according to its dimensions, duration, and intensity. If this standard be applied, Confucius was one of the greatest of men. For even at the present day, after the lapse of more than two thousand years, the moral, social, and political life of about one-third of mankind continues to be under the full influence of his mind.[1]

Confucius has indeed been the maker of the Chinese people, but he himself did not spring from an uncivilized world. The date of the beginning of Chinese history is unknown, but it is certain that China has existed as a nation for at least six thousand years. The first legendary emperor, Pao Hsi, or Fu Hsi, is placed 2402 years before the Confucian era (2953-2839 B. C.). After the period of the Five Emperors, came the period of the Three Kings of as many dynasties, and it was during the Chou dynasty, the last of these three, that Chinese civilization reached maturity. It was after long periods of so-called sage rulers who were regarded as the heads of both religion and government, at the highest development of Chinese civilization under the Chou dynasty, and in the most cultured state of the Duke of Chou, that Confucius appeared. Confucianism, the new religion founded by Confucius, is therefore not the religion of a primitive tribe, but the religion of a civilized people.

While this was the general stage of development preceding the advent of Confucius, it must not be imagined that actual conditions during his time were so perfect as to make the work of a reformer unnecessary. The age of Confucius was quite remote from that of the sage rulers. With

[1] *Confucius und seine Lehre*, p. 4 *et seq.*, quoted in Friedrich Hirth's *The Ancient History of China*, *pp.* 242-3.

the beginning of Ping Wang's reign (219 B. K.[1] or 770 B. C.), the Chou dynasty had practically fallen, and all the emperors of the Eastern Chou line were without real power. It was the age of feudalism. Each feudal estate was an independent nation, each prince of each nation fought for its supremacy, and the power of the princes was greater than that of the emperor. During Confucius' time, the power of the prince in each state had generally fallen into the hands of a few noble families, and the government had become a form of oligarchy. Sometimes the private officials of these families took public affairs into their own hands. The confusion and disorder brought about by the ruling class extended over the whole empire, while the common people, who were not sufficiently educated to help themselves, were entirely neglected.

Although the great mass of the people in Confucius' time was uneducated, there was a middle class which had educated itself. Since China had been civilized for so long a time, the people were naturally developed to some extent. During the period of the Eastern Chou dynasty, although the power of the imperial government declined, the intellectual growth of the people increased. The greater importance acquired by the different independent states with the diminishing power of the emperor gave rise to much peaceful diplomatic intercourse as well as to many hostile military expeditions, and these forms of contact had an educative influence upon a considerable class of the people. Further, as the political power was shifting from class to class and from person to person within each state, some noble families had been ruined, and some common people had risen. Thus the profession of learning was also shifted

[1] We use the forms B. K. and A. K. to avoid confusion with the C. in the western chronology, as in B. C. The Chinese form of the name, Confucius, is K'ung Fu Tzŭ.

and more widely diffused. Moreover, in such a struggle, every one had absolute freedom of movement and of speech. It was a condition very favorable to the development of the minds of the people.

Such was the time in which Confucius was born. But the birthplace of Confucius was no less important than his time. His family had settled in the state of Lu, which was the state of the Duke of Chou. As the Duke himself remained with the imperial government, he gave the administration of his estate over to his son, who conducted it according to his father's principles and under his direction. Lu had become the center of Chinese civilization. About Confucius' time, Lu, although subordinate to the great states in military force, was supreme in art, literature, philosophy and morality.

Among Confucius' ancestors was Ch'êng T'ang, the founder of the Yin dynasty (1215-1203 B. K. or 1766-1754 B. C.). After the fall of this dynasty, Wei Tzŭ, brother of the fallen emperor, was enfeoffed by Chou Ch'êng Wang in the dukedom of Sung. The tenth ancestor of Confucius resigned his dukedom to his younger brother, and thus it passed out of the direct line of Confucius. Five generations later, K'ung-fu Chia, the sixth ancestor of Confucius, invented the surname of K'ung from his adult designation indicating separation from the house of the duke in conformity with the ancient custom. On account of some political trouble, the great-grandfather of Confucius fled from Sung to the state of Lu, and became mayor in the city of Fang. Confucius' father, Shu-liang Ho, was mayor in the city of Tsou, and distinguished himself as a brave soldier. Since on reaching the age of sixty-four he had no heir who could be his successor, he was obliged to marry a young girl, Yen Chêng-tsai, who became the mother of Confucius.

The year of Confucius' birth, according to the Commentaries of Kung-yang and Ku-liang, was the twentieth year of Chou Ling Wang's reign (552 B. C.); but the beginning of the Confucian era is dated one year later (551 B. C.) on account of a mistake made by Ssŭ-ma Chien, the greatest historian.[1] His birthday, according to the present Chinese calendar, is the twenty-first day of the eighth month. His birthplace is in the present district of K'ühfeu, Shantung province. K'ung was his family name; Ch'iu, his personal name; and Chung-ni, his adult designation. The word Confucius has come from three Chinese words, K'ung Fu Tzŭ, *Fu Tzŭ* meaning master.

Confucius was powerful in body and keen in mind. He studied under many masters and in many places, becoming a many-sided and versatile man.

The greatest service of Confucius to his contemporaries was as a teacher. Opening his school at the age of twenty-two,[2] he taught continuously to the time of his death. When he was thirty-five, a noble of one of the leading families of Lu, on his death-bed, ordered his two sons, Mêng Yi-tzŭ and Nan-kung Ching-shu, to become pupils of Confucius, and these two noble pupils undoubtedly increased his influence. When at this time he wished to visit the imperial capital, Nan-kung Ching-shu advised the Marquis of Lu to furnish a carriage, two horses and a servant for him, and himself accompanied his teacher. During this visit a very significant interview occurred between Confucius and Lao Tzŭ, the earliest philosopher of the Chou dynasty, then keeper of the imperial archives, and later regarded as the founder of Taoism. Confucius consulted this learned man concerning the rites, questioned Chang Hung, a high im-

[1] He began to write the *Historical Record* in 448, and finished it in 455 (104-97 B. C.).

[2] *Canonical Interpretation of the Ts'ing Dynasty*, vol. xxxiii, ch. i.

perial officer, about music, and studied many other things. After his return home, his pupils increased in number.

One year later, on account of a civil war, Confucius went to the neighboring state of Ch'i. The Marquis of Ch'i wished to confer upon him a territory, but this was objected to by a courtier named An Tzŭ. As he could not hold a good office there, Confucius returned, at the age of forty-two, to Lu.

After his return, he devoted himself exclusively to teaching and writing for a period of ten years. At forty-eight, he prepared the Canons of *Poetry*, of *History*, of *Rites* and of *Music*. Many pupils now came to him from remote regions. But he was so anxious to secure political power in order to reform the Chinese world that he even considered accepting the invitations of the rebels. At fifty-one, when Kung-shan Fu-jao, who held the city of Fei in rebellion against the minister of Lu, invited him to come, Confucius was disposed to comply. He said that if any one would employ him, he might create a new dynasty of Chou in the East.[1] Ten years later, at sixty-one, he also considered accepting the invitation of Pi Hsi, who rebelled with the city of Chung-mou against the minister of Tsin.[2] Although he did not go to see these two rebels at all and refused their invitations, it is clear that his love and faith were directed much more toward the general public than toward any personal ruler.

The political career of Confucius, although not an important part of his life, is proof of his practical talents. At fifty-two, he was appointed magistrate of the city of Chung-tu by the Marquis of Lu. His administration was very successful, and the princes of neighboring states took it as a

[1] *The Chinese Classics*, vol. i, pp. 319-20.

[2] *Ibid.*, p. 321.

model.[1] At fifty-three, the Marquis appointed him Minister of the Interior, and then Minister of Justice. A courtier of the state of Ch'i, which was jealous of its neighbor Lu, warned his prince that the increasing influence of the latter state under the administration of Confucius would endanger the balance of power. His prince, therefore, invited the Marquis of Lu to come to a friendly meeting in order to catch him and make him prisoner. Confucius accompanied his prince as substitute for the prime minister. He defeated the treacherous plot through his speeches and through a show of military force, so that Ch'i was obliged to apologize and as a mark of friendship to restore the former conquests which it had made from Lu. At fifty-five, Confucius strengthened the ruling house by having the walls of the cities of the noble families pulled down. Reaching the height of civil greatness, he became, at fifty-six, the acting prime minister. Within seven days, he ordered the execution of a great demagogue, Shao-chêng Mao, as being dangerous to the public welfare. Within three months, his moral influence prevailed over the whole state. But the neighboring countries began to fear that under Confucius' reformation, Lu would overtop and subdue them all. To prevent this, the Marquis of Ch'i, above referred to, sent eighty beautiful dancing girls and one hundred and twenty fine horses as a gift to the prince of Lu for the purpose of bringing about a separation between him and Confucius. The result was the demoralization of the government, as both the prince and the real prime minister neglected their duties. Confucius lost his influence, and soon left his native country for travel.

Confucius' travels were in the nature of missionary work. He aimed to establish his kingdom in the actual present

[1] *Cf.* the *Historical Record*, ch. xlvii, on which this chapter is based.

world through the influence of a government. He was not a narrow patriot. He presented himself for official employment before seventy-two princes, and even in the barbaric state of Ch'u. But he was not able in any case to realize his purpose. He was satirized by many of his contemporaries who felt the world to be evil and kept aloof from it. Confucius' declaration is at once sane and pathetic: "The bird and beast," said he sorrowfully, "cannot be in the same society with us. If I do not associate with my fellow-men, with whom shall I associate? Had the world been perfect, I would not care to change it!"[1] This was the spirit of Confucius: to love the world, to serve the world, and to busy himself restlessly in his mission.

Upon four different occasions during his travels, his life was placed in jeopardy. First, at fifty-seven, he was imprisoned by the people of the city of K'uang for five days. His pupils were fearful, but he said: "After the death of Wên Wang, was not the cause of truth lodged here in me? If God had wished to let this cause of truth perish, then I, his successor who later must die, should not have been placed in such a relation to that cause. But so long as God does not let the cause of truth perish, what can the people of K'uang do to me?"[2] Again, at fifty-eight, when with his pupils he was performing religious ceremonies under the shade of a large tree, Huan Tui, the minister of war of the state of Sung, who wished to kill him, had the tree cut down. Then his pupils warned him to go away at once. "God has produced," said he, "the virtue that is in me.

[1] *Classics*, vol. i, p. 334.

[2] Confucius here indentifies himself with the line of the great sage rulers to whom God had intrusted the instruction of men. In all the six centuries between himself and Wên Wang (673-584 B. K.), he does not admit of such another. *Ibid*, pp 217-8

What can Huan Tui do to me?"[1] It is clear that he felt that God had committed to him the right way, and that he bore a charmed life until his work was done. Again, at fifty-nine, he was stopped by the rebels in the city of Po. But one of his pupils, Kung-liang Yü, who was following his master with five private chariots, fought bravely for him, and he was allowed to proceed. Once more, at sixty-four, he was surrounded by the officials of the states of Chên and Tsai. He was without food for seven days, and his pupils were so sick as to be unable to rise. But he never stopped preaching, reading, playing on the harp and singing. Finally he was rescued by the military force of the state of Ch'u.

When he arrived at Ch'u, the king wished to confer upon him a territory of seven hundred square miles. But the prime minister objected, because he feared Confucius' power and virtues, saying that the latter's pupils were much better than any of their own officials, and that if Confucius could occupy any territory, he himself would eventually be a real king and this would not be good for their state.

Having spent fourteen years in traveling abroad, Confucius was now, at sixty-nine, called back by the government of his native state. But the government did not finally employ him, and he himself at this period had no desire to be employed. About this time, his son died; his wife had died two years previously.

Confucius was destined, however, not chiefly to serve his own immediate period, but to influence endless ages of the future. He now spent all his time in writing, and this was, in the final analysis, his greatest work. As he had at the age of forty-eight already prepared the greater part of the Canons of *Poetry,* of *History,* of *Rites,* and of *Music,*

[1] *Classics,* vol. i, p. 202.

he now finished them, and also the *Canon of Changes*. The *Spring and Autumn* was written at the age of seventy-two.

What he wrote was very much the same as what he was teaching to his three thousand pupils, particularly the Canons of *Poetry, History, Rites* and *Music*. Those who graduated in the six arts—rites, music, archery, charioteering, writing and mathematics—which were all prescribed courses for each person, were seventy-two in number. His best students were those who specialized in morality, oratory, politics and literature. There were many special students. Therefore, the number of his followers amounted to sixty thousand.

Confucius was already an old man when he finished his writings; they were the product of his most mature wisdom. He now felt that his work was done. One morning, he got up early, and as he walked back and forth before his door with his hands behind his back dragging his staff, he sang the following words:

> The Tai Mountain must crumble!
> The strongest beam must break!
> The wisest man must fade!

Seven days later, the death of "The Perfect Holy Man" took place.[1] He was seventy-four years old (479 B. C.).

The highest honors were bestowed upon him after his death. The Marquis of Lu came to pass eulogy upon him. He was buried in what is now called the Forest of K'ung, to which the trees were originally brought from different states by his pupils. His pupils stayed there until the end of three years' mourning, but Tzŭ-kung (his pupil) alone built a house near his tomb and lived there for three years more. Some of his pupils and some of the people of Lu,

[1] According to the present Chinese calendar, the corresponding date is the eleventh day of the second month.

more than one hundred families in all, moved to the vicinity of his tomb and formed what was called the Village of K'ung. The people sacrificed to his tomb for many generations, and the Confucian scholars also practised different ceremonies about it. His house was then converted into a temple in which his clothes, hats, harp, carriage and books were stored. The first emperor who came to worship him was Han Kao Ti (357 A. K. or 195 B. C.). When new princes and governors first came to the state, they always worshiped him before they took up their official duties. Since 504 A. K. the descendants of Confucius have been a permanent nobility. The present duke of his descendants is in the seventy-sixth generation from him. In 610 A. K. (59 A. D.), Han Ming Ti first ordered the Imperial University and all the government schools in each district to worship Confucius. Since that time the school houses have been at the same time Confucian churches, and they have been established throughout the whole empire.

In conclusion, then, we may say that Confucius was a great philosopher, a great educator, a great statesman, and a great musician; but, above all, that he was the founder of a great religion. This is well stated by Tzŭ-kung when he says: "Certainly God has endowed him unlimitedly as a great sage, and, moreover, his ability is various." [1] Yu Jo, pupil of Confucius, said, "From the birth of mankind till now, there never has been one so complete as Confucius," and the same statement is also given by Tzŭ-kung and Mencius (180-263 A. K. or 372-289 B. C.).[2] In the *Analects,*[3] Confucius, by tacit implication, compares himself with God, and in the "Doctrine of the Mean," [4] Confucius is

[1] *Classics,* vol. i, p. 218.

[2] *Classics,* vol. ii, pp. 194-6.

[3] *Classics,* vol. i, p. 326.

[4] *Ibid.,* p. 429.

called "the equal of God". The Chinese worship him not from any superstitious idea, but on the philosophical ground that "the individual possessed of the most complete sincerity is regarded as divine",[1] and that "when the sage is beyond our knowledge, he is what is called divine."[2] Although Confucius died about twenty-five centuries ago, the Chinese believe that his fundamental teachings will remain true forever. This is because, on the one hand, the teachings, based on the doctrine of the mean, never go to extremes; and on the other, being subject to the doctrine of changes, they easily adapt themselves to the environment. Confucius is called by Mencius "The Sage of Times". In fact, the teachings of Confucius are based on the nature of man,[3] and as long as we are human beings, no matter in what age or in what region we may live, we can learn from him. Hence, the Chinese believe that there has been no other man so great as Confucius.

[1] *Classics,* vol. i, p. 418.

[2] *Classics,* vol. ii, p. 490.

[3] *Classics,* vol. i, p. 393.

CHAPTER II

The Fundamental Concepts of Confucius

Having reviewed the more important facts of Confucius' life, we pass now to the fundamental concepts of the whole Confucian philosophy. There are two general classes of these concepts, one class based on the law of variety, and the other on the law of unity; the one, changeable with the needs of the times, the other unchangeable, rooted in the nature of man. Of the first type are the principle of the Three Systems and the principle of the Three Stages; of the second is the principle of love, which is to be practised on the basis of reciprocity.

I. THE THREE SYSTEMS

Confucius is like a great physician, and his teachings are like prescriptions. Just as the great physician never gives a single kind of medicine as a remedy for all diseases, so Confucius never gives a single form of teaching as the law of all ages. In the *Spring and Autumn,* he sets forth the principle of the Three Systems, and we meet this principle in all his writings. The Three Systems are represented by the Three Dynasties, Hsia, Yin and Chou, and he makes everything in three different forms. For example, the new year begins with either the first month, or the second, or the third; the new day begins either in the morning, or in the middle between morning and midnight, or at midnight; the principal color is either black, or white, or red. There is not a certain form, but the one is as good as the others. Hence the principles of the Three Dynasties are as in a cycle,

—the one succeeds the other, whenever the former principle does not work well. The fundamental concept is that all human civilization and social life are necessarily changed in order to reform the evil of the past and meet the need of the present. Any good thing must come to a period of decay and become an evil. Civilization may run through a long course to the original principle and then start again, although such a principle may not take exactly the original form. Or, in different places, different civilizations and institutions may exist at the same time.

II. THE THREE STAGES

A principle more important than the Three Systems is the Three Stages. In the first of these, the Disorderly Stage, primitive civilization is just arising from chaos, and the social mind is still very rude. There is a sharp distinction between one's own country and all other civilized countries. Hence attention is paid more to conditions at home than abroad, and, except the great powers, the small countries are neglected. In the second, the Advancing Peace Stage, there is a distinction only between all the civilized countries and the barbarians. The limit of civilization is broader, and the friendship of nations is closer; by the equal right, even the small countries can have their representatives. In the third, the Extreme Peace Stage, there is no distinction at all. The barbarians become civilized countries, and obtain the same title in the diplomatic circle. Whether the nations are remote or near, small or great, the whole world is as one unit, and the character of mankind is on the highest plane.

The principle of the Three Stages, illustrated by the international relation, is established in the *Spring and Autumn*.[1]

[1] It is very strange that Professor James Legge apparently does not know the international view of Confucius at all. He says: "Confucius

But we can find this principle in all Confucius' writings, whatever the subject. For example, in politics, despotism, constitutionalism and anarchism are three stages; in religion, polytheism, monism and atheism are three stages. The three stages can be subdivided into nine, eighty-one, and so on. It is simply the theory of progress, or evolution. But we must remember this principle in order to understand that the teachings of Confucius, although sometimes apparently inconsistent, are all fitted to different stages, and that we must not make the mistake of applying the theories of the low stage to the advanced stage.

The Advancing Peace Stage is also called the Small Tranquillity, and the Extreme Peace Stage, the Great Similarity. The marked difference between these two stages is described by Confucius himself. It is a most important passage, and

makes no provision for the intercourse of his country with other and independent nations. He knew indeed of none such. China was to him 'The Middle Kingdom,' 'The multitude of Great States,' 'All under Heaven.' Beyond it were only rude and barbarous tribes." (*Chinese Classics*, vol. i, pp. 107-8.) This statement is quite misleading. Confucius has made many provisions for the intercourse of his country with other and independent nations; and we can compile the International Law of Confucius even from the *Spring and Autumn* only. In Confucius' time, China was divided up into many nations. The number of leading nations was twelve, and the total number of nations was over one hundred. Therefore, his country was not China, but Lu. Since Lu had intercourse continuously with other and independent nations, why should Confucius know nothing about them? These nations were called "The multitude of Great States" and "The Middle Kingdom." This was the international society, and the term Middle Kingdom was like the term Christendom. Beyond this, there were at this time only rude and barbarous tribes, so far as the Chinese knew This was the condition under which Confucius lived. By the term "All under Heaven," however, Confucius really meant the whole world, and it included not only the multitude of great states, but also all the barbarous tribes. Although it was sometimes used to cover only the Chinese world, such a term, everyone can see, could never mean a national state. In fact, Confucius always keeps the whole world in his mind.

we must quote it fully. In the "Evolution of Civilization," Confucius says:

When the Great Principle [of the Great Similarity] prevails, the whole world becomes a republic; they elect men of talents, virtue, and ability; they talk about sincere agreement, and cultivate universal peace. Thus men do not regard as their parents only their own parents, nor treat as their children only their own children. A competent provision is secured for the aged till their death, employment for the middle-aged, and the means of growing up to the young. The widowers, widows, orphans, childless men, and those who are disabled by disease, are all sufficiently maintained. Each man has his rights, and each woman her individuality safe-guarded. They produce wealth, disliking that it should be thrown away upon the ground, but not wishing to keep it for their own gratification. Disliking idleness, they labor, but not alone with a view to their own advantage. In this way selfish schemings are repressed and find no way to arise. Robbers, filchers and rebellious traitors do not exist. Hence the outer doors remain open, and are not shut. This is the stage of what I call the Great Similarity.

Now that the Great Principle has not yet been developed, the world is inherited through family. Each one regards as his parents only his own parents, and treats as his children only his own children. The wealth of each and his labor are only for his self-interest. Great men imagine it is the rule that their estates should descend in their own families. Their object is to make the walls of their cities and suburbs strong and their ditches and moats secure. Rites and justice are regarded as the threads by which they seek to maintain in its correctness the relation between ruler and minister; in its generous regard that between father and son; in its harmony that between elder brother and younger; and in a community of sentiment that between husband and wife; and in accordance with them they regulate consumption, distribute land and dwellings, distinguish the men of military ability and cunning, and achieve their work with a view to their own advantage. Thus it is that selfish schemes and enterprises are constantly taking their rise, and war is inevitably forthcoming. In this course of rites and justice, Yü, T'ang, Wên, Wu, Ch'êng Wang and the Duke of Chou are the best examples of good government. Of these six superior men, every one was attentive to the rites, thus to secure the display of justice, the realization of sincerity, the exhibition of errors, the exemplification of benevolence, and the discussion of courtesy, showing the people all the constant virtues. If any ruler, having power and position, would not follow this course, he should be driven away by the multitude who regard him as a public enemy. This is the stage of what I call the Small Tranquillity.[1]

This is the most important statement of all Confucius' teachings. The stage of Great Similarity or Extreme Peace is the final aim of Confucius; it is the golden age of Confucianism. If we make a comparison between the Great Similarity and the Small Tranquillity, we may get a clear view. Every one knows that Confucianism has five social relations and five moral constants: ruler and subject, father and son, elder and younger brothers, husband and wife, friend and friend, make up the five social relations; love, justice, rite, wisdom and sincerity, make up the five moral constants. But, according to the statement of Confucius himself, they belong only to the Small Tranquillity. Every one knows that Confucianism is in favor of monarchical government and of filial piety. But they are good only in the Small Tranquillity. In the Great Similarity, the whole world is the only social organization, and the individual is the independent unit; both socialistic and individualistic characters reach the highest point. There is no national state, so that there is no war, no need of defence, nor of men of military ability and cunning. Men of talents, virtue,

[1] *Li Ki*, bk. vii, pp. 365-7. "The exhibition of errors" refers to wisdom, and "the discussion of courtesy" to rites.

and ability are chosen by the people, so that the people themselves are the sovereign, and the relation between ruler and subject does not exist. Man and woman are not bound by the tie of marriage, so that the relations between husband and wife, between father and son and between brothers, do not exist. The only relation that remains is friendship. There is no family, so that there is no inheritance, no private property, no selfish scheme. There is no class, so that the only classification is made either by age or by sex; but whether old, middle-aged, or young, whether man or woman, each satisfies his needs. The Great Principle of the Great Similarity prevails, so that everyone is naturally as good as every one else and the distinction of the five moral constants is gone. Each has only natural love toward others, regardless of artificial rites and justice. Speaking of the Small Tranquillity, Confucius gives six superior men as examples, but for the Great Similarity, he does not mention any one, because it has never existed. In the *Canon of History,* Confucius takes up Yao and Shun to represent the stage of Great Similarity as they did not hand down their thrones to their sons, yet he does not mention them here. The principle of the Three Stages is the principle of progress; we must look for the golden age in the future; the Extreme Peace or the Great Similarity is the goal.

III. LOVE

Both the Three Systems and the Three Stages come under the law of variety in accordance with external conditions; the law of unity is based on the inner nature of man. It is the principle of love. From the religious point of view, the unity is called God; from the philosophical point of view, it is called *Yüan;* from the ethical point of view, it is called love.[1] These three names are based on the same principle, because it is a unity. The unity of the universe is nothing but love. The cement of the universe is called God or *Yüan,* and that of society is called love. Confucius says " Love is man ", and Mencius repeats the same words.[2] If we put it into negative form, any one who does not conform to the principle of love is not a man.

IV. RECIPROCITY

There is a question as to how we should practice the principle of love. After Confucius said to Ts'êng-Tzŭ, his pupil, " My doctrine is that of an all-pervading unity ", Ts'êng-Tzŭ explained to other pupils that the unity is simply faithfulness and reciprocity.[3] Confucius himself says: " Faithfulness and reciprocity are not far from the way. What you do not wish when done to yourself, do not do to others." [4] We can see, therefore, that faithfulness and reciprocity both make up the unity, but faithfulness is included in the principle of reciprocity. When Tzŭ-kung asked, " Is there one word which may serve as a rule of practice for all one's life? " Confucius said, " Is not reciprocity such a word? What you do not want done to yourself, do not do to others." [5] Stating this golden rule positively, Confucius says: " The man who practices the principle of love, wishing to establish himself, seeks also to establish others; wishing to develop himself, he seeks also to develop others. To be able to take one's inmost self for

1 See *Yi King,* pp. 408, 415. Legge's translation is obscure. The word *Ch'ien* means God, and also the word *Yüan,* " the great and originating." The word benevolence is love.

2 *Classics,* vol. i, p. 405; and vol. ii, p. 485.

3 *Classics,* vol. i, pp. 169-170.

4 *Ibid.,* p. 394.

5 *Ibid.,* p. 301.

the judging of others may be called the art of applying the principle of love."[1] This principle makes egotism and altruism into one and the same thing, and makes one regard others as oneself. In short, the principle of love is the end, and the law of reciprocity is the means. This is the unity of Confucianism.

[1] *Classics*, vol. i, p. 194.

CHAPTER III

Writings of Confucius and His Disciples

I. WRITINGS OF CONFUCIUS

We have said that the work of Confucius is no greater than his writings. Let us now consider what his writings are. Since they are called the Holy Bible,[1] and are the oldest and best literature of the Chinese, they occupy the first department of the Chinese library. The study of them is very difficult; many good scholars, spending their whole lives, study thoroughly merely a part of them; yet their principles can never be exhausted. The writings on the subject of the Confucian Bible, therefore, are most numerous. But we shall give the essentials in the most condensed way.

[1] Since the Chinese word for "Bible" was mistranslated by Professor James Legge into the word "Classic," there has been much misunderstanding of the nature of Confucius' writings. It must be contended that these writings are regarded as divinely inspired, because Confucius himself is considered to have been divinely sent and appointed. (*Cf.* passage from the *Adjunct to the Spring and Autumn,* quoted in the *Annotation of Kung-yang,* 14th year of Duke Ai). An account given in the *Adjunct to the Canon of Filial Piety,* in which Confucius is represented as reporting to God the completion of his writings and as receiving divine approval in the form of a red rainbow coming down from above and transmitting itself into yellow jade with words sculptured upon it, would seem to give to the religion and writings of Confucius in the minds of the Chinese people the same claim to a sacred character as other religions and Bibles possess for the people who accept them. But the real value of the writings of Confucius is not based on such a story.

All the different writings of Confucius himself are called Bibles. But as the word is not ordinarily used in the plural in English, we are obliged to adopt the word "Canon." Originally, the Chinese called them *Ching,* which means Bible. We shall review them according to their original order, as follows:

1. The *Canon of Poetry* contains three hundred and five poems. Except the first two poems of "The Odes of Pin," they were all written by different authors in the Chou dynasty (about 631-47 B. K. or 1182-598 B. C.), but they are edited by Confucius according to his own principles. How many corrections have been made by him we do not know, but we are sure that he must have changed the original words in some way. The poems are divided into three kinds: the *Fêng,* spirits of different nations; the *Ya,* politics of the imperial government; the *Sung,* praises in the temples. Because politics is concerned with great and small questions, the *Ya* is divided up again into Small *Ya* and Great *Ya.* Hence, this Canon has four parts. All the poems are the expression of human nature; the description, narration, or criticism of social and political conditions. Their character is somewhat like that of a newspaper, and they serve as a comparative study of political science. This Canon is also a song book, as all the poems can be sung in harmony with music.

2. The *Canon of History* has twenty-eight books. It covers the history of China from Yao (1806-1707 B. K. or 2357-2258 B. C.) to Duke Mu of Ch'in (108-70 B. K. or 659-621 B. C.), and gives all the most important documents of this period. These documents were written by different authors, and edited by Confucius. But the labor Confucius put on this Canon is evidently greater than that put on the *Canon of Poetry.* The "System of Yao," the "Tribute of Yü," the "Great Model," and the "Code of

Po," are apparently the works of Confucius himself, because their style is different from that of the other documents and similar to the style of Confucius. This Canon is a study of history and political science.

3. The *Canon of Rites* has seventeen books, and describes the details of the eight rites. These eight rites are: (1) capping for the indication of maturity, (2) marriage, (3) funeral, (4) sacrifice, (5) district-drinking, (6) game of archery, (7) diplomatic intercourse, and (8) visiting of the emperor by the princes. These eight rites are the rules governing the five social relations: The rites of capping and marriage govern the relation of husband and wife; the rites of funeral and sacrifice, that of father and son; the rites of district-drinking and archery, that of seniors and juniors; the rites of diplomatic intercourse and visiting of the emperor, that of ruler and minister. For the relation of friends, there are the third book on social intercourse, the twelfth book on feasting, and the fifteenth book on the rites of entertaining great officials by a prince. Moreover, through all the different rites there must be two parties, host and guest; hence the relation of friend to friend is within all the rites. Such rites are the old customs and manners, but they are collected and prescribed by Confucius. This Canon is now miscalled *Yi Li.*

4. The *Canon of Music.* Since the songs are all in the *Canon of Poetry,* and the different uses of music are prescribed in the *Canon of Rites,* there was no need to have a canon for music like the other *Five Canons.* But there must originally have been a *Canon of Music,* though different in form from the others, having notes instead of words. Unfortunately it was lost during the Han dynasty, (after 636 A. K. or 85 A. D.). Therefore, we generally speak only of the *Five Canons.*

5. The *Canon of Changes.* Although Pao Hsi first drew

the eight trigrams, and Wên Wang multiplied them into sixty-four hexagrams, the text of this Canon is virtually the exclusive work of Confucius. It is divided into two parts, and has sixty-four books. The first two books of the first part refer to heaven and earth respectively; those of the second part, to the relation between husband and wife; the last two books of this Canon are called " Success " and " Failure ". Heaven and earth are the basis of the universal system, and husband and wife that of the social system. As the world never comes to the stage of perfection, and everything must have an end, this Canon ends at the book of Failure. The thought is mystical; the words are figurative; the illustrations are mathematical. The word "changes" has three distinct meanings: easy, changeable, unchangeable; and the principles of this Canon have these three qualities. In fact, the *Canon of Changes* is the doctrine of evolution, and we may adopt the word evolution instead of changes.

6. The *Spring and Autumn.* This Canon was originally the annals of Lu, but Confucius changed them into the present form. It covers the period of two hundred and forty-two years (171 B. K.-71 A. K. or 722-481 B. C.), and records the events during the reigns of twelve dukes. For the preparation of this Canon, Confucius sent fourteen pupils to get the sacred books from one hundred and twenty nations It is an inductive work, written entirely by Confucius himself. This Canon is the most important of all his works. It is not historical in character; the words drawn from history are but the figures by which Confucius has illustrated his principles. " I should like to convey my ideas as pure theories," said he, " but it is deeper, truer, clearer, brighter, to represent them through the actions of men." He claims the rights of a king, represents his kingdom under the name of Lu, and gives numerous laws along

with historical events. Censuring the emperors, abasing the princes, and attacking the great officials, he establishes his kingdom on earth through the *Spring and Autumn*. On this account, Confucius said: "It is only the *Spring and Autumn* which will make men know me, and it is only the *Spring and Autumn* which will make men condemn me." [1]

Of the *Five Canons*, the *Canon of Changes* and the *Spring and Autumn* are the most important. The Canons of *Poetry*, of *History*, and of *Rites* contain materials drawn from the ancients and remodeled by him, but the *Canon of Changes* and the *Spring and Autumn* are written entirely in his own words. The other three are his ordinary teachings; these two, his most important teachings. The *Canon of Changes* is a deductive work, beginning with abstract principles and proceeding to their practical application, while the *Spring and Autumn* is inductive, coming to the general theories through the analysis of facts.[2]

Both the inductive and the deductive method are employed by Confucius. He recognizes the equal importance of them, and points out the dangers of using either exclusively. He says: "Learning without thought is labor lost; thought without learning is perilous." [3] The word learning means induction, and the word thought, deduction. They must be combined and neither one can get along without the other. He tells us from his own experience that the single method of deduction is useless. He says: "I have been the whole day without eating, and the whole night without sleeping—occupied with thinking. It was of no use. The better plan is to learn."[4] Again, he speaks of his

[1] *Classics*, vol. ii, pp. 281-2

[2] *Historical Record*, ch. cxvii.

[3] *Classics*, vol. i, p. 150.

[4] *Ibid.*, pp. 302-3.

inductive method as follows: "There may be those who write something without the knowledge of it. I have no such fault. Hearing much, and selecting what is good and using it; seeing much, and selecting what is good and writing it down: this way of getting knowledge is second only to having knowledge by birth."[1] From these two passages, it seems that he is more in favor of induction than of deduction.

We must understand, however, that since Confucius was not a historian, but the founder of a religion, his writings are not of a historical but of a religious character. All the data given in his writings, although often true, are primarily figurative illustrations of his own ideas, and he did not necessarily regard them as facts. In the *Analects* he says:

> I can describe the civilization of the Hsia dynasty, but the state of Chi cannot sufficiently prove my words. I can describe the civilization of the Yin dynasty, but the state of Sung cannot sufficiently prove my words. It is because of the insufficiency of their literature and scholars. If those were sufficient, I could adduce them in support of my words.[2]

This passage indicates that Confucius himself fails to find historical data on which to base his doctrines, and that the descriptions of the ancient civilization given by him are simply from his own mind. In the "Doctrine of the Mean,"[3] and in the "Evolution of Civilization,"[4] Confucius gives passages similar to the above, so that we are assured that he creates the ancients out of his own mind. Moreover,

[1] *Classics*, vol. i, p. 201.

[2] *Ibid.*, p. 158.

[3] *Ibid.*, p. 424.

[4] *Li Ki*, bk. vii, p. 368.

when Mencius was asked by Pei-kung Yi about the arrangement of dignities and emoluments determined by the Chou dynasty, he replied, " The particulars of that arrangement cannot be learned, for the princes, disliking them as injurious to themselves, have all made away with the records of them." [1] We can see, therefore, that in Confucius' time, not only the civilization of the Hsia and the Yin dynasties had no authentic history, but also that of the Chou dynasty was without complete records. How much more doubtful were the things beyond these three dynasties to which he refers? Yet Confucius describes many matters which refer not only to the Three Dynasties, but also to the legendary periods.

When we compare his writings with those of other schools, we find no agreement among the different writers as to the facts, because they all utilize the ancient kings as figures to portray their own theories. Chuang Tzŭ (a pupil of the disciple of Confucius, who, however, turned to Taoism), is such a writer of the extreme type, and Confucius is one of the moderate type. Mo Tzŭ, a young pupil of Confucius, and later the founder of the rival school of Moism, said, " Between two philosophers, their words condemn each other, and their actions oppose each other. Yet they both say, 'I transmit from the ancients the principles of Yao, Shun, Yü, T'ang, Wên, and Wu.' " [2] Han Fei Tzŭ (died 319 A. K. or 233 B. C.), the greatest philosopher of the Law School, formerly a Confucian, said, " Confucius and Mo Tzŭ both speak of Yao and Shun, but what they select or reject is different. Yet they both claim to be the true representatives of Yao and Shun. As Yao and Shun cannot be alive again, who can be sent to determine the truthfulness of Confucius and Mo Tzŭ? " [3] Han Fei Tzŭ, living

[1] *Classics*, vol. ii, p. 373.

[2] Bk. xxv.

[3] Bk 1.

near to the age of Confucius, yet failed to assert whether the things ascribed by Confucius to the ancient kings were true or not; how can we assert such things to-day? It is evident that Confucius creates them himself.

The reason Confucius uses the names of the ancient kings to father his theories is told by himself, when he says to Ts'êng Tzŭ, "I humble myself in order to avoid danger, and refer to the ancient kings in order to borrow authority."[1] On the one hand, he escapes danger from the princes, and on the other, he wins the confidence of the people. Moreover, as China had a glorious history long before his time, and he was a great scholar, it was natural for him to utilize historical materials for his own purpose. But at bottom, all his writings are the fruit of his own mind and for his own religious teachings.

Some people think, however, that Confucius was "a transmitter and not an originator, believing in and loving the ancients," and quote this phrase from his own words in the *Analects*.[2] But these words simply express the characteristic modesty of the Chinese, a quality which Confucius shows in extreme form. Yet he was not always so modest, sometimes confessing that he was an originator. In the *Adjunct to the Spring and Autumn,* he said, "A sage is never born to do nothing; he must produce something in order to show the mind of God. I am 'the wooden-tongued bell', and make laws for the world." In the *Adjunct to the Canon of Filial Piety,* he said, "I am the law-making lord." Confucius was the real creator of his new religion, although incidentally transmitting some elements from the ancients.[3]

[1] *Adjunct to the Canon of Filial Piety.*

[2] *Classics,* vol. i, p. 195.

[3] *Cf. Research on the Reformation of Confucius*, published in 2449 (1898 A. D.) by Kang Yu-wei.

II. WRITINGS OF THE DISCIPLES OF CONFUCIUS

The *Five Canons* do not give all the teachings of Confucius. So if we wish to learn his teachings, besides studying his own works, we must study also the writings of his disciples. For they are very closely related to each other, and both together make up the religion of Confucianism. If we neglect the writings of his disciples and take up only his own writings, it means that we omit a great part of his teachings, and that therefore we cannot understand him so well, or do him justice.

We shall now point out the names of the writings of his disciples, calling them Records and Commentaries, in order to distinguish them from the Canons of Confucius.

1. *Records and Commentaries*

1. The *Analects*. This is a record of the monologues and conversations of Confucius and his disciples. It was written by his disciples, Chung-kung, Tzŭ-yu, Tzŭ-hsia, and others.

2. The *Canon of Filial Piety*. This may have been written by the pupils of Ts'êng Tzŭ, and it serves as the gateway to the *Five Canons*.

3. The twelve "Records" and the "Commentary of Mourning." These Records are the complements to the twelve books of the *Canon of Rites,* which were written by the pupils of Confucius. The Commentary explains the mourning system prescribed in the Canon itself, and in the Record, and was written by Tzŭ-hsia alone. Both these Records and the Commentary are now contained in the *Canon of Rites.*

4. *Elder Tai's Record of Rites*. It was compiled by Tai Tê. The number of its original books is disputed. It has thirty-nine books now.

5. *Younger Tai's Record of Rites*. . It was compiled by Tai Shêng, second cousin of Tai Tê. This has forty-nine

books now, but its original number is also disputed. It is now called the *Record of Rites* (*Li Ki*).

There was originally a compilation entitled *The Records of the Seventy Disciples and Their Followers,* which included all the books written by the disciples of Confucius, even the *Analects* and the *Canon of Filial Piety*. The number of books was two hundred and four. But the scholars of the *Canon of Rites* took many books out of it, and formed a particular encyclopaedia on the subject of rites. The Elder Tai and the Younger Tai, both great scholars of the *Rites* during the reign of Han Hsüan Ti (479-503 A. K. or 73-49 B. C.), compiled these two Records, and they are later called the *Records of Rites.*

6. The "Appendix" of the *Canon of Changes* was written by the disciples of Confucius, and is now contained in the *Canon of Changes* just after the sixty-four books of this Canon.

7. *Kung-yang's Commentary*. In order to understand the principles of the *Spring and Autumn,* nay, in order to understand the principles of Confucius at all, it is necessary to study *Kung-yang's Commentary*. Fearing the injury which the princes would do to his writings, Confucius omitted all detailed explanation in the *Spring and Autumn,* and such explanation is given by this Commentary, which records the oral teachings of Confucius. In fact, it is the keystone of Confucianism. It and the Canon are now contained in a single book.[1]

8. *Ku-liang's Commentary* is also a commentary on the *Spring and Autumn,* and a record of the oral teachings of Confucius. This Commentary is inferior to that of Kung-yang. It also is compiled with the Canon in a single book. These two Commentaries were written by the disciples of Tzŭ-hsia.

[1] The *Annotation of Kung-Yang* given by Ho Hsiu (680-733, or 129-182 A. D.) is very valuable and reliable.

9. The *Seven Adjuncts*. They were seven separate books, each of them supplementing respectively the *Six Canons* and the *Canon of Filial Piety*. The Canons are the warp, the Adjuncts the woof. Some scholars say that they were written by Confucius himself.[2] Since they appeared in the Former Han dynasty, and their interpretations agree with the Canons and the Modern Literature School, they are very valuable, because they give many oral teachings of Confucius. We are sure that they were written by his disciples, although many statements were added to them by the Confucians of the Former Han dynasty. In character, they were religious, mystical and prophetical. Unfortunately, they were prohibited by several emperors, and burned entirely by Sui Yang Ti (about 1156, or 605 A. D.). To-day, there is only a collection of their fragments.

2. *Independent Works*

There is another kind of writing, which is not the record of the words of Confucius, nor the commentary on his works. Such a kind is called *tzŭ* philosophy. It is a name given to the works either of the founders of different schools, or of the most prominent followers of any school. There are some original and independent thoughts in such writings. Among the Confucians, the most important works of this kind are those of Mencius and Hsun Tzŭ.

1. *Mêng Tzŭ* is the work of Mencius himself, and has seven books.

2. *Hsun Tzŭ* is the work of Hsun Tzŭ (218-339, or 334-213 B. C.), and has thirty-two books.

Although these two books are the independent works of the authors, they are exponents of the principles of Confucius. Therefore, they are not the exclusive products of

[1] *History of Sui*, ch. xxxii

Mencius and Hsun Tzŭ, and form a part of the religion of Confucius.

III. CONCLUSION

Passing through the Ch'in dynasty and the Former Han dynasty, to the time of Liu Hsin (died 574, or 23 A. D.), all the Confucian literature remained the same as the original works of Confucius and his disciples. Unfortunately, when the political usurper, Wang Mang, came to power (551-574, or 1 B. C.-23 A. D.), there was also a religious usurper named Liu Hsin. At that time, books were scarce. Liu Hsin in 545 (7 B. C.) succeeded his father, Liu Hsiang,[1] as the reviewer in the imperial library. Both he and his father were great scholars; but he, under such favorable conditions, made many corruptions in the whole Confucian Bible in order to satisfy his literary purpose and the political purpose of Wang Mang. In 560 (9 A. D.) he was made by Wang Mang the National Teacher. He changed the order of the *Six Canons*—the *Canon of Changes* first, the *History* second, the *Poetry* third, *etc.* Since he had no way to destroy the Bible, he changed the original text somewhat and put some spurious words, statements, chapters, and books into it. Then he wrote or compiled many books for the interpretation of his spurious Bible. He found an ingenious pretext to help him. There had been a burning of literature by the Ch'in Dynasty (339 A. K. or 213 B. C.), but the existence of the Confucian literature was not affected. Yet Liu Hsin pretended that the existing Confucian literature was not complete on account of that fire, and that his spurious books were the only

[1] Liu Hsiang (473-544, or 79 B. C. to 8 A. D.) became the reviewer in the imperial library in 526 (26 B. C.), and his son, Liu Hsin, was his assistant. He was the author of the *Park of Narratives*, the *New Narration*, the *Biography of Noteworthy Women*, *etc.* He was one of the greatest authorities in the Modern Literature.

old texts rediscovered, in the period between 397 and 423 (155-129 B. C.), which had escaped this burning. Hence, he called his spurious books the Ancient Literature.

Liu Hsin's chief works are these: 1. He compiled the *Official System of Chou* under the feigned name of the Duke of Chou, making the Duke a rival to Confucius. 2. He wrote the spurious *Tso's Commentary*, formed from the greater part of Tso-ch'iu Ming's *Narratives of Nations*, in order to interpret the *Spring and Autumn*. This was a great calamity.[1]

Opposing this spurious Ancient Literature are the true Canons interpreted by the great authorities of the Former Han dynasty. These interpretations are called the Modern Literature. Of course, it is very difficult to distinguish the true Canons from the spurious Canons, especially as many of the books of the Modern Literature have been lost.[2] But,

[1] Although the *Official System of Chou* and *Tso's Commentary* are the compilations of Liu Hsin, they give much information about the old customs, institutions and facts, because the materials of the *Official System of Chou* are drawn from the old books, and the *Narratives of Nations* is a history. Therefore, for the sake of mere facts, we cannot help making use of these two books.

[2] Chêng Hsüan (678-751, or 127-200 A. D.) was the chief figure among all the Confucians of the Han dynasty. He studied both the Modern and the Ancient Literature, but his works were based on the latter more than on the former. He was a very good man, and a very good scholar, though he mixed up the Modern and the Ancient Literature. He commented on nearly all the canonical books, taking up the interpretations from both the Modern and the Ancient Literature, but he used the text of the Ancient Literature for his annotation. Therefore, when his annotations were generally accepted, nearly all the Modern Literature was lost, but the Ancient Literature remains. From the time that Liu Hsin made the Ancient Literature, there had always been a bitter rivalry between the two schools, who had never come to any compromise. If such a condition had lasted forever, the Modern Literature would never have been lost. But, since Chêng Hsüan mixed up the two, a great confusion had been interwoven through them, and it is very difficult to distinguish them. Through his influence, the

since some still remain, and since there are many collections of the fragments of the Modern Literature, a most careful study has determined what the true Canons are. While every word cannot be made out, still the *Five Canons* are at least ninety per cent authentic.

Both these two classes of books—the Canons of Confucius, and the Records, Commentaries and the independent works of his disciples—are sources from which we have learned the principles of Confucius. In addition to these authorities, we use many interpretations suggested by the Confucians of different ages, from the Han dynasty to the present day, and information supplied by different philosophers from the Chou dynasty to the Former Han dynasty. But these need not be mentioned here. The details of distinguishing the Modern Literature from the Ancient Literature are very complex, and we have not space to discuss them here.[1] We have been very careful to base this study on the works of the School of Modern Literature, to leave out entirely spurious passages and books, and to present the principles of Confucius with all possible accuracy.

It should be noted that the influence of the writings cited above is exceedingly great. Nearly all Chinese institutions are based upon them. This appears from a consideration of the great events in Chinese history in their chronological order. The abolition of the feudal system, the abolition of

forged books of Liu Hsin were diffused and accepted. The people read him, and through him believed Liu Hsin. Therefore he was unconsciously a strong supporter of Liu Hsin, and a betrayer of Confucius. Despite this, he was a great authority, and from him we learn some of the oral teachings of Confucius. His chief works which remain are the *Annotation of the Canon of Peotry,* the *Annotation of the Canon of Rites,* the *Annotation of the Record of Rites,* and the *Annotation of the Official System of Chou.*

[1] The best book for it is the *Research on the False Bible of the School of Hsin,* published in 2442 (1891 A. D.) by Kang Yu-wei.

hereditary officials, the election system, the educational system, the adoption of the calendar of the Hsia dynasty, the three years' mourning, the distribution of the public land—all these were the products of Confucius himself. The theories of these writings are called by the Chinese "canonical principles," and they are of value not only for study, but even more in their application to practical affairs. Therefore, even a single word or a single phrase may be of great importance in the solution of problems of the day. For example, the Chinese want constitutional government, but they refer to Confucius for the support of their demand. Confucius is the chief authority, and it is the habit of the Chinese to seek from these writings sanction or guidance in the determination of important questions. It is necessary to bear these facts in mind in order to understand the significance of the quotations from these writings, no matter how short or how figurative they may be.

It should be noted also that Confucius was not primarily an economist. He was a general philosopher, interested in many things. Throughout all his writings, there is scarcely a single book treating exclusively of economic subjects. But there are many passages and chapters referring to economic life and giving economic principles. When we combine these two classes of writings, we find that economic principles are quite abundant. But the difficulty is that they are scattered through all the writings, and in such a chaotic way that they are not easily collected and arranged. Moreover, when there is an economic principle, it is generally mixed up with something else. Therefore, in bringing together the economic teachings of Confucius from these writings, we shall arrange them in the order of modern economists. That is to say, that while materials are old, the arrangement is quite new.

For the interpretation of these writings, we shall, so far

as possible, pick out the best from among the many old scholars. But, if we are not satisfied with the old interpretation, we are obliged to make a new one according to the original texts. Therefore, while the author does not pretend to any originality, he does claim to have discovered some new truths contained in the old texts.

CHAPTER IV

Historical Movements of Confucianism

Confucianism is the name of the new religion founded by Confucius. The word Confucianism in Chinese is called *Ju,* which may be applied both to the religion of Confucius and to his followers. Since Confucianism has been made the state religion, and practically every Chinese has been a Confucian, the word *Ju* is used narrowly as equivalent to scholar or litterateur,[1] but in its original sense it signifies simply those who believe the teachings of Confucius. Among the whole body of *Ju,* there are still many different classes. Confucius said to Tzŭ-hsia: "You shall be a great man of *Ju,* and shall not be a small man of *Ju.*"[2] Hsun Tzŭ[3] classifies the people as these:—the common people, the common *Ju,* the regular *Ju,* and the great *Ju.* In the time of Hsun Tzŭ, Confucianism did not yet rule the whole Chinese people, so that the heathen of Confucianism were called common people. But even within the limit of *Ju,* there were still varying degrees. For the governing of his people, Confucius sets forth the "Conducts of Ju"[4] as the Confucian creed.

Confucianism is the new religion of China, but what was

[1] James Legge says: "We must bear in mind that the literati in China do in reality occupy the place of priests and ministers in Christian kingdoms. Sovereign and people have to seek the law at their lips." *Chinese Classics,* vol. ii, p. 53.

[2] *Classics,* vol. i, p. 189.

[3] Bk. viii.

[4] *Li Ki,* bk. xxxviii, pp. 402–410.

her old religion? Her old religion was polytheism, and had no special name. According to the *Official System of Chou*[1] there were four classes of spirits—the spirits of heaven, of earth, of the dead, and of all material things—but above all there was a Supreme God. For the communication between the spirits and men, rose the priesthood, which was a body of scholars. They divided their profession into six departments:—(1) astrology, (2) the almanac, (3) the five elements (water, fire, wood, metal and earth), (4) milfoil and tortoise, (5) miscellaneous foretelling (dream-interpreting, devil-driving, prayer, *etc.*), (6) physical laws (the features of geography, of cities, of building, of human beings, of animals, of things, *etc.*). The *History of Han*[2] puts these six professions into the class of "magic", but they were really a mixture of magic and science which is unintelligible and forgotten to-day.

Under this old religion, the whole empire was ruled by superstition. Confucius was a great religious reformer who swept away the old and established the new. He did not like to talk about extraordinary things and spiritual beings.[3] "To give one's self earnestly," said he, "to the duties due to men, and, while respecting spiritual beings, to keep aloof from them, may be called wisdom."[4] In Confucianism, there is no prayer. Confucius being very sick, Tzŭ-lu, his pupil, asked leave to pray for him. The master said: "My praying has been for a long time."[5] In other words, he had no need of prayer. The *Canon of Poetry* speaks of "seeking for much happiness by yourself,"[6] which Mencius explains as meaning, "Calamity and happiness are in all

[1] Chs. xviii, xxvii.
[2] Ch. xxx.
[3] *Classics*, vol. i, p. 201.
[4] *Ibid.*, p. 191.
[5] *Ibid.*, p. 206.
[6] *Ibid.*, vol. iv, pt. ii, p. 431.

cases of man's own seeking." [1] Confucius frees all mankind from supernatural power, and lays stress on the independent cultivation of one's own personality. Any individual, who has reached the highest standard of the means and harmony, can fix the Heaven and Earth and can nourish all things.[2] In fact, such a religion not only was new to China in ancient times, but is also new in the Western World to-day, where it is only now appearing in such forms as the Ethical Culture Society, though we find its essentials also in the teachings of Aristotle and of the stoics.

Confucianism is a religion of the highest development, so we must not think Confucius unreligious. In the *Canon of Changes,* Confucius said, "The sages took the spiritual way to establish religion, and hence the world submitted to them." [3] "To combine ghost and spirit," said Confucius, "is the good form of religion. . . . The sages framed distinctly the names of ghost and spirit, to constitute a pattern for the black-haired race; and all the multitudes were filled with awe and the myriads of the people constrained to submission." [4] All this shows that Confucius recognized the usefulness of the old religion, and so did not destroy it entirely. In his writings, we still find some of the old elements. Because he knew that the world could not attain the final stage at once, he did not carry his ideal too far, and this was one reason why Confucianism was accepted as the state religion of China. From the beginning of Chinese history, the old religion had been combined with politics, and the sage rulers had been the heads of both government and church; but ever since the new religion arose, Confucius,

[1] *Classics*, vol. ii, p. 198. [2] *Ibid.*, vol. i, p. 385.

[3] *Yi King*, p. 230. The two words "spiritual way" in Chinese are pronounced *shên tao*. Hence, the Japanese call their religion Shêntaoism.

[4] *Li Ki*, bk. xxi, pp. 220–221.

coming from an ordinary family, has been "The Throneless King," and religion has been separated from politics—the great sage was not necessarily to have a crown.

We must not think, however, that Confucianism was to become a state religion without a struggle for supremacy. In the periods of Spring and Autumn (171 B. K.-71 A. K. or 722-481 B. C.) and of Warring States (149-331 A. K. or 403-221 B. C.), great philosophers with creative genius were numerous, and each fought for his own doctrines. According to the *History of Han*,[1] there were nine sects: (1) Confucianism, (2) Taoism, (3) Spiritualism (the old religion), (4) The School of Law, (5) The School of Logic, (6) Moism, (7) The School of Diplomacy, (8) The School of Generalization, (9) The School of Agriculture. The most powerful of these were Confucianism, Taoism and Moism. Yang Chu was a great disciple of Lao Tzŭ, and he made Taoism a religion of extreme egoism, while Mo Tzŭ established his own school, which was one of extreme altruism. Yang was like Epicurus, and Mo was like Jesus. During the time of Mencius, the doctrines of Yang and Mo ruled the whole empire, and endangered the existence of Confucianism.[2] A little later, however, as society would not accept the doctrine of Taoism, now made extremely egoistic by Yang Chu, the only rivals were Confucianism and Moism. At the end of the Chou dynasty and the beginning of the Han dynasty, the names of Confucius and Mo Ti had equal prominence, and a life and death struggle between the two coming religions was now going on.

Let us consider the fate of Confucianism. After the death of Confucius, his pupils scattered over the whole empire. Some became teachers and ministers in the govern-

[1] Ch. xxx.

[2] *Classics*, vol. ii, pp. 282-3.

ments of different states, some private teachers. In 145 A. K. (407 B. C.), the Marquis Wên of Wei accepted the Confucian Bible from Tzŭ-hsia. This was the first time that Confucianism was recognized as a state religion. About 231 A. K. (321 B. C.), the Marquis Wên of Têng put Confucianism into practice on the advice of Mencius.[1] During this same period, we find that five states—Lu, Ch'i, Wei, Sung, and Ch'in—had established the Board of Great Scholars, (*Po Shih*), the government professorship of Confucianism. Confucianism attained this dominance largely because of the achievements of its disciples. According to *Han Fei Tzŭ*,[2] Confucianism was at that time divided up into eight branches. But the greatest Confucians fighting against all other schools were Mencius and Hsun Tzŭ. When the First Emperor of the Ch'in dynasty consolidated the whole empire, and Li Ssŭ, pupil of Hsun Tzŭ, became the prime minister, Confucianism was made in 339 (213 B. C.) a universal religion throughout the Chinese world, although this tyrannical emperor did not give religious freedom to the people, but confined authority of interpretation to the government.[3] The life of the Ch'in dynasty, however, was short, and the influence of the different schools was still felt during the beginning of the Han dynasty. It was not until 412 (140 B. C.) that Han Wu Ti accepted the proposal of Tung Chung-shu, the greatest Confucian of the Han dynasty, to abolish all other religions and to establish Confucianism as the only one. Then all the other schools, including Moism, died out, and the supremacy of Confucianism was complete.

During the Han dynasty (346-771, or 206 B. C.-220 A. D.), the influence of Confucianism was so great that its

[1] *Classics*, vol. ii, pp. 235–247.

[2] Bk. I.

[3] *Cf. Classics*, vol. i, pp. 7–9.

Bible served not only as a religious book, but also as a legal code. The whole Confucian school in this dynasty may be styled the canonistic school. During the Latter Han dynasty (576-771, or 25-220 A. D.) especially, the moral influence produced by Confucianism was the best in Chinese history. Personal honor and personal liberty were the first considerations; and, during the decay of this dynasty, the students fighting against the bad government sacrificed even their lives. The moral standard of society as a whole was very high. In fact, the Han dynasty, although not following the best principles of Confucius, proved the applicability of Confucianism to practical as well as theoretical problems.

After the Han dynasty, Confucianism fell into a period of decline. Tsao Tsao, the founder of the Wei dynasty, in 761 (210 A. D.) openly decreed official employment of bad men, and destroyed the moral influence that Confucianism had exerted. During the Wei and the Tsin dynasties (771-867, or 220-316 A. D.), Taoism was powerful; and during the Southern and the Northern dynasties, and the Sui and the Tang dynasties (868-1458, or 317-907 A. D.), Buddhism prevailed. Confucianism, although remaining nominally the state religion, had lost its supremacy. Nevertheless, the governments, especially those of the Northern Wei, the Northern Chou and the Tang dynasties, did apply some Confucian principles to political and economic problems, so that the people still enjoyed some of its benefits. There was only one scholar, Han Yü (1319-1375, or 768-824 A. D.), who fought for Confucianism, and against Taoism and Buddhism. Han Yü, not a deep philosopher, but the greatest writer since the Han dynasty, gave a death-blow to Taoism and Buddhism by attacking them from the economic standpoint. But the popular study of this period was literature in the narrow sense, and the Confucian philosophy was the study of but few. Then came the age of the Five Dynasties (1458-1511, or 907-960 A. D.) which, for Confucianism, was worst of all.

But such a decline had to come to an end, and during the Sung dynasty there were many great Confucians. The greatest of these was Chu Hsi (1681-1751, or 1130-1200 A. D.), who was the Martin Luther of Confucianism and whose influence is still strong at the present time. He, however, was a one-sided reformer who emphasized the ethical teachings of Confucius, and omitted his religious views; laid stress on individual character and neglected social welfare. In this dynasty, there was a great statesman named Wang An-shih (1572-1637, or 1021-1086 A. D.), who tried to change the whole of society by economic reforms. There was also a school called Yungchia (about 1714-1775, or 1163-1224 A. D.), that advocated material welfare as well as moral cultivation. But both failed to overcome the general influence of public opinion, and the scholars usually paid much attention to philosophical controversies and forgot practical problems. Passing through the Yüan and the Ming dynasties, the learning was not different from that of the Sung dynasty, although in the Ming dynasty there was Wang Shou-jen (2023-2079, or 1472-1528 A. D.) who was rival to Chu Hsi. For this period (1511-2194, or 960-1643 A. D.) the whole Confucian school may be styled the philosophical school.

In the present dynasty, beginning in 2195 (1644 A. D.), Confucianism has been in the period of renaissance. There were three great Confucians at the beginning of this dynasty: Ku Yen-wu (2163-2232, or 1612-1681 A. D.), Huang Tsung-hsi (2160-2246, or 1609-1695 A. D.), and Wang Fu-chih (2178-2230, or 1627-1679 A. D.). They did not belong to any particular school, but were great in many lines. Then came the school of the canonists. First (about 2287-2371, or 1736-1820 A. D.), they turned from the learning of all the mediæval and modern dynasties to the school of Ancient Literature of the Latter Han dynasty. Second (about 2372-2425, or 1821-1874 A. D.), they went back to the school of Modern Literature of the Former Han dynasty, and new thoughts sprang up. Kung Tsi-chin (born in 2343, or 1792 A. D.) and Wei Yüan (died in 2407, or 1856 A. D.) were the representatives of this movement. In the present day, the greatest exponent of Confucius is Kang Yu-wei, the personal advisor of Tê Tsung in the political reforms of 2449 (1898 A. D.).

We may roughly sum up the historical movements of Confucianism under six heads: (1) the school of the doctrine of Great Similarity, emphasizing liberty, handed down from Tzŭ-yu, Tzŭ-ssŭ to Mencius; (2) the school of the doctrine of Small Tranquillity, emphasizing government, handed down from Chung-kung to Hsun Tzŭ. Li Ssŭ applied it to the government of the Ch'in dynasty (331, or 221 B. C.), and it has lasted to the present day; (3) the theological school, drawn from the whole Bible, and especially from the "Great Model" of the *Canon of History,* the *Canon of Changes,* and the *Spring and Autumn.* Tung Chung-shu and Liu Hsiang were conspicuous representatives, but this school was practically ended after the Han dynasty; (4) the ethical school, the chief element of Confucianism, and highly developed in the Sung and the Ming dynasties; (5) the historical school, based on the *Canon of History* and the *Spring and Autumn.* Ssŭ-ma Chien and other great historians were the representatives; (6) the school of literary research and scientific study, set forth by Confucius, and popularly, but narrowly, applied in the present dynasty.

So far as we can see, we have not yet come to the best principles of Confucius. There have been many causes for this, but the influence of the government on religion has been the most important one. With a few exceptions, the mind of the great mass of students has been controlled by the direction of the government and this has greatly hampered the natural development of Confucianism. As soon as the Chinese shall have established a constitutional government, and secured perfect freedom of thought, Confucianism must enter on a new life. Then we may hope to have the stage of Great Similarity for the whole world.

BOOK II RELATION OF ECONOMICS TO OTHER SCIENCES

CHAPTER V

Economics and Other Sciences in General

I. DEFINITION OF ECONOMICS

The equivalent of the English term "economics" in Chinese is "administering wealth." Such a term explains itself, and calls for no definition. Let us, however, trace the origin of the term. It occurs first in the "Appendix" of the *Canon of Changes* as follows: "That which enables men to live collectively, is wealth. Administering wealth, formulating rules, and prohibiting the people from doing wrong—this is called justice."[1] Since the "Appendix" was written, the Chinese have usually used the term "administering wealth" for the art of political economy, and also for the science of economics. But the modern Japanese has adopted another Chinese term, *ching chi,* for the word economics; and Herbert A. Giles has put this term, *ching chi,* in his *Chinese-English Dictionary* for "political economy". The term *ching chi,* however, has a very broad meaning, and is not a good equivalent for the word economics. It generally means statesmanship, and covers the whole field of governmental action. It thus belongs to politics rather than to economics. It will be well, there-

[1] *Yi King*, p. 381.

fore, to keep the old term " administering wealth " as the equivalent of economics, since it is much more accurate and comprehensive than the term *ching chi.*

As we have taken the scientific term from the Confucian text, let us also adopt its definition. The term " administering wealth " covers the whole field of economics. " Formulating rules " and " prohibiting the people from doing wrong " refer respectively to the ethical and political life. All three of these aspects of life should be directed by the principle of justice, and their relations will be stated later. But we must remember that the object of " administering wealth " is man. Our reason for administering wealth is simply that men are living collectively and need wealth to support them. Man is our end, and wealth our means. From this we get as a definition: Economics is the science administering wealth according to the principle of justice, for the sake of men who live collectively.

II. GENERAL RELATION TO OTHER SCIENCES

From the above-quoted passage from the " Appendix " of the *Canon of Changes,* we can understand not only the meaning of economics, but also its relation to other sciences. Since the chief object of " administering wealth " is man, and man living collectively, when we administer wealth, we must deal with the whole body of men. Thus economics is very close to sociology. All the social sciences relate to man, so they all are also connected with economics. But there are two groups, most closely related to economics, that is, the moral and the political sciences. We cannot administer wealth in society without " formulating rules " as to what is right and what is wrong. The way to " formulate rules " is through moral teachings, and under this heading come the sciences of language, education, ethics and religion. We cannot administer wealth in a society without "prohibiting the people from doing wrong". This we must do by political organizations, and in this group come the sciences of politics and law. All of these sciences —economics, ethics, and politics—are part of the science of justice, and they form a single group. But of them all, economics comes first, and is the most important. If we cannot maintain our economic life, we do not care to formulate our rules, and moral science is useless; we do not fear the prohibition of wrongdoing, and political science is without force. If there is to be any ethics or politics, there must be economic life before them. The "Appendix," therefore, tells us not only the close connection of economics with other sciences, but also the relatively higher importance of economics.

In the "Great Model" contained in the *Canon of History*, there are eight objects of government: "The first is called food; the second, commodities; the third, sacrifices; the fourth, the minister of works; the fifth, the minister of education; the sixth, the minister of justice; the seventh, the entertainment of guests; and the eighth, the army." [1]

These eight objects of government are simply the eight objects of human activities. We can understand their relation to each other from their order. First of all, food is most important, to satisfy hunger; and this word indicates agricultural life. The word commodities includes all other economic goods, among which money holds a prominent place, and indicates commercial and industrial life. These two words, "food and commodities", represent the whole economic life, and they stand first before any other human activities. After the material wants are satisfied, religious worship begins. Then comes in the minister of works, to improve the physical environment; the minister of education,

[1] *Classics*, vol. iii, pt. ii, p. 327.

to develop the intellectual and moral power; and the minister of justice, to enforce the law. Now, the life of polite society is developed, and this is called the entertainment of guests. Finally, the army is maintained to keep the whole society in peace.

If we compare the eight objects of the "Great Model" with the seven sciences that Roscher groups together—language, religion, art, science, law, the state and economy—we may say that art and science are included in the functions of the minister of works and the minister of education, that language is implied in education, and that the state is represented by all eight objects. If we compare them with the eight groups of Prof. R. T. Ely—language, art, education, religion, family life, society life, political life, economic life—we may say that the family life is a concern of the minister of education. It is remarkable that the statement of the Confucian Bible is so similar to that of the modern economists.

It should be noted that all the great historians, except Ssŭ-ma Chien, have entitled all the economic histories of different dynasties "Record of Food and Commodities". This shows what great influence Confucianism exercises upon the economic thought of the Chinese.

From the "Great Model," we have seen the relation of economics to other sciences in general; and from the "Appendix", we have seen the relation of economics to sociology, politics and ethics in particular. Now, we shall study the relation of economics to these three sciences separately.

CHAPTER VI

Economics and Sociology

I. ECONOMICS AS THE BASIS OF SOCIOLOGY

SINCE economics is the science which administers wealth within human society, we shall consider first the relation between economics and sociology. In order to understand this relation, we must first raise the question, How does society come to exist? For the answer to this question, the "Appendix" has given the statement quoted above, "That which enables men to live collectively, is wealth." Therefore, sociology is dependent upon economics. If there were no wealth, men could not live collectively, and there would be no society. Before many men can live collectively, man must live individually. The individual man cannot live without wealth, but can live without society, because he can get wealth from nature instead of men. Therefore, economics precedes sociology.

For the explanation of the fundamental cause of the formation of co-operative groups, Hsun Tzŭ gives a good sociological theory, and it answers the question as to why society comes to exist. He says:

> The water and fire have breath, but without life. The herb and wood have life, but without knowledge. The bird and beast have knowledge, but without justice. Man has breath, life, knowledge, and also justice; hence he is the noblest being in the world. His strength is not equal to that of the bull, and his running is not equal to that of the horse; yet the bull and horse are subjected to him. Why? It is because man

is able to be social and they are not. How is man able to be social? It is by the principle of individual right. How can the individual right be realized? By justice. Therefore, justice and individual right make men harmonious. Since men are harmonious, they form one unity. Since they form one unity, they increase their strength. Increasing their strength, they become strong. Since they are strong, they conquer the natural things. Hence, the house can be secured for their safety. Hence, they arrange the four seasons, master all things, and benefit the world universally. It is for no other cause than that man possesses right and justice. Therefore, when man is born, he cannot get along without society. But if society did not distribute the individual right justly, men would quarrel. If they were to quarrel, society would be disorderly. If society were disorderly, men would be disunited. If men were disunited, they would be weak. If they were weak, they could not conquer natural things. Hence, the house could not be secured for their safety. All of which means that rites and justice cannot be left out for a moment.[1]

According to the theory of Hsun Tzŭ, society is based on legal rights, and legal rights are based on ethical justice. But the reason men form a society is simply because they want to unite in order to conquer the natural things through their collective activities. Therefore, the struggle between men and animals is the chief cause for the formation of society. Having society, they are strong enough to conquer these things, otherwise they cannot; and so men survive through being social—a foreshadowing of the principle of "natural selection" in explaining the development of sociality. Indeed, in men's economic needs is found the primary cause of the formation of society.

Pan Ku (583-643 A. K. or 32-92 A. D.) says:

Imitating the manner of heaven and earth, embracing the

[1] Bk. ix.

nature of the five moral constants, man, who is wise, subtile and pure, is the most intelligent being of all the species. His finger nails and his teeth cannot supply his wants. His running cannot escape dangers. He himself has no fur nor feather against heat and cold. He must enslave natural things in order to provide for his nourishment. Trusting to intellectual power and not to physical strength, he is the noble being. Therefore, if men did not love each other, they could not be social. If they were not social, they could not conquer natural things. If they could not conquer natural things, their nourishment would be insufficient. When they gather together, but their nourishment is insufficient, the warring spirit arises. The great sage first superexcellently practises the virtues of respect, deference, and universal love, so that the mass of people love and follow him. If the people follow him and form a society, he is the ruler. If the people come and go to him, he is the king.[1]

According to the theory of Pan Ku, society is based on love. But why should men love each other and form a society? This is simply because men have to conquer nature for their nourishment. Here, Pan Ku gives the same reason for the formation of society as that which is given by Hsun Tzŭ, namely, economic utility. But Hsun Tzŭ mentions the house because he emphasizes the struggle for safety, while Pan Ku mentions nourishment, because he emphasizes the struggle for subsistence. Yet their fundamental point is the same.

The social constitution is established not always according to the idea of the sages, but mostly through the historical development of actual conditions. And this actual condition is based on economic causes, namely, the struggle

[1] *History of Han*, ch. xxiii. The word "society" and the word "ruler" in the Chinese language are both pronounced *chün*, and the words "go" and "king," *wang*. In the Chinese characters, the words in each pair have also marked similarity in form.

for existence. In his " Essay on Feudalism ", Liu Chung-yüan (1324-1370 A. K. or 773-819 A. D.) says:

In the beginning man is born at the same time with other things. The vegetable kingdom is wild, and the animal kingdom is cruel. Man cannot fight with his hand and eat with his mouth, as can the beast. He also has no feathers, as has the bird. He is unable to be self-supporting and self-protecting. Hsun Tzŭ has said that he must borrow some material things from outside for his use. Generally, if he borrows some material things from outside, struggle or war must arise. If the war is ceaseless, he must come to one who can decide the dispute, and must obey his dictate. Those who are the wise men must have a great number of subjects. When the wise men tell them what is right and they do not correct themselves, punishment must be used to increase their fear. In this way, the ruler, the leader, laws and politics arise. Therefore, the men of the neighborhood organize themselves into a society. But, when the society is formed, the division is sharper, and the war must be greater. When the war is greater, military force and personal virtue are more important. If there are those who possess the greater virtue, the leaders of various societies will come to them and obey their dictate, in order to keep their members peaceful. Hence, the class of feudal lords exists; but the war is still greater. If there are those who possess still greater virtue, the feudal lords will come to them and obey their dictate, in order to keep their territory peaceful. Hence, some sort of leading princes exist; but the war is still greater. If there is a man whose virtue is greatest of all, the leading princes will come to him and obey his dictate, in order to keep all the people peaceful. Then the whole world is united into one. Therefore, there must be first the masters of towns, then the magistrates of districts. Having the magistrates, then come the feudal lords. Having the feudal lords, then come the leading princes. Having leading princes, then arises the emperor. From the emperor to the town-master, if their virtue has impressed the mind of the people, the people certainly support their posterity, after their death, in holding their office through hereditary right. Therefore, feudalism is not the idea of the sages, but only the necessity of the condition.

According to Hsun Tzŭ, society is based on justice; according to Pan Ku, on love; and according to Liu Chung-yüan, on necessity. These three theories—legal, ethical and historical—are correct, although they are from different points of view. But why does society come to exist? On this point, they give the same answer. Man is physically weaker than other animals. If he wants to conquer other things, or enslave them, or borrow them from outside, he must make himself stronger. If he wants to make himself stronger, he must co-operate with his fellows. If he cooperates with his fellows, such a society must be based on justice, love and necessity to avoid war and keep peace. Therefore, society is the result, but economic life is the cause. Had the human being had no economic needs, society would not exist. Why do men regard social justice and observe individual right? Why do men love each other and restrain the warring spirit? Why do men make war against each other before society is formed, and why is the war still greater when that society is larger? Why do the warlike animals subdue their passions and come to the arbitrator, obey the law of the ruler and keep peace among themselves? It is simply for their own interest. But their own interest is nothing greater than the economic interest In a word, society is an organization carrying on the struggle for existence in collective form. Ethics and law, religion and politics, love and hatred, peace and war, justice and injustice, all of them are the results of economic causes. Indeed, economic interest is the basis of everything. According to Liu Chung-yüan, war continues among the diferent sizes of societies, and it ceases only in the unification of the whole world. It is the doctrine of "great uniformity" of Confucius. But, in the past, the world from the Chinese point of view was fictitious; in the present, the world is the real one. By the application of "great uniformity" to the real world, the whole world will be equalized into a single economic unit, and industrialism instead of militarism will dominate the globe. In short, world economy is the solution of the problems of world sociology, and it is the step to the stage of Great Similarity.

II. ECONOMICS AS THE BASIS OF RELIGION

As religion is a great force in social life, we may ask how it comes to exist. The answer to this question is given by Confucius, who says:

> The first development of religion began with food and drink. Primitive people roasted millet and pieces of pork on heated stones; they excavated the ground in the form of a jar, and scooped the wine from it with their two hands; they fashioned a handle of clay, and struck with it an earthen drum. Simple as this economic life was, they yet seemed to be able to express by these things their reverence for spiritual beings.[1]

That is, food and drink follow heaven and earth, and worship follows food and drink. This means that immediately after the creation of heaven and earth, as soon as there is a man, there must be economic life; and that the religious life comes next. The "Great Model," therefore, puts "sacrifices" next only to "food and commodities". Indeed, economic satisfaction is the condition necessary for the development of religion.

[1] *Li Ki*, bk. vii, p. 368.

III. ORIGIN OF MAN

Since economics and sociology are interdependent, we should study the sociological teachings of Confucius in order the better to understand his economic teachings. Among all his sociological teachings, there is nothing more important than the doctrines of the fatherhood of God and the brotherhood of man. With these doctrines as a basis, there arise the principle of universal love, the principle of universal equality, and the principle of individual independence. We may designate these doctrines by a phrase—the origin of man. One cannot understand the foundations of society until he knows the origin of man, but he cannot think of the origin of man until he satisfies his economic wants.

We have already said that the word *Yüan* is similar to the word God and that they are different only from different points of view. However, we shall discuss them more fully, and take up the doctrine of *Yüan* first. The word *Yüan* is the first word of the *Spring and Autumn,* and it is the chief principle of Confucius' philosophy. Ordinarily, one says the first year of the reign of so and so, but Confucius says, "*yüan* year" instead of the first year. Ho Hsiu comments: "*Yüan* is the infinite breath, from which the immaterial things arise and the material things are separated. It creates heaven and earth, and it is the beginning of heaven and earth." This is the theory of creation in Confucianism. The *Many Dewdrops of the Spring and Autumn* [1] says: "Only the holy man can relate the myriad of things to one and subject them to the *Yüan*. . . . *Yüan* means the origin. . . . *Yüan* is the root of everything, upon which the origin of man depends. Where is the origin of man? It precedes heaven and earth." The

[1] Written by Tung Chung-shu, bk. xiii.

Canon of Changes says: "How great the masculine *Yüan* is! All things owe to it their beginning. It governs the heavens."[1]

Yüan is the ruling power governing the whole universe. It is interpreted most clearly by Ho Hsiu, who says, "*Yüan* is the infinite breath." In fact, it is the natural and originating force of everything. In the "Evolution of Civilization," it is called Grand Unity.[2] In the "Appendix," it is called Grand Summit.[3] But the name of Grand Unity can be changed into the word Heaven in the "Evolution of Civilization," and the word Heaven is identified with the word God in many places. Therefore, the word *Yüan* is identified with the word God. The reason Confucius prefers the word *Yüan* to the word God is because *Yüan* is infinite, while God is personal. Indeed, Confucius writes from the philosophical rather than from the religious point of view.

Since *Yüan* is the origin of everything, the origin of man must be derived from it. But it is not only the origin of man, but also the origin of the heavens. Therefore, man may originally have come from *Yüan* either at the same time with the heavens, or afterward, or even before them. This doctrine is the highest theological stage. It makes every man free from supernatural power, and dependent upon his own conscience. According to this doctrine, we may call *Yüan* our father, instead of God; and we may call not only all men our brothers, but even all the heavens. Wearing the heavens, and standing upon the earth, how noble is man! All that man can do and all that he ought to do are merely the duties of man, and nothing else. The object of man is simply to be a man. Man is not only the son of God, but also his assistant and his co-ordinate.

[1] *Yi King*, p. 213.

[2] *Li Ki*, bk. vii, p. 386.

[3] *Yi King*, p. 313.

We now come to the doctrine of the fatherhood of God proper, stated very clearly in *Ku-liang's Commentary,* which says:

The female alone cannot give birth; the male alone cannot give birth; and God alone cannot give birth. The three must unite together, then there is a birth. Therefore, we may call anyone either the son of his mother, or the son of God. But, according to his social position, the honorable person takes the honorable designation, while the common people take the common one. That some one is called king is simply because the people come to him.[1]

This is the doctrine of the trinity in the Confucian religion; it means that the union of father, mother, and God, gives birth to everyone. The *Many Dewdrops of the Spring and Autumn* says: "There never has been a birth without the influence of God. God is the father of everything."[2]

The doctrine of the brotherhood of man has already been included in the doctrine of the fatherhood of God. But we may quote two passages showing this doctrine separately. Confucius says: "All within the four seas are brothers."[3] Again he says: "A holy man is able to make the whole world as one family, and the Middle Kingdom as one person."[4] Therefore, from Confucius' point of view, the whole world is but a single family, and all the men are brothers of this same family.

The best explanation for the principle of universal love is given by Chang Tsai, a great Confucian in the Sung dynasty (1571-1628, or 1020-1077 A. D.). He says:

The virtue of Heaven is called our Father, and the virtue of Earth is called our Mother. Although we are small beings, we

[1] 3rd year of Duke Chuang. [2] Bk. lxx.

[3] Quoted by Tzŭ-hsia, *Classics,* vol. i, p. 253.

[4] *Li Ki,* bk. vii, p. 379.

are their mixture and stand firmly in the middle. Therefore, the full breath of Heaven and Earth is our body, and the strong spirit of Heaven and Earth is our mind. All people are our brothers, and all things are our companions. The great ruler is the heir of our Parents, and the great minister is his steward. To respect the seniors of the world is to honor our older brothers, and to pity the weak is to help our younger brothers. The holy men are those who possess virtue equal to that of our Parents, and the wise men are the leaders of ourselves. All the unfortunate persons of the world, through physical weariness, old age, severe sickness, the brotherless, childless, widowers and widows, are calamitous and helpless brothers of our own.[1]

As to the principle of universal equality, we may look at it from two aspects. First, from the religious aspect, not only the founder of a religion is the son of God, but everyone is the son of God. On this point, Confucianism is more democratic than Christianity, because the Confucians never say that Confucius is the "only begotten son" of God. Mencius says: "The holy man and we are the same in kind."[2] The Confucian religion gives full freedom of thought to everybody,[3] and promotes everybody to the highest position, equal to God. The Confucian church has never had such a head as the pope, and the Chinese emperor is not the head of the church. Throughout the whole of Chinese history, no blood has ever been shed on account of religious controversy. In a word, China enjoys complete religious freedom.

Second, from the political aspect, not only is the emperor the son of God, but every one is the son of God. In Confucianism, there is no such thing as the "divine right" theory. Five hundred and seventy-one years be-

[1] *Correction of the Youth*, ch. xvii.

[2] *Classics*, vol. ii, p. 405.

[3] *Yi King*, p. 389.

fore Confucius, Chou Wu Wang cut off the head of the Emperor Chou, and put it on the top of a flag. Confucius said that the revolution of Wu Wang was in accordance with the will of God.[1] Mencius also said that the act of Wu Wang was not that of a regicide, but simply the execution of an outcast.[2] From 343 to 350 A. K. (209-202 B. C.) China had as great a revolution as had France in 2341 A. K. (1790 A. D.). By this great revolution, the common people began to rule the empire. Hence, China has been at the stage of democracy since this revolution, although in many respects she did not change the monarchical form. The *General Discussion in the White Tiger Palace*[3] says: "The nomination, 'The Son of God,' [emperor], is merely an honorable title." Indeed, China has been the most democratic country of the world, with the exception of the really constitutional states at the present time.

The best illustration of the principle of individual independence is given in the *General Discussion in the White Tiger Palace*. It says:

> Why should a father be executed for killing his son? "Among all the lives given by Heaven and Earth, that of man is the noblest." All men are the children of God, and are merely born through the breath of father and mother. The emperor should nourish and teach them. Hence the father has no absolute power over his son.[4]

This is a very important principle of Confucius. Unless we understand it, we might make the mistake of thinking that in accordance with the teachings of Confucius a father has the power of life and death over his son, and the son has no independence. But this is not the case. In a family,

[1] *Yi King*, p. 254. [2] *Classics*, vol. ii, p. 167.
[3] Written by Pan Ku in 630 (79 A. D.), bk. i. [4] Bk. v.

one is the son of his father; in a state, he is the citizen of the emperor; in the universe, he is the son of God. Therefore, according to the *Canon of History,* the punishment for the unkind father is equal to that for the undutiful son, and no member of the family is responsible for the crime of any other member.[1]

This is personal liberty. But we should consider also personal responsibility. Confucius puts great emphasis on the cultivation of personality. The "Great Learning" says: "From the emperor down to the mass of the people, all must consider the cultivation of personality the root of everything besides."[2] Ts'êng Tzŭ says: "One cannot be a student without breadth of mind and vigorous endurance. His responsibility is heavy and his way is long. He assumes universal love as his own responsibility;—is it not heavy? Only with death does his way come to an end;—is it not long?"[3] This is the type of student from the Confucian standpoint. After Mencius, Lu Chiu-yüan (1691-1743 A. K. or 1140-1192 A. D.) and Wang Shou-jen distinguished their school on the basis of personal liberty and personal responsibility. The teachings of Lu Chiu-yüan are as follows: "Even if I do not know a single word, I must try my best to become a man gloriously." "While above is heaven and below is earth, man lives in the middle. Unless he is able to become a man, his life is of no use." Indeed, the Confucians put a great deal of emphasis on personal responsibility, since man is the son of God and is independent.

IV. POSITION OF WOMAN

Next to the origin of man, the most important question is the position of woman. Since man and woman are the

[1] *Cf. Classics,* vol. iii, pt. ii, pp. 392-3.

[2] *Classics,* vol. i, p. 395. [3] *Ibid.,* pp. 210-211.

two component parts of society, her position is very important, not only for the social life, but also for the economic life. Therefore, we shall study her position from the point of view of Confucius.

First, according to the teachings of Confucius, the position of woman is equal to that of man. From the emperor to the common people, the wife of each is his equal. Therefore, the word wife means equal. And the *Canon of Changes* even says that with the repression of the one for the satisfaction of the other, man is placed below woman in relative position.[1] Hence, the relation of husband and wife is called "brothers" by Confucius.[2] And the *Canon of Poetry* also says: "Love your bride as your brothers."[3]

For the equality of man and woman, Confucius prescribes the rite of "personal receiving" as a necessary ceremony for marriage, that is, the bridegroom must go to the bride's home to receive her personally. This rite is necessary for all classes, not excepting even the emperor. In the *Canon of Poetry* and the *Spring and Autumn*, there are many condemnations of those who do not observe this rite. Confucius was asked by Duke Ai of Lu if to wear a crown for the exercise of "personal receiving" would be too ceremonious. Confucius answered him by saying that an emperor must pay respect to his wife.[4] Indeed, the rite of "personal receiving" is to indicate the principle of respect for woman. Mo Tzŭ attacked Confucius on this point by saying that one is as respectful and humble as a servant to his wife; that the ceremony of taking her to the carriage is like the service due to one's parents; and that all the

[1] *Yi King*, p. 238.

[2] *Cf. Li Ki*, bk. v, p. 320. But it is incorrectly translated.

Classics, vol. iv, pt. i, p. 54.

[4] *Li Ki*, bk. xxiv, pp. 264–6.

ceremonies of marriage are as solemn as those of sacrifices.[1] From the argument of Mo Tzŭ, we know clearly that Confucius raised the position of woman very high.

Another example illustrating the equality of man and woman is that the married woman preserves her own name after marriage. We shall see that Confucius regards the name of anyone as very important as it identifies the personailty and is dearer even than life.[2] If anyone cannot have his own name, it means that he loses his personality and cannot leave any mark upon the world. This is the worst of calamities. Europeans and Americans are proud of the high position of their women, but the married woman must give up her own name, and adopt the name of her husband, being known as Mrs. So-and-so. This means that she cannot keep her individuality and is merely a dependant of her husband; whereas, among the Chinese, the married woman has her individual name. In the *Spring and Autumn,* Confucius always gives the name of the women themselves, such as Po-chi, Shu-chi, Chi-chi, Chung-tzŭ, Ch'êng-fêng, *etc.* It shows that woman does not lose her individuality after marriage, and that she is equal to man.

Second, we shall consider the separation of the two sexes. This was an old custom, and was recognized by Confucius. The "Details of Rites" says:

Man and woman should not sit together in the same apartment, . . . nor let their hands touch in giving and receiving. A sister-in-law and brother-in-law do not interchange compliments about each other. . . . When a young lady has been engaged, . . . no man should enter the door of her apartment, unless there be some grave occasion [such as great sickness, or death, or other great calamity]. When a married aunt, or sister, or daughter, returns home on a visit, no brother of the

[1] Bk. xix. [2] See *infra*.

family should sit with her on the same mat or eat with her from the same dish. Even father and daughter should not occupy the same mat. Man and woman, without the intervention of the matchmaker, do not know each other's name. Unless the engagement has been accepted, there should be no communication or affection between them.[1]

Since human nature is universally the same, the social life of the Far East cannot differ very much from that of the West. Therefore, the separation of the two sexes was not the original plan in China. In the *Canon of Poetry,* there are many poems describing a social life quite like that of the West to-day. We may select two stanzas from two poems for examples. The one reads this way:

> The Tsin and the Wei,
> Now present their broad sheets of water.
> Ladies and gentlemen
> Are carrying flowers of valerian.
> A lady says, "Shall we go to see?"
> A gentleman replies, "I have already been."
> "But let us go again to see.
> Beyond the Wei
> The ground is large and fit for pleasure."
> So the gentlemen and ladies
> Make sport together,
> Presenting one another with small peonies.[2]

The other reads as follows:

> [The girl] goes out on a fine morning;
> Then [the boy and girl] proceed together.
> "I look on you as the flower of the thorny mallows;
> You give me a stalk of the pepper plant!"[3]

[1] *Li Ki*, bk. i, pp. 77–8.

[2] *Classics*, vol. iv, pt. i, p. 148.

[3] *Ibid.*, p. 207.

From what has been described by the two stanzas, the reader may not find any difference in the social life of the West and China; and he may not see any wrong in such a gathering of the two sexes. But Confucius puts them in the *Canon of Poetry* as bad examples of a lewd custom. The separation of the sexes was indeed generally approved by the ancient Chinese, but such a theory was strengthened very much by Confucius.

The separation of the sexes was developed on historical facts. Formerly, when the princes called on each other, the princess came out with her husband for the "great entertainment" of the guests. But, the Marquis of Yang, on such an occasion, killed the Marquis of Mu, and stole away his wife. This is something like the story of the Trojan War, when Paris visited the Spartan king, Menelaus, and took away secretly his wife, Helen. According to Confucius, the abolition of the practice of making a princess part of the "great entertainment" was due to the Marquis of Yang.[1] From this instance, we can see that the sexes were not formerly separated so severely as in later times. But such a custom was gradually developed in many cases, even long before the age of Confucius.

The simple reason for the separation of the sexes is for the preventing of illicit intercourse. Confucius says:

> The ceremonial usages prevent the people from excesses; they display the separation which should be maintained between the sexes; and they make the people free from suspicion, in order to define the relations of the people. Therefore, man and woman do not make friendship when there is no go-between, and they do not meet together when there is no ceremonial present;—these are for the distinction between the two sexes.[2]

[1] *Li Ki*, bk. xxvii, p. 298.

[2] *Ibid.*, p. 297. But its translation has left out a few sentences.

Although the separation of the two sexes has raised the standard of morality, it has retarded economic development. Montesquieu says:

> The society of the fair sex spoils the manners and forms the taste; the desire of giving greater pleasure than others establishes the embellishments of dress; and the desire of pleasing others more than ourselves gives rise to fashions. This fashion is a subject of importance; by encouraging a trifling turn of mind, it continually increases the branches of its commerce.[1]

From this statement of Montesquieu, we may understand why the economic condition of China has been stationary for so long a time. The chief reason for it is that the Chinese woman has been separated from the man, so that social life is dry and commercial development slow. Setting aside the question of right and wrong, woman is, indeed, the spice of society, and the promoter of economic progress. But the ancient Chinese, although they might have realized the economic advantage of letting woman share society with man, were afraid of the moral disadvantage, her possible loss of chastity.

We must understand, however, that the separation of the sexes does not mean that woman is not the equal of man. Of course, in a paternal society, woman inevitably suffers many disadvantages. But, as far as the separation is concerned, woman is equal to man. Though women cannot join the social gatherings of men, and so lose a great amount of social pleasure, on the other hand, men cannot share the social gatherings of women, and they, too, suffer the loss of such social pleasure. On this point, man never can have more privileges than woman,

[1] *Spirit of Laws*, vol. i, p. 318. Bohn's Library, George Bell & Sons, 1906.

although he belongs to the more fortunate sex and may enjoy some things which woman cannot have. Thus, the fundamental principle of equality is not altered by the separation.

Third, we shall see that Confucius has sanctioned the social intercourse of man and woman. According to his *tsing tien* system, during the winter, from the tenth month to the first, men and women should work together at weaving in the same street from evening to midnight. This is an extremely unusual example of the commingling of the sexes and the promotion of social intercourse. Moreover, during these four months, whenever men and women have any dissatisfaction, the two sexes may sing together to express their discontent.[1] This affords great freedom of social contact of the two sexes.

Again, according to the principles of *Spring and Autumn,* the queen and princess must have teachers and nurses. The teachers, who are selected from the old great officials, look after their conduct. The nurses, who are selected from the wives of the great officials, look after their physical welfare.[2] This principle is quite significant. As soon as the old great officials can be selected as the teachers of the queen and princess, the separation of men and women is destroyed. Therefore, separation is not the ideal of Confucius, but only a necessary custom for the time being.

Fourth, the political rights of woman are given to her by Confucius, and these rights are indicated in the instance of holding office. This principle is one of the most valuable things mentioned in the *Spring and Autumn.* Under the *tsing tien* system of Confucius, if the women have no children at the age of fifty, they are to be given clothes and food by the government; and they are to be appointed

[1] The *Annotation of Kung-yang,* 15th year of Duke Hsüan.

[2] 30th year of Duke Hsiang.

commissioners for the collection of poetry from the people.[1] This shows that Confucius thinks that women are qualified to hold government office. Since the commission of collecting poetry is equal to the imperial commission of to-day, it is quite different from inferior service. Moreover, it implies that the education of women should be very high, otherwise they could not take the office and could not understand poetry. This principle will have great importance in the future.

Fifth, we may learn that the absolute independence of woman is the final stage of the doctrine of Confucius. We have already seen that in the Great Similarity there is no marriage, but we shall discuss this more fully here. The stage of Small Tranquillity accepts all the present institutions, but that of Great Similarity does not. The fundamental difference between these two stages is the independence of woman, and it forms the basis for the changes from Small Tranquillity to Great Similarity. Therefore, in the Small Tranquillity, Confucius mentions all the family relations, such as father and son, brothers, husband and wife. But, in the Great Similarity, he does not mention them at all, and says that " men do not regard as their parents only their own parents, nor treat as their children only their own children." Here Confucius does not use the words husband and wife, but uses the words man and woman. " Each man has his rights, and each woman her individuality safeguarded," are the two fundamental bases of Great Similarity. But how can this be? It is simply that they have to abolish the institution of marriage.

What Confucius means by " each woman has her individuality safeguarded " is that she is not the wife of any man. She has her individual personality, and in all things

[1] 15th year of Duke Hsüan.

depends upon herself. She does not lose any individuality on account of sexual relations to man. When she loves a man, it is simply like the act of shaking hands or dancing with a man, and she does not become the property of man. Kang Yu-wei, in the fifth book of his *Book on the Great Similarity*,[1] has given a very good explanation of this principle. His theory is something like this. The institution of marriage is changed to a legal agreement of love, and the names of husband and wife are abolished. Such an agreement must be limited to a certain length of time. When it expires, the contracting parties may either dissolve immediately, or renew it successively until the end of their life, or dissolve first and renew it again in later times. In fact, there is perfect freedom for them to do what they want in accordance with their true love. The time limit of an agreement is not longer than one year, nor shorter than one month.

If the tie of marriage is destroyed, however, the functions of the family must be handed over to the state. Therefore, the sixth book treats of the substitution of the state for the family. In the Great Similarity, the state is a world republic. All the people are cared for by the state. As soon as a woman is pregnant, she must go to the " school of gestatory education " in order to teach the child before he is born. At the age of twenty, the child's education is completed, and he is independent and may go his own way. After the age of sixty, he can live in the " house of old age " until he dies. Indeed, the state is the large family for everybody. Only in this way can woman get absolute independence.

Apart from the doctrine of Great Similarity given by Confucius, the ancient Chinese never talked of the abolition

[1] This book has not been published yet, but Kang Yu-wei kindly sent the author a duplicate of the manuscript.

of marriage. The only exception to this was Lieh Tzŭ, a philosopher in the period of Warring States. He describes a Utopian state called Extreme North, where everything is very happy and pleasant. As to the social relations, he gives the following four sentences: "The old and young live equally; there is no ruler, nor minister. The men and women ramble together; there is no matchmaker, nor engagement."[1] This is a picture somewhat like that of the Great Similarity.

In conclusion, the position of woman is this: fundamentally woman is the equal of man. But, in the Disorderly Stage, the separation of the two sexes is advisable; in the Advancing Peace Stage, social intercourse between the sexes is suitable; in the Extreme Peace Stage, the absolute independence of woman is most lovely and just. All these are harmonious with the doctrine of the Three Stages of Confucius.

[1] Bk. v.

CHAPTER VII

Economics and Politics

I. ECONOMICS AS THE BASIS OF POLITICS

In order to understand the relation between economics and politics, let us take the " System of Yao," the first book of the *Canon of History,* written by Confucius to represent his political program. According to this, the whole government is divided into nine departments. The first one is the department of water and earth, the interior department assigned to the prime minister; the second, that of agriculture; the third, that of education; the fourth, that of justice; the fifth, that of labor; the sixth, that of natural resources, charged with the forests, the animals and the mines; the seventh, that of religion; the eighth, that of music; the ninth, that of communication, the mediator between the emperor and the people. Of the nine departments, none is for personal service to the emperor, showing the principle of democracy, and none for the preparation of war, indicating the principle of peace. But four departments out of the nine—the first, the second, the fifth and the sixth—are charged with economic functions. From the second book of the *Canon of History,* it appears that the functions of commerce are included in the first department.[1] Therefore, the whole government is, in large part, a tool for economic development. Indeed, if there were no economics, there would be no politics; the government exists chiefly for

[1] See *infra.*

economic reasons. It is not a military, but an industrial society.

In the *Analects,* also, there is a chapter showing very clearly the relation between economics and politics. When Yen Yüan, Confucius' best pupil, modestly puts his question with reference to the government of a state, he really asks how the government of a universal empire should be administered. The answer of Confucius is:

> Adopt the calendar of the Hsia dynasty. Ride in the state carriage of the Yin dynasty. Wear the crown of the Chou dynasty. Imitate the music of Shao and Wu. Banish the tunes of Chêng, and keep far from specious talkers. The tunes of Chêng are licentious; specious talkers are dangerous.[1]

This chapter has been highly praised by all scholars through all ages, but none has understood the meaning of it. Its exact meaning is similar to that of the last chapter of the "Great Learning." The subject of that chapter is the governing of the state and the equalizing of the whole world, and there are only two ways to realize such a purpose, namely, administering wealth and employing the best men. This chapter has exactly these two principles. Keeping far from specious talkers is the negative form of stating the principle of employing the best men. All the four positive rules are economic principles. The calendar of Hsia is most seasonable; to adopt it means to keep the agricultural works in the best time. The carriage of Yin is most economical and lasting; to ride in it means to promote commerce by means of economical and lasting transportation. The crown of Chou is most beautiful; to wear it means to raise the standard of workmanship. These three things, calendar, carriage and crown, refer to agri-

[1] *Classics*, vol. i, pp. 297–8.

culture, commerce, and industry respectively. These three sentences are more concerned with the production of wealth than with its consumption, while the fourth sentence, which mentions music, refers to consumption. The music of Shao belonging to Shun and that of Wu belonging to Wu Wang, both are the best music of the ancients; to imitate them means to better the standard of life in the most refined stage, while to banish the tunes of Chêng is simply to prevent excess of pleasure. Therefore, Confucius gives Yen Yüan six rules, four positive and two negative; but five rules out of the six are economic principles. In fact, the first way of governing either a state or a universal empire is to reform economic life, and the second way is to employ good men. These are the essential meanings of this chapter, although Confucius uses figures of speech. Unless we understand that Confucius refers to economic principles, how can we explain how a calendar, a carriage, and a crown have anything to do with the governing of a state or a universal empire? According to the old interpretation, the answer of Confucius has no significance. But according to our interpretation, it means that the chief concern of a government is economic life.

Mencius also recognizes that economics is the chief object of politics. When the Marquis Wên of Têng asks him about the proper way of governing a state, he replies: "The business of the people should not be remissly neglected." What he means by the business of the people is their economic life. Then he explains the importance to the people of permanent property as that which he has told the King Hsüan of Ch'i,[1] and his conclusion for the betterment of their economic condition is the *tsing tien* system.[2] The answer of Mencius is quite significant. What

[1] See *infra*.

[2] *Classics*, vol. ii, pp. 239–245.

the Marquis asks about is the business of the state—politics. But what Mencius discusses in his answer is the business of the people—economics. It seems that Mencius does not answer directly the question of the Marquis. But he really answers him from the fundamental point of view. For the business of the people is the chief business of the state; and if a ruler can attend to such business earnestly, he will govern the state well. In short, besides economics, there is no politics, and true politics is economics.

II. POLITICS AS THE PROMOTER OF ECONOMIC LIFE

While economic forces form the basis of political organization, political organization in turn promotes economic development. Mencius says: "Without the great principles of government and its various activities, wealth will not be sufficient."[1] Therefore, the economic needs are the causes for the existence of government, and a good government is also the cause of successful economic life.

The simplest reason for the economic development of a good government is given in the "Great Commentary":

> When a ruler attaches importance to the state, he loves the people. When he loves the people, punishments and penalties are just. When punishments and penalties are just, the people are peaceful. When people are peaceful, wealth is sufficient. When wealth is sufficient, all purposes can be realized.[2]

Judging from this reasoning, economic development is based on legal development. When legal development comes to the stage of just punishments and penalties, the people can engage peacefully in different occupations, and the production of wealth may be sufficient. This is the type of

[1] *Classics*, vol. ii, p. 483.

[2] *Li Ki*, bk. xiv, p. 67.

patriarchal government. But, even in the democratic government of modern time, economic development is still based on legal justice. If there were no good law, there could not be great industries. Therefore, good government is necessary for economic development, and politics paves the way for economics.

III. GENERAL PRINCIPLES OF GOVERNMENT

Since politics paves the way for economics, we should study the political teachings of Confucius in order to understand the background for his economic principles. Therefore, we shall study first his principles of government in general, and then his system of instruction in particular. If we take these as illustrating Confucius' political views, we shall understand the economic principles in his mind.

1. *Imperial Democracy*

According to Confucius, the external form of government is monarchical, but the fundamental principle of it is democratic. The four parts of the *Canon of Poetry* all begin with Wên Wang, who represents the type of constitutional monarchy. The *Canon of History* begins with Yao and Shun, who represent the type of republic. The *Spring and Autumn* begins with Wên Wang and ends with Yao and Shun. These are enough to show that in the ideal government of Confucius the sovereign power is in the hands of the people. Of course, Confucius teaches the people to be loyal to their ruler; but what he means by a ruler is the man who has the best character and talents The "Great Learning" gives a very good definition of the patriarchal government of Confucius. It says: "Loving what the people love, and hating what the people hate: this is he who is called the parent of the people." As soon as the people turn away from their ruler, he is no longer to be a ruler, but a single fellow. If he is a bad man, according to the

"Great Learning," he will be executed by the people of the whole world.[1] Tyrannicide is recognixed as a great deed by all great Confucians, because they do not recognize the tyrant as a ruler.

Confucius himself has the revolutionary idea; in the *Canon of Changes,* he gives a book entitled "Revolution." He says: "Heaven and earth are revolutionary, so that the four seasons complete their functions. The revolutions of T'ang and of Wu were in accordance with the will of God and in response to the wishes of men. Great indeed is what takes place in a time of revolution."[2] When Confucius reads the *Poetry* about the revolution changing the Yin dynasty to the Chou dynasty, he exclaims: "If there were no revolution, what could make the emperor and princes take precaution, and what could make the common people keep up their ambition?"[3] From this exclamation, we know that Confucius does not regard the king as sacred, and that he gives the common people the right of being king. The reason Confucius is sometimes in favor of imperialism or absolute monarchy is because, for the time being, he wants to do away with feudalism; but his fundamental idea is democracy.

The principle of democracy is most clearly set forth by Mencius as follows: "The people are the most important element; the state is the next; and the ruler is the least. Therefore, to gain the mass of people is the way to become emperor; to gain the emperor is the way to become a prince of a feudal state; and to gain the prince is the way to become a great official."[4] By this statement, Mencius means that

[1] *Classics*, vol. i, p. 374.

[2] *Yi King*, p. 254.

[3] *History of Han*, ch. xxxvi.

[4] *Classics*, vol. ii, pp. 483-4.

the emperor should hold his place by popular consent, and the prince should be appointed by the emperor, and the great official by the prince. Since the appointive governor of the province took the place of the hereditary prince of the feudal state, the last two things have been realized in China; but the first never has been realized, except in the negative form of revolution. But that the sovereign power is in the hands of the people is the fundamental concept of the Confucians.[1]

2. *State Government*

For the government of the feudal state, Confucius gives the following general principles: "To rule a state of a thousand chariots, there must be reverent attention to business, and sincerity to the people; economy in expenditure, and love for the people; and the employment of the people at the proper seasons."[2] These principles are the theories of Confucius' political economy. Under such a government, the people are encouraged to work and enjoy their occupations, to care first for public, and then for private welfare.

3. *Local Government*

By the *tsing tien* system of Confucius, a village is a unit of political division, which consists of eighty families. In a village, the people elect aged and virtuous men called patriarchs, and eloquent and strong men called justices. The official rank of the patriarchs is equal to that of the subordinates of the educational department, and that of the justices is equal to that of the common people who are employed about the government offices. Both of them receive double shares of land, and ride on horseback. They are the people themselves; but at the same time, they are offi-

[1] *Classics*, vol. ii, pp. 354-9.   [2] *Ibid.*, vol. i, p. 140.

cials among the people. Therefore, their administration is so efficient in detail as to extend from the morning to the midnight, from the field to the town, from the man to the woman, and from the physical to the intellectual and moral life. These numerous things can be done only by the system of self-government.

4. *Freedom of Speech*

In an imperial democracy, the government is really ruled by public opinion, and the way to get public opinion is by freedom of speech in the form of poetry. According to the *tsing tien* system of Confucius, from the tenth month to the first month, the people live in town. If they have any cause for dissatisfaction, men and women sing together to express their discontent in the form of poetry. Those who are hungry sing about their food; and those who are tired, about their business. Indeed, their economic conditions are their principal subjects. They have, however, the absolute freedom of choosing any subject, referring either to themselves or to the court and government. The principal thing is the style in which the reproof is cunningly insinuated. The authors of the poetry give no offence, but the hearers of it are warned.

Men at the age of sixty and women at that of fifty, if they have no children, are supported by the government, and are appointed commissioners for the collection of poetry. In the first month, when the people are about to leave the town for the field, the commissioners ring out the wooden-tongued bell along the roads in order to collect poetry from the people. From the village, the poetry is transferred to the town; then to the capital of the feudal states; and at last it comes to the imperial government. After the Grand Music-master arranges the poetry according to its style and tune, it is presented to the emperor.

Therefore, even if the emperor does not go out of the door, he understands all the grievances of the empire; and even if he does not come down from the palace, he knows about the four quarters. Hence poetry forms the basis of government.

In the *Canon of Poetry,* the three hundred and five poems are the remainder of ancient poetry edited by Confucius. Their functions are equal to those of newspapers; both are the description of daily life of the people and the expression of public opinion. That the poetry had fulfilled such functions shows that there had been freedom of speech.

5. *Morals v. Law*

Under the *tsing tien* system, people can live sufficiently well, so that they can understand what is honor and what is dishonor. As their virtue has been refined, they become moderate in their concern for wealth, and are complaisant toward others. Hence, there is no dispute nor litigation. Men are governed not by the legal code, but by the moral law. Such a society is higher than the so-called law-governed society, because there is self-respect without the need of law. The legal code must be limited to a certain number of acts, and the people may escape the law when it does not literally specify the act; but the moral law is unlimited and is a matter of spirit rather than letter. Legislation is enforced by external power after the deed is done, and prevents only the bad act, while moral law is enforced by internal conscience. Not only does it prevent the bad thought, but it also makes them good. Therefore Confucius says: "In hearing litigations, I am like any one else. What is necessary, however, is to cause the people to have no litigations." [1] Again, Confucius says:

If the people be led by laws, and uniformity be sought to be

[1] *Classics*, vol. i, p. 257.

given them by punishments, they will try to avoid the punishment, but have no sense of shame. If they be led by virtue, and uniformity be sought to be given them by the rules of propriety, they will have the sense of shame, and moreover will become good.[1]

In fact, in the government system of Confucius, there is much legislation, but more emphasis is laid on the moral than on the legal side.

IV. SYSTEM OF INSTRUCTION

The system of instruction is the fountain of democracy in the political system of Confucius. The reason we use the word instruction instead of education is because the former is broader in sense than the latter. We may divide the word instruction into three great branches, namely, education, religion, and election. They are all together the same stream. Education is one source, and religion is the other, while election is the flow. In Confucianism, religion is really included in education, because the word education itself means intellectual education, while the word religion means ethical education. For the convenience of our readers, however, we may put religion in a separate section in order to make a comparison between China and the West. The only thing we should remember is that the system of instruction is a whole. According to the political system of Confucius, the *tsing tien* system and the instruction system are the two greatest things, and they must go together, although the former precedes the latter. Therefore, if we are going to study the economic system of Confucius represented by *tsing tien,* we should know something about his system of instruction.

1. *Universally Free Education*

After the people can make their living and thus satisfy

[1] *Classics*, vol. i, p. 146.

their physical needs, development of mind and character is necessary. Then the educational system arises. According to Confucius, in the center of a village which contains eighty families, there is a schoolhouse. The aged and virtuous men are elected " patriarchs ", and are teachers of the school; usually, they come from the retired officials of the government. Such a school of a village is called a local school. It opens in the tenth month when the agricultural work has been finished, and closes in the first month, when this work begins again. At eight years of age, the children begin to go to school, and study reading and writing, mathematics and geography, and the ethical rules of family and society. This is the most popular education, and is the basis of all the higher schools.

There are different grades of schools. The local school of the village is the lowest grade. Then come successively the district school, the provincial college, and the national university. The highest one is the imperial university. The local school is in every village; the district school, in every district; the provincial college, in every province; the national university, in every capital city of every feudal state; and the imperial university, in the imperial capital.[1] Thus educational institutions exist over the whole empire. They are all public schools and are maintained by the different governments; hence they are all free. The school system was an actual system of the ancients, although it may not have been so complete as the Confucians prescribe. In ancient times, the different institutions were used not only as schools, but also as churches, and for political meetings, social gatherings, and even military councils.[2]

Regarding the training of the different schools, all those below the imperial university are called small learning; the

[1] *Li Ki*, bk. xvi, p. 83.

[2] *Ibid.*, bk. iii, p. 220.

latter is called great learning. The lowest age for the great learning is fifteen, and the highest is twenty. The subjects of study are the different civilizations of the ancients and the social and political institutions of the present. The "Record of Education" says:

> Every year new students may enter the imperial university, and every alternate year there is a comparative examination. At the end of the first year, the examination is to see whether they can read the texts intelligently, and what the individual taste of each is; in the third year, whether they are reverently attentive to their work, and what companionship is most pleasant to them; in the fifth year, how they extend their studies and seek the company of their teachers; in the seventh year, how they can discuss the subjects of their studies and select their friends. They are now said to have made some small accomplishments. In the ninth year, when they know the different relative subjects and have gained general intelligence, establishing themselves firmly so that they cannot be moved, they are said to have made some great accomplishments.[1]

In every one of these five examinations, the students are examined from two points of view: one is knowledge, and the other is character. To balance mental and moral training is the Chinese system of education, handed down from Confucius. In fact, the educational system of Confucius has been partially carried out in different periods.

2. *Social Religion and Freedom of Belief*

In the Chinese language, the word religion is not exactly the same as in English. The Chinese word *chiao* means instruction; hence it stands for education as well as for religion. But the word *chiao* in the religious sense of the Chinese means moral teachings; sometimes it in-

[1] *Li Ki*, bk. xvi, pp. 83-4.

cludes even the whole of civilization. Therefore, what the Chinese call religion is moral, social and philosophical rather than spiritual. As the word *chiao* means both education and religion, an educational institution is a church as well as a school. According to Mencius, the object of all the schools of the Three Dynasties is to illustrate the human relations.[1] Even in the present day, in the Confucian Churches over the whole empire, there is a hall called "Illustrating-Human-Relations Hall"; and the Chinese call the Confucian Church by the name of Holy Temple, or Civil Temple, or School House. This is the reason why under the *tsing tien* system there is no church, because the religious function is absorbed by education. The patriarchs, although the teachers of the school, are like the pastors or fathers of the church. But what are the subjects of their sermons? According to Mencius, the most important teachings of the schools are the filial and fraternal duties; and their results are that the gray-haired men do not need to carry any burdens on their backs or on their heads along the roads.[2] Therefore, we can see that the Chinese religion has been directed toward man more than toward God. Indeed, the religion of Confucius is based on sociology rather than on theology. Hence, China has given full freedom of belief to the people, since spiritual worship has not been the essential of the Chinese religion.

In modern times, there is a conflict between religion and science, but this can never be the case in Confucianism. Confucianism is based on scientific principles. When Confucius teaches Tzŭ-lu what knowledge is, he says: "When you know a thing, to hold that you know it; and when you do not know a thing, to allow that you do not know it—this is knowledge."[3] In the *Spring and Autumn,* "to leave out

[1] *Classics*, vol. ii, p. 242.

[2] *Ibid.*, vol. ii, pp. 131–2.

[3] *Ibid.*, vol. i, p. 151.

the doubtful points" is a great principle. With such a scientific nature, Confucianism differs from all other religions, and is a religon of the highest type. On this account, the Chinese can identify religion with education, and church with school; and there will never be any conflict between science and Confucianism, because Confucianism itself is also a science.

In modern times, there is also a conflict between religion and politics, but this is not the case in Confucianism. The Roman Catholics have a pope who assumes political power as an emperor, and the ecclesiastical body forms a specially-favored class exercising political privileges over and against the common people. This is an unnatural and unjust thing. Therefore, conflict between church and state arises, and European and American statesmen separate church from state. How is this in the religion of Confucius? He did not choose a special successor, and no one dared to call himself the only successor of Confucius. In fact, Confucianism is a democratic religion, and has no such monarchical idea. Confucius did not distinguish his followers from the common people, and they never formed such a special class as the priesthood. Therefore, the Confucians never got political privileges. Although the student class always has more access to the government than the common people, it is through educational qualifications, and not through religious privilege. Therefore, since the Confucians have never taken any political power from the state, the state has no trouble with the Confucian religion at all, and there is no need to separate it from the state.

Moreover, Christianity is a simple religion, and has nothing to do with government; hence it can be separated from the state. But Confucianism is a complex religion, and has very much to do with government; hence it can never be separated from the state. The missionary work of Confucius himself was mostly in court; he taught the people not on the subject of theology, but on that of social relations; he taught his pupils not in order to make priests of them, but to make them statesmen and teachers. His teachings are at least half on political subjects; and the whole Chinese society is built up under his teachings, although not under the best of them, and even opposing some of them. In a word, China never can separate Confucianism from the state, unless she would destroy her whole civilization. It is not only unwise and unnecessary, but also impossible. This is the main characteristic of the religion of Confucius.

4. *Educational Election as a System of Popular Representation*

As regards politics, Confucius lays much stress on the power of man. He says:

> The principles of the government of Wên and Wu are always displayed in the records—the tablets of wood and bamboo. But, when there are the right men, such a government flourishes; while without such men, such a government decays and ceases. With a good quality of men, the growth of government is rapid, just as vegetation is rapid in land of good quality. Thus a government is like an easily-growing rush. Therefore, the administration of government depends upon man.[1]

Having such a theory of government, Confucius thinks that to get good men is the fundamental thing for a good government. But how shall we get them? By the system of educational election.

According to Confucius, the school is not only a system of education, but also a system of election; hence, it combines politics with education. His political doctrine is

[1] *Classics*, vol. i, p. 405.

democratic, and no aristocracy is allowed. The *Record of Rites* says: "Even the eldest son of the emperor by his legitimate queen is only as an ordinary student. In the world, there is nowhere such a thing as being born noble." [1] In the *Spring and Autumn*, Confucius denies the hereditary right of aristocracy, and gives educational election as a substitute.[2] This was at that time a revolutionary idea in social life; it was realized by the recommendation of Tung Chung-shu (412 A. K. or 140 B. C.). According to the "Royal Regulations," the sons of the emperor, the princes, and the officials, are to study at the same university with the students chosen from among the common people; and their classes are to be divided up, not by ranks, but by ages.[3] Hsun Tzŭ says: "Even among the sons of the emperor, the princes, and the great officials, if they were not qualified to rites and justice, they should be put down to the class of common people; even among the sons of common people, if they have good education and character and are qualified to rites and justice, they should be elevated to the class of ministers and nobles." [4] In short, under the system of Confucius, there is no distinction of classes; and education is the only determining force in social standing. We may say that there is an educational aristocracy, but such an aristocracy is unavoidable, unless human characteristics be equal by birth. The only thing that human power can do is to make education universal and free, in order to give everyone equal opportunity; and this is the way of Confucius.

The way Confucius combines politics with education is something like this: the best students of the local school are elected and transferred to the district school; the best of the

[1] *Li Ki*, bk. ix, p. 438.

[2] Third year of Duke Yin.

[3] *Li Ki*, bk. iii, p. 233.

[4] Bk. ix.

district school, to the provincial college; and the best of the provincial college, to the national university. Every three years, the feudal princes send the best students from their national universities to the emperor, and let them study at the imperial university. The best students of the imperial university are called "complete scholars". If their conduct and capability are equal, they are distinguished by archery. Then titles are conferred upon them. In this way, the students promote themselves by their capability; and the emperor appoints the officials by the examination of their merit.[1] This sytem may be called educational election.

The system of educational election may also be called a system of representation. Since the students elected from the common people become high officials, the different institutions are really the places where the representatives of the people are elected. As the elections are held in schools and the representatives are confined to the body of students, education is the exclusive qualification. The educational test takes the place of universal suffrage. But choosing education as a qualification is much better than choosing anything else, especially when education is universally free. Although there is no popular vote, this should not be far from popular sentiment, because those chosen are the best students. Since they come from different political divisions, although there is no legal responsibility between them and their native localities, they should be regarded as the representatives of the people as a whole. The *Great Commentary of the Canon of History*[2] speaks thus of the election of students. " It lets the wise men have their way to come up, and co-operate with their ruler in the government. It

[1] *Annotation of Kung-yang*, 15th year of Duke Hsüan, *etc.*

[2] Written by Professor Fu of the Ch'in dynasty, the oldest and greatest authority on the *Canon of History*.

shows that a ruler alone should not control the government. This is the way to give the greatest importance to the people."

What we have mentioned is the ideal system of Confucius, and it has been essentially carried into effect. But the system of representation was also a fact of the ancients, although it may not have been so perfect as the Confucians describe. The *Official System of Chou* says: "Let the people elect the virtuous to be their leaders outside, and let them also elect the able to be their governors inside."[1] "Outside" means the central government out of their province, and "inside" means the local government, the word leaders meaning representatives. In ancient times, the students were at the same time the farmers, so that the farmers could easily elect the students among themselves. The *Canon of Poetry* tells how the prince goes to the field to preside over the election: "Now, I go to the south-lying acres, where some are weeding and some gather the earth about the roots. The millets look luxuriant. And in a spacious resting place, we elect our eminent students."[2] From this poem, we can understand that the farmers, outside of the school, still had the right to choose their representatives, although the election was controlled by the government.

Historically, the system of representation was changed from election by the people into selection by the government, that is, civil-service competitive examinations. Even by this change, the graduates who passed examinations still had the qualifications of representatives, because the number of graduates was proportionate to the population and the amount of taxation of their native province. So China had the representative system. But the great trouble was that China did not develop a legal organi-

[1] Ch. xii.

[2] *Classics*, vol. iv, pt. ii, p. 377.

zation of the representative body to assume the sovereign power. In ancient times, although there was a popular council of the people in the central government,[1] it had not been legally well organized. And so those representatives were only the advisors of the ruler.

According to the ideal of Confucius, before the officials take office, there is an educational election; and after they come to office, there is also an examination of merit every three years. Hence, there can be no corruption. The examination is based entirely on the economic conditions of the people. After three examinations, officials are either degraded or promoted according to the value of their service to the people. They are required to have such conditions that not only is capital increased, but also labor is improved. In short, economic prosperity is the only test of a good government, and it is the chief task of the officials who are subjected to the examination of merit. Ho Hsiu says: "The wise ruler gives reward to the officials according to their obvious service, so that the undeserving cannot be promoted by popular praise; and gives punishment to them according to their obvious guilt, so that the innocent cannot be dismissed by popular slander."[2] This principle has been put into actual law.

In conclusion, the word representatives includes all the officials of the government. Although there are three powers—legislative, administrative and judicial—they are not sharply divided into distinct branches. Therefore, the representatives of the people, the students, may take office in any branch of the government, not being confined to legislative power only.

[1] *Cf. Classics*, vol. iii, pt. i, pp. 41, 224, 233-4. F. Hirth's *The Ancient History of China*, p. 124. *Kuan Tsu*, bk. lvi.

[2] Third year of Duke Yin.

Under the influence of Confucius, the Chinese government has been that of imperial democracy, and everyone has the chance to be prime minister, although it is not necessary that everyone should have the ambition to be emperor. In China, " linen prime minister " and " white house duke and minister " have become popular terms. " Linen " and " white house " indicate the poor conditions from which they arise to the highest office. Indeed, China has been the most democratic country of the world in this point. Even in the United States, a republican government, it is difficult for one to hold an elective public office, no matter how high or how low, unless he is an active member of one of the two great parties. This means that many good men are excluded from the government, and it tends to make men lose their personality, and to deny them the opportunity for showing their political ability in rendering public service. Although the form of the American government is republican, it is very tyrannical in this respect; or at least it is something of an aristocracy. How much worse are the monarchical governments of the world! All the modern European countries and Japan are only now doing away with aristocracy; and in most of them the nobility is still a great element in their government. But China had largely destroyed the nobility with the election system of the Han dynasty (418 A. K. or 134 B. C.), and has extinguished it entirely since the *Chin Shih* examination of the Sui dynasty (1157 A. K. or 606 A. D.). In the present day, all the titles of nobility are merely nominal honors, and have no political power whatever attached to them. The only material gain they bring is the hereditary salary received in the form of pension. Even the members of the imperial family have no political power, unless they are officials. Any student, poor in the economic sense, studying quietly and even laboring hard, may expect to become prime minister and carry out his principles. He does not need to spend his time, energy and money in self-advertisement.

If the ruler should always be as good as Confucius requires, the system of educational election would be perfect. But, since the ruler is not always good, and the world has been progressive, China is going to change her absolute to a constitutional government. As soon as she shall have a constitutional government, she will have a party government. And as soon as she has a party government, she will have party elections, and modern aristocracy will grow in China. But, as the educational election is a system peculiar to the Chinese, they should keep the best of their own, and adopt only the best of their neighbors' systems, without their defects. By extending the principle of popular suffrage to just the right point, China will have a governmental system which surpasses the most sanguine hopes of American civil service reformers.

The election system of Confucius is the chief weapon for the destruction of class interests. This was appreciated by the physiocrats. They hold up as the ideal of political government, not Switzerland or England, but China,[1] because in other countries one did not find individual interest coming to the front. In England the political system gives too much power to the merchants; on the other hand, democracy gives too much power to the lower classes, and aristocracy, too much power to the higher classes. In China alone no one class tends to become dominant. This view of the physiocrats is very true. It is doubtless true that Quesnay was theorizing, and used China as a model because it was far away and he knew little about it, but in this instance his theory was justified by the facts.

[1] *Cf.* Quesnay's *Despotisme de la Chine*, first published in the *Éphémérides du Citoyen* in 1767 and reprinted in *Oeuvres Économiques et Philosophiques de Quesnay*, ed. Oncken, 1888, pp. 563–660.

CHAPTER VIII

ECONOMICS AND ETHICS

I. ECONOMICS AS THE BASIS OF ETHICS

IN the Confucian system, there are two great principles. One is called love, or humanity; the other, justice, or righteousness. It may be interesting to notice that, according to the Chinese etymology, the word love is formed from the word denoting man, or others, and the word justice from the word denoting self. Thus the primary meaning of the word love is a relation between persons; and that of the word justice is an aspect of the self. We love others, but we justify ourselves. Hence we should strictly control ourselves, according to the highest standard of morality, and treat others liberally, according to the ordinary level of human nature. Confucius says: "The superior man reasons about theoretical principles from the standpoint of himself, but lays down practical laws from the capabilities of the people."[1] Therefore, regarding ourselves, Confucius puts ethical teaching above economic life,—in some cases, life itself should be sacrificed for the sake of virtue; but regarding society as a whole, he puts economic life before ethical teaching.

The best illustration of this principle is given in the *Analects*. When Confucius went to Wei, Jan Yu acted as driver of his carriage. Confucius observed, "How numerous are the people!" Jan said, "Since they are thus nu-

[1] *Li Ki,* bk. xxix, p. 333.

merous, what more shall be done for them?" "Enrich them," was the reply. "And when they have been enriched, what more shall be done?" Confucius said, "Instruct them".[1]

Before we can instruct the people, we must enrich them, no matter how few or many they are. This is a universal principle. The *Canon of Poetry* repeats three times the following two sentences: "Give them drink and give them food. Instruct them and teach them."[2]

If we understand in the beginning that Confucius gives two principles for the two classes of men, one for the officials and students, the other for the mass of common people at large, we shall avoid confusion. For the higher class, ethical life is first, but for the lower class, economic life is first. Confucius says: "The mind of great men is conversant with justice; the mind of small men is conversant with profit."[3] In speaking of great men and small men, he refers to their social standing. This theory is very clearly stated by Tung Chung-shu when he says: "Busily seeking for wealth and profit, and fearing only the condition of want, this is the mind of common people; busily seeking for love and justice, and fearing always that they could not influence the people, this is the mind of ministers and great officials."[4] Such a statement, of course, is only a theory, not fact. Yet we must understand that Confucius has these two classes in his mind, and sets forth two different principles for them. On the one hand, he forbids the higher class, from emperor to student, to seek private gain. They should confine themselves to the ethical life. On the

[1] *Classics,* vol. i, pp. 266-7.

[2] *Classics,* vol. iv, pt. ii, pp. 418-420.

[3] *Classics,* vol. i, p. 170.

[4] *History of Han,* ch. lvi.

other hand, he allows the lower class to make profit, and thinks that they ought to do so. Hence, for the governing of society, Confucius takes up the economic life of the people for the first consideration. The "Great Learning" describes the effects of a good government as follows: "The common people find pleasure in what they call their pleasure, and find profit in what they call their profit." [1] We are sure that Confucius, in the program of his reformation, feels that economic betterment is the first item.[2]

Unfortunately, since the Confucians of the Sung dynasty did not wholly understand the principles of Confucius and thought that he did not approve even talking about profits, the teachings of Confucius failed to be considered of great importance in the practical world, and the Chinese suffered a great deal through need of economic reforms. They made such a great mistake because they misunderstood the statements of Mencius and Tung Chung-shu. Mencius tells the King Hui of Liang: "Why must your Majesty use that word profit? What I am provided with are counsels concerning the principles of love and justice, and these are my only topics." [3] Tung Chung-shu tells the Prince of Kiang-tu: "The man of perfect virtue is thus: following strictly justice, not for the sake of profit; discussing thoroughly principle, not with the expectation of success." [4] This simply means virtue for virtue's sake. These two statements given by Mencius and Tung Chung-shu are quite good in themselves, but they do not mean that the economic problems should be entirely left out. They have their own writings, and we can find their economic principles even from the

[1] *Classics,* vol. i, p. 364.

[2] *Classics,* vol. ii, p. 131.

[3] *Classics,* vol. ii, p. 126.

[4] *History of Han,* ch. lvi.

quotations of this treatise. They are talking to the king and the prince, and such men, of course, are forbidden by Confucius to talk about profits. We never expect to use the same prescription for everybody; why should we apply those statements to every one? Neither Confucius, nor Mencius, nor Tung Chung-shu, nor any great Confucian before the Sung dynasty, has ever said that the common people should not talk about profits. Moreover, the Confucians of the Sung dynasty did not distinguish the public profits from private profits, and left them both out of consideration This has been a great obstacle to the economic development of China.

II. HARMONY OF ECONOMICS AND ETHICS

The reason the Confucians of the Sung dynasty fear to talk about profit is because they make the distinction between profit and justice too sharp, and think they are necessarily opposed to each other. But true Confucianism harmonizes economics and ethics, and identifies profit with justice. A true profit, it holds, is justice, and the immediate profit which opposes justice is, in the long run, not a profit at all. The essential of these two words, profit and justice, is the same thing, but expressed in different terms.

As Confucius lived in the stage of feudalism, and generally talked with princes, he did not like to mention the word profit, but used the word justice for its substitute. Since princes, as we know, generally care for profit, but not for justice; for wealth, but not for virtue; why should Confucius talk to them about profit instead of about justice? But, if Confucius only says to them that justice is good, and does not say that justice is a profit, they will not believe him, and will not practice justice. Therefore, Confucius points out very clearly that justice is a real profit, and that to prefer the immediate profit is only a suicidal policy

This principle is thus set forth in the "Great Learning":

The superior man will first take pains about his own virtue. . . . . Virtue is the root, and wealth only the result. If he make the root his secondary object, and the result his primary, he will only wrangle with his people, and teach them rapine. Hence, the concentration of wealth is the cause of driving the people away, and the diffusion of it among them is the way to collect the people. And hence, . . . the wealth, got by improper ways, will take its departure by the same. . . . The virtuous man, by means of his wealth, makes his personality more distinguished. The vicious man accumulates wealth at the expense of his life. Never has there been a case of the sovereign liking love, and the people not liking justice. Never has there been a case where the people have liked justice, and the affairs of the sovereign have not been carried to completion. And never has there been a case where the wealth in such a state, collected in the treasuries and arsenals, did not continue in the sovereign's possession.

For the explanation that the real profit of a state is not pecuniary profit, but justice, it quotes from Mêng Hsien-tsŭ: "It is better to have an officer who steals, than to have one who collects unjust imposts from the people." Indeed, losing wealth is better than losing justice.

The conclusion of the "Great Learning" is this:

When he who presides over a state or a family makes wealth his chief business, he must be under the influence of some mean fellow. He may consider this fellow good; but when such a person is employed in the administration of a state or family, calamities from nature and injuries from men will befall it together. And, although a good man may take his place, he will not be able to remedy the evil. This illustrates the saying, that a state does not take the pecuniary profit as a real profit, but takes justice as a real profit.[1]

The same principle is also given by Mencius. When he

[1] *Classics*, vol. i, pp. 375-381.

meets King Hui of Liang, he first rejects the word profit, which is mentioned by the king, and supplies the two words love and justice. Then he points out that profit in the common sense is not a profit. If the king, the great officials, the students and the common people, all try to snatch this profit the one from the other, the state will be endangered. He says: "If justice be put last, and profit be put first, they will not be satisfied without snatching all."

Now, he turns to the real profit of love and justice, and says: "There never has been a man who practiced the principle of love and neglected his parents. There never has been a man who practiced the principle of justice and made his sovereign an after-consideration.[1]

What has been said in the "Great Learning" and by Mencius is for princes or for the government. But the principle that justice is a profit holds true among all mankind. The Chinese take this principle as the fundamental law of economics, and carry it into practice in daily life. This is why the Chinese merchants have the highest moral standard. Indeed, "honesty is the best policy." If justice is not a profit, the morality of man would be as low as that of the beast. But to-day, as human progress has risen to the present stage, it proves that justice is a profit. The more just we are, the more we shall prosper.

Since justice is a profit, why do not the Confucians use the word profit as often as the word justice? Human nature is already selfish, and society is already a profit-seeking society. The people know profit in the narrow sense by birth, and do not need any more teaching about it. If a great teacher like Confucius were to talk constantly about profit, it would make the people think about profit still more and about justice still less. They would care much more for money than for character. They would excuse them-

[1] *Classics*, vol. ii, pp. 125-7.

selves on the ground of the teachings of Confucius, and would use Confucius' word for their pretext. Therefore, Confucius does not use the word profit very often, but uses the word justice for its substitute. This idea is very well explained by Adam Smith. He says:

> Those principles of the human mind which are most beneficial to society are by no means marked by nature as the most honorable. Hunger, thirst, and the passion for sex are the great supports of the human species, yet almost every expression of these excites contempt. In the same manner, that principle in the mind which prompts to truck, barter, and exchange, though it is the foundation of arts, commerce, and the division of labor, yet it is not marked with anything amiable. . . . The plain reason for this is that these principles are so strongly implanted by nature that they have no occasion for that additional force which the weaker principles [*e. g.*, generosity] need.[1]

Moreover, social profit is harmonious with social justice, while individual profit is not always harmonious with individual justice. Confucius says: " Riches and honors acquired by injustice are to me as a floating cloud." [2] He recognizes that there are some individual profits without the principle of justice. Yang Hu was a bad officer at the time of Confucius, but Mencius quotes his words as follows: " He who seeks to be rich will not be benevolent. He who wishes to be benevolent will not be rich." [3] Mencius thinks that there is sometimes a contradiction between economic gains and ethical principles. Hence, Confucius speaks of the superior man as one who, when he sees gain, thinks of justice.[4] And hence, the *Record of Rites*

[1] *Lectures of Adam Smith,* p. 232.

[2] *Classics,* vol. i, p. 200.

[3] *Classics,* vol. ii, p. 240.

[4] *Classics,* vol. i, p. 314.

says: "When you find wealth within your reach, do not try to get it by improper means."[1]

III. CHOICE BETWEEN ECONOMIC LIFE AND ETHICAL LIFE

Even though the economic principles are finally harmonious with those of ethices, under some circumstances economic life cannot exist along with ethical life. Hence, we shall see how Confucius makes a choice between these two things.

When Tzŭ-kung asks Confucius about government, Confucius says: "The requisites of government are that there be sufficiency of food, sufficiency of soldiers, and the faith of the people." Tzŭ-kung says: "If it cannot be helped, and one of these must be dispensed with, which of the three should be foregone first?" "The soldiers", says Confucius. Tzŭ-kung again asks: "If it cannot be helped, and one of the remaining two must be dispensed with, which of them should be foregone?" Confucius answers: "Part with the food. From of old, death has been the lot of all men; but if the people have no faith in their hearts, there is no standing for any one."[2]

This dialogue is very important and very interesting; the questions and the answers are both very good. The word food includes all economic life; the word soldiers, all military forces and equipments; and the word faith, all religious and ethical life. So far as we have seen, Confucius emphasizes economic life as the first thing in society. And even in this dialogue, he puts food before the other two. But, when the economic life and ethical life cannot both be preserved, economic life must be sacrificed. This seems a foolish policy, and an impracticable theory. Moreover, it seems contradictory to his own principle that economic

[1] *Li Ki,* bk. i, p. 62.

[2] *Classics,* vol. i, p. 254.

life should come before ethical life. In reality, however, there is great harmony here. In the primary stage, when the people do not know much about faith, and their immediate need is food, if you talk to them on any subject, such as religion or ethics, before they can satisfy their hunger, they will not listen to you. Food, therefore, must come before all other things. In the advanced stage, when they have built a society as high as a state, they must know something about faith, and faith is the strongest social tie. If the getting of food were their sole aim, or escaping from death their highest ideal, they would do anything in any way for the sake of their lowest self. Without faith, the world would be a wilderness; no one would trust others, and every one would be an enemy to others. Society could not exist; and at last, not even the individual could exist. Only the strongest would survive. In the beginning, the people would sacrifice their faith to escape death; but ultimately, they would fall together into death because they had no faith. A great teacher like Confucius must prefer faith to food. Or, in other words, he must choose to die with faith rather than to live without it. Food is the primary means of building up society, but faith is the final end in maintaining it. These two theories of Confucius are not contradictory. Hence, this policy is not only honest, but also wise. Nor is it impracticable.

To show that the ethical life should be preferred to the economic life, Mencius cites this concrete case, and shows that every one has such conscience. He says:

We desire fish, and we also desire bear's paws. If we cannot have the two together, we will let the fish go and take the bear's paws. So, we desire life, and we also desire righteousness. If we cannot keep the two together, we will let life go and choose righteousness. We desire life indeed, but there is that which we desire more than life, and therefore we will not seek to possess it by any improper ways. We dislike death indeed, but there is that which we dislike more than death, and therefore there are occasions when we will not avoid danger. . . .

Therefore, men have that which they desire more than life, and that which they dislike more than death. They who have this conscience are not men of distinguished talents and virtue only. All men have it; what distinguishes such men is simply that they do not lose it.

Here are a small basket of rice and a platter of soup, and the case is one in which the getting them will preserve life, and the want of them will be death; if they are offered with an insulting voice, even a tramp will not receive them, or if you first tread upon them, even a beggar will not stoop to take them.[1]

This statement of Mencius, that even the tramp or the beggar still cares for his personal honor, and that he preserves it even at the expense of his life, is very true. Hence, there is really no such man as may be called the purely economic man, and the ethical motive is rooted in human nature as well as the economic motive. For this reason, we can harmonize the economic life with the ethical life.

IV. ACCEPTANCE OF WEALTH

When we discuss economics and ethics, the important question is the acceptance of wealth. As men are living in society, they have to give and receive wealth in daily life. But what are the principles which govern those matters? On this question, it is best to look at the teachings of Mencius. For the principles of both giving and receiving wealth, he says: "When it appears proper to take a thing, and afterwards not proper, to take it is contrary to moderation. When it appears proper to give a thing, and after-

[1] *Classics,* vol. ii, pp. 411-3.

wards not proper, to give it is contrary to kindness." [1] Again, when he speaks of Yi Yin, he says that Yin would neither have given nor have taken a single straw, if it were contrary to justice and principle.[2] Therefore, he wants the people to act in the proper way not only in their taking, but also in their giving; foolish generosity and unwise alms are not approved by Mencius.

But the principles governing the taking of wealth are more important than those governing the giving of it, because human nature is more often too covetous, rather than too liberal. For the taking of wealth, Mencius gives this general principle: if there be not proper ground for taking it, a single bamboo-cup of rice may not be received from a man; but if there be such proper ground, then Shun's receiving the empire from Yao is not to be considered excessive.[3] Therefore, the taking of wealth, no matter how great or how little, must be governed by moral considerations.

The greatest difficulty, however, is to determine what is proper and what is not. On this point, there is no certain rule. But we may refer to concrete cases and take them as examples. When Mencius was in Ch'i, the king sent him a present of 2000 taels of fine gold, and he refused it. But he accepted a present of 1400 taels when he was in Sung, and accepted one of 1000 taels when he was in Hsieh. Chen Tsin, his pupil, asked him if there were not something wrong in one of the two cases. But Mencius said that they are all right. When he was in Sung, he was about to take a long journey. It is a custom of the Chinese to present a traveler with a traveling present. Therefore, the message of the prince was the sending of such a present. Why

[1] *Classics*, vol. ii, p. 328.

[2] *Ibid.*, p. 362.

[3] *Ibid.*, p. 269.

should he have declined the gift? When he was in Hsieh, he was apprehensive for his safety, and taking measures for his protection. The message was, "I have heard that you are taking measures to protect yourself, and send this to help you in procuring arms." Why should he have declined the gift? But when he was in Ch'i, he had no occasion for money. To send a man a gift when he has no occasion for it, is to bribe him. How is it possible that a superior man should accept a bribe? [1] These are concrete cases showing the principles of accepting and declining wealth.

There is a most interesting discussion between Mencius and Wan Chang, his pupil, about the acceptance of wealth. The point of Mencius is that, when the donor offers his gift on a reasonable ground and in a manner in accordance with propriety, even Confucius would have received it. "Here now," says Wan Chang, "is one who stops and robs people outside the city gates. He offers his gift on a ground of reason and in a proper manner;—would it be right to receive it when so acquired?" The answer of Mencius is, of course, negative. "The princes of the present day," pursues Wan Chang, "take from their people just as a robber despoils his victim. Yet if they put a good face of propriety on their gifts, the superior man receices them. I venture to ask you to explain this." Here Wan Chang alludes to Mencius himself. Mencius answers:

Do you think that, if there should arise a truly imperial sovereign, he would collect the princes of the present day and put them all to death? Or would he admonish them, and then, if they did not change their ways, put them to death? Indeed, to call every one who takes what does not properly belong to him a robber is pushing a point of resemblance to the utmost

[1] *Classics*, vol. ii, pp. 215-6.

and insisting on the most refined idea of righteousness. When Confucius was in office in Lu, the officials struggled together for the game taken in hunting, and he did the same. If that struggling for the captured game was proper, how much more may the gifts of the princes be received![1]

According to the reasoning of Mencius, we may receive a gift offered on a reasonable ground and in a proper manner, and need not push the idea of absolute justice to the extreme. For instance, we may receive donations from a trust in a proper way, and need not regard the trust as a robber. Although the trust may take what does not properly belong to it, we cannot call it a robber because the whole structure of present society is not an ideal society. Under present conditions, we cannot judge every one according to the ideal standard. We should need to change the condition itself first. This is the explanation of Mencius, and it may be also the principle of Confucius.

V. THREE DOCTRINES DIRECTLY OPPOSED TO ECONOMIC MOTIVE

Confucius has very many teachings on the subject of ethics, but we shall leave them out entirely, and take up only three doctrines which are directly against the economic motive. The first is the doctrine of fate; the second is the doctrine of name; and the third is the doctrine of soul. All are very important teachings of Confucius.

1. *Doctrine of Fate*

In order to understand the doctrine of fate, we must ask first what is meant by the word fate. Here is a definition given by Mencius: "That which is done without man's doing is from Heaven. That which happens without man's causing is from fate."[2] These two words, Heaven and

[1] *Classics,* vol. ii, pp. 379-383. [2] *Ibid.,* p. 359.

fate, are interchangeable. According to the *Adjunct to the Canon of Filial Piety*, there are three kinds of fate. Doing good and getting good is called receiving fate; doing good but getting evil is called encountering fate; doing evil and getting evil is called following fate. Therefore, Mencius says: "There is a fate for everything. A man should receive submissively what may be correctly ascribed thereto."[1] Indeed, the word fate has three points of view. From the religious viewpoint, it is a supernatural power predetermining everything. From the philosophical viewpoint, it is the law of necessity. From the ethical viewpoint, it is the right principle, doing the right thing at the right moment and in the right way. The doctrine of fate of Confucius embraces these three points of view; hence he says that without recognizing fate, it is impossible to be a superior man.[2]

Believing in fate and having no anxiety to acquire wealth, Confucius gives himself as an example. He says: "If the search for riches were sure to be successful, though I should become a groom with whip in hand to get them, I should do so. As the search may not be successful, I will follow after that which I love."[3] What he loves is the study of truth, and not the search for wealth. Hence he says: "Death and life have their fate; riches and honors depend upon Heaven."[4] The word Heaven and the word fate are the same thing expressed differently.

Since man's fate is determined in Heaven, and his nature is also given by Heaven, how can he harmonize these two things when his nature has wants and his fate cannot satisfy them? According to Confucius, man should subject

[1] *Classics,* vol. ii, p. 449.

[2] *Classics,* vol. i, p. 354.

[3] *Ibid.*, p. 198.

[4] Quoted by Tzŭ-hsia, *ibid.*, pp. 252-3.

his nature to fate. He says: "The superior man proclaims the doctrine of fate as a barrier against material wants."[1] As the human wants rooted in nature are very numerous, and never can be completely controlled by anything, he proclaims the fate which is in Heaven and beyond the power of man, in order to prevent unlawful ambition and to lessen unlimited desires. Mencius gives the same principle. He says:

> For the mouth to desire sweet tastes, the eye to desire beautiful colors, the ear to desire pleasant sounds, the nose to desire fragrant odors, and the four limbs to desire ease and comfort: these wants are of human nature. But there is fate in connection with them, and the superior man does not say of his pursuit of them, "It is my nature."[2]

Mencius recognizes what human nature is, but he teaches men to respect fate and not to excuse their pursuit of gratification on the pretext of nature. Therefore, the doctrine of fate is an ethical teaching directly modifying the economic wants.

From the doctrine of fate spring two policies. The first policy is negative, passive, taking everything when it comes, but not running risks to get it. This is primarily for the weakening of economic wants, and especially so in the individual case. For the individual himself, if he takes the natural course and does not try to get anything by improper means, frees his mind from physical desires, and enjoys a great amount of happiness. It is said in the "Appendix" of the *Canon of Changes* that a sage rejoices in Heaven and knows fate, hence he has no anxieties.[3] This is the view

[1] *Li Ki*, bk. xxvii, p. 284.

[2] *Classics*, vol. ii, p. 489.

[3] *Yi King*, p. 354.

of optimism. If one does not believe in fate, he will be the slave of passion and the hunter of fortune. Therefore, Confucius says: "The superior man lives in safe ways in order to wait for fate, while the mean man walks in dangerous paths in order to catch luck." [1]

But we must not misunderstand and think that the passive policy excludes the principle of self-help. When one dies in the discharge of his duties, it is a regular fate; but when one dies of his own fault, it is not a regular fate. Therefore, Mencius says that the one who knows fate will not stand beneath a precipitous wall.[2] Therefore, according to the principle of rites, those who die either from an unreasonable attack which they do not wisely escape, or through the fall of some dangerous thing, or by drowning through heedlessness, should have no condolence offered for them.[3] Indeed, if anyone does not help himself, fate never can help him, and he would be punished by his own fault. Fate is the final cause which operates after man has tried his best, but not a mere chance for the careless man. "Trust in God and keep your powder dry" is the real meaning of waiting for fate. The only difference between those who recognize fate and those who do not is that the former do everything morally, legally, reasonably, and that the latter do the opposite thing. But fate does not make men do nothing. Mencius says: "The superior man performs the law of right, and thereby waits simply for fate." [4]

The second policy is positive, active, trusting one's own principles, and disregarding all circumstances. This is primarily for the fulfillment of ethical duties, and especially

[1] *Classics,* vol. i, p. 396.

[2] *Classics,* vol. ii, p. 450.

[3] *Li Ki,* bk. ii, p. 131.

[4] *Classics,* vol. ii, p. 496.

so in the social case. In the social relations and conditions, it is usually very difficult for men to carry out their ethical principles; and there is fate. But we should be true to our nature, and should not discourage ourselves by saying that there is a fate.[1] The spirit of Confucius is that although he knows the impracticable nature of the times, yet will he be striving to do something.[2] He makes himself responsible for the betterment of the world, and exhausts all his mental powers. This is the principle of "establishing fate."

The active policy is not to disregard fate, but to believe it, and such a belief makes the character of man very strong. When Confucius was in the state of Wei, he lived with Yen Ch'ou-yu, a worthy of Wei. But Mi Tzŭ, an unworthy favorite of the court, informed Confucius through his pupil, that if he would lodge with him, he might obtain a position as a minister. The answer of Confucius was that there is fate. Mencius comments as follows: "Confucius went into office according to propriety, and retired from it according to righteousness. In regard to his obtaining office or not obtaining it, he said: 'There is fate.'"[3] When Confucius was informed that Kung-po Liao, an officer of Lu, slandered Tzŭ-lu to Chi-sun, the prime minister, Confucius said: "If my principles are to be carried out, it is fate. If they are to fall to the ground, it is fate. What can Kung-po Liao do to fate?"[4] Therefore, the doctrine of fate makes man believe firmly his own principles, and not move on account of anything outside of himself. Even the question of life and death cannot affect him,—how

[1] *Classics,* vol. ii, pp. 489-490.

[2] *Classics,* vol. i, p. 290.

[3] *Classics,* vol. ii, p. 365.

[4] *Classics,* vol. i, p. 289.

can the question of obtaining office or wealth affect him? Mencius says: "When neither a premature death nor long life causes a man any double-mindedness, but he cultivates his personal character, and waits for whatever issue;—this is the way in which he establishes fate."[1] Every one has his own fate; if he does not believe it, he will be disturbed and changed by even very little things, and he destroys by himself what he has done before. This is a lack of self-confidence. Therefore, the doctrine of fate is good not only for those who discharge their ethical duties, but also for those who carry on their economic business. Indeed, it applies to the problems of daily life.

The doctrine of fate is accepted by Taoism, but rejected by Moism. Mo Tzŭ gives three books against this doctrine, but he cannot attack it on any exact point. He says that by the doctrine of fate, the ruler and officer must be lazy regarding the works of government, and the men and women must also be lazy regarding production of wealth.[2] But this is not the doctrine of fate at all.

2. *Doctrine of Name*

The second principle directly against the economic motive is the doctrine of name. The name of a man is the identification of his personality, and what a man cares for is not merely the name but the merits which make the name famous. Confucius says: "The superior man hates that his name will not be praised after his death."[3] Since the name is the invariable concomitant of merit, and no one can have been a superior man without his name being remembered, the name is necessary to the superior man. This does not mean that he should seek for his name from others,

[1] *Classics,* vol. ii, p. 449.

[2] Bk. xxxvii.

[3] *Classics,* vol. i, p. 300.

but that he should make his name for himself. Again, he says: "When we have established our personality and diffused our principles, so as to make our name famous in future ages, and thereby glorify our parents: this is the end of filial piety." [1] From this statement, we know that Confucius regards the name as the final aim of ethical life. It is said by Ssŭ-ma Chien that establishing a name is the highest of conduct.[2]

The doctrine of name is to make the ethical motive stronger than the economic motive, and to make people disregard their economic conditions through attachment to virtue. Confucius says:

> Riches and honors are what men want. But, if they are obtained in an improper way, they should not be held. Poverty and low estate are what men hate. But, even though they befall one who does not deserve them, they should not be evaded.
>
> If a superior man abandon the virtue of love, how can he completely make his name? The superior man does not, even for the space of a single meal, act contrary to the virtue of love. In moments of haste, he cleaves to it. In times of danger, he cleaves to it.[3]

This is the ethical teaching which directly opposes economic wants. What we must cling to is the virtue of love, and it is the means by which to make our name complete. Therefore, we must cleave to the virtue of love and must not prefer riches to poverty. This is the way of making a name.

Since desire for riches and hatred of poverty are very strong human motives, how can Confucius make men indifferent to these two conditions and careful for their name? In order to preach the doctrine of name, not only are ethical theories needed, but also historical facts. Hence, Confucius

[1] *Sacred Books of the East,* vol. iii, p. 466.

[2] *History of Han,* ch. lxii.

[3] *Classics,* vol. i, p. 166.

gives these facts to show that a name is independent of riches, and that it is much more lasting and important. He says:

The Duke Ching of Ch'i had a thousand teams, each of four horses, but on the day of his death, the people did not praise him for a single virtue. Po-yi and Shu-ch'i died of hunger at the foot of the Shou-yang mountain, but the people, down to the present time, praise them. "It is certainly not on account of material wealth, but merely on account of personal distinction"—is not that saying illustrated by this?[1]

The rich prince cannot live longer than the day of his death, and all his riches cannot be of any use to him; but the two starved men can live forever by their names. This is proof that the name has much more value than riches, and man should not deceive himself when he makes a choice between them. Therefore, Chia Yi (352-384 A. K. or 200-168 B. C.) says: "The coveteous man dies for the sake of wealth, but the heroic man dies for the sake of his name."[2]

Some people would say that the doctrine of name is based on selfishness, and that it is not the highest principle of ethics. This might be somewhat true, but we must discuss it further. To care for the name may be a form of selfishness, but we never can get away from selfishness in that sense, no matter how perfect the ethical principle. The highest principle is that virtue is for virtue's sake. Confucius says: "The determined scholar and the man of virtue will not seek to live at the expense of injuring their virtue, but will sacrifice even their lives to preserve their virue complete."[3] This is the highest type of man. But

[1] *Classics*, vol. i, p. 315.

[2] *Historical Record*, ch. lxxxiv.

[3] *Classics*, vol. i, p. 297.

when we ask why they sacrifice their lives to preserve their virtue complete, it must be explained that in this way they satisfy their ethical wants. It is a feeling that they cannot withstand, and for the satisfaction of this feeling they sacrifice even their lives. This may be selfishness, but how can we get any better than this? In fact, man is a living creature with feelings and wants, and he never can be an absolutely unselfish man from this point of view, unless he is not a man.

Since men are generally very anxious to make profit, Confucius cannot weaken such an economic interest without arousing the ethical interest; hence he preaches the doctrine of name as a substitute for profit. Human nature is so weak that it does not want to do good unless there is some gain either in the form of profit or in that of name. Confucius says: "In the whole world, there is only one man who loves what is proper to humanity without some personal object in the matter, or who hates what is contrary to humanity without being apprehensive of some evil." Again, he says: "The philanthropist practices the virtue of humanity easily and naturally; the wise man practices it for the sake of advantage which it brings; and those who fear the guilt of transgression practice it by constraint." [1] We should not expect all men to be philanthropists practicing virtue without aiming at any advantage, and we should give some reward to anyone who practices this virtue. If we taught the people not to make profit, and denied them also the interest of making a name, it would be too cruel, and unjust, and human society would not progress at all. Therefore Confucius establishes the doctrine of name in order to draw the people away from the economic world to the ethical world, and to give them ethical gain instead of economic gain.

[1] *Li Ki,* bk. xxix, pp. 332-3.

According to Confucius, the name has two kinds of use, one for reward and the other for punishment. In the *Spring and Autumn*, he exercises his authority to praise and to condemn men, from the emperor to the common people, by the use of name. When he praises a name, even a single word is more honorable than the position of emperor; and when he condemns a name, even a single word is more severe than the death penalty. Therefore, when he speaks of Wu Wang, he says that he does not lose his famous name in the world.[1] Mencius says: "If a ruler is called after his death by the name of the Dark or the Cruel, even though he may have filial sons and affectionate grandsons, they will not be able to change his bad name even after a hundred generations."[2] Hence, the people are impelled to do good in the hope of getting a good name, and are afraid to do wrong for fear of getting a bad name. This illustrates the usefulness of the doctrine of name.

Taoism destroys the doctrine of name. Lao Tzŭ raises the following question: "Which is dearer to you, your name or your life?"[3] He means that the life is dearer than the name, and that we should not care for our name at the expense of our life. Taoism is egoistic, and Yang Chu carries it to the extreme. His doctrine is that everyone must come to the same end, death, no matter how good or how bad he may be. The good men have a good name after their death, but they lose enjoyment during their life; the bad men have a bad name after their death, but they have the enjoyment of gratifying their wants during their life. Both the good name and the bad name are no more to the dead than to the trunk of a tree or a clod of earth; they do not know either the praise or the condemna-

[1] *Classics,* vol. i, p. 400.

[2] *Classics,* vol. ii, p. 293.

[3] *Tao Tê King,* ch. xliv.

tion. How can a name do any good to the rotten bones?[1] Such a doctrine is extreme Epicureanism, and it is directly against Confucianism. But it was swept away by Mencius.

3. *Doctrine of Soul*

The third principle directly against the economic motive is the doctrine of soul. With the word soul, we must include its synonyms. In the "Great Learning," soul is also called "brilliant virtue"; in the "Doctrine of the Mean," it is called "the nature of Heavenly endowment", "the virtuous nature", and "sincerity"; in the "Evolution of Civilization", "intelligent spirit"; in the "Appendix" of the *Canon of Changes*, "essential spirit"; in *Mêng Tzŭ* (Mencius), it is called "the spirit of the greatest and strongest", "the good conscience", "the good mind," "the original mind", and "mind". According to Confucianism, we can look at soul from two points of view. From the ethical viewpoint, there is the soul of the living which is the best part of the mind. From the religious viewpoint, there is the soul of the dead which is apart from the body. It is the same soul, only in different times of the life. If we can keep our soul here in the ethical way, we shall preserve it hereafter as the essential spirit shining in Heaven; if we cannot keep it right, it will be dissolved and changed.[2]

To contrast it with the economic motive, we shall discuss the doctrine of soul only from the ethical point of view. On this account, the teachings of Mencius are best fitted to our purpose. He usually employs the word mind instead of the word soul, but its meaning is the same. He first points out that the spiritual wants are just as strong as the physical wants. To illustrate this principle, he indicates that the senses of the mouth, the ears and the eyes all have standards of taste, of sound and of beauty. Why should

[1] *Cf. Classics*, vol. ii, pp. 93-7. [2] *Yi King*, p. 354.

the mind alone have no standard at all? The standard of the mind is one of reason and justice. Therefore, reason and justice satisfy the needs of our mind just as the best foods satisfy the needs of our appetite.[1]

Now, Mencius is going to show that the soul is more important than the body. He says:

There is no part of the person which a man does not love, and as he loves all, so he must nourish all. . . . But some part of the person is noble, and some ignoble; some great, and some small. The great must not be injured for the small, nor the noble for the ignoble. He who nourishes the little belonging to him is a little man, and he who nourishes the great is a great man. . . . The man of only eating and drinking is counted mean by others, because he nourishes what is little to the neglect of what is great.[2]

What he means by the noble and great part of the person is the soul; and by the ignoble and small part, the body. A man should love both his soul and his body, and he should nourish them both. But he should nourish the soul more than the body. He who cares more for the body is a little man. What Mencius calls "the man of only eating and drinking" is what we may call the economic man who cares only for the body. According to the principle of Mencius, the chief object of man is the soul and not the body, and he should subject the economic life to the ethical or spiritual life.

The question arises as to how he can make the soul more important than the body, or in other words, how he can use the soul as the master of the whole body. Why does not every one take more care for his soul than for his body? To answer this question, Mencius gives a very good principle which is the key to the ethical religion of Confucius. He says:

[1] *Classics,* vol. ii, pp. 405-7.

[2] *Ibid.,* pp. 416-7.

The senses of hearing and seeing do not think, and are obscured by external things. When the external things come into contact with the senses which are also only things, as a matter of course they lead them away. To the mind belongs the office of thinking. By thinking it gets the right view of things; by neglecting to think it fails to do this. Both the senses and the mind are what Heaven has given to us. If a man can first establish the supremacy of the nobler part of his constitution, the inferior part will not be able to take it from him. It is simply this which makes the great man.[1]

From this statement, we know that the superiority of the mind over the senses is that the mind can think about anything and the senses cannot. Although both are the endowments of Heaven, the one is nobler than the other. The mind is like the sovereign, having the full powers of will and reasoning, while the senses are like the ordinary officials, performing their functions only in a passive way. The senses are material things themselves, and of course they are subjected to the material things outside. But the mind is the soul, which has the power of thinking and is independent of anything. If a man can make his soul supreme, how can the senses snatch it away? But how can he establish the supremacy of the soul? Simply by thinking, and thinking is sufficient to make a great man. It is said in the *Canon of History* that the effect of thinking is perspicacity, and that perspicacity becomes the quality of the holy man.[2] Therefore, thinking is the way of establishing the soul, and establishing the soul is the way of controlling economic wants. In fact, the doctrine of soul is an ethical teaching, but it is practiced in the economic life. Hence, according to Confucianism, we can live in the economic world, and yet we can be holy men.

[1] *Classics,* vol. ii, p. 418.

[2] *Classics,* vol. iii, pt. ii, pp. 326-7.

BOOK III GENERAL ECONOMIC PRINCIPLES

CHAPTER IX

Economic Development as the Chief Cause of Progress

I. ECONOMIC DEVELOPMENT

We have already seen that Confucius is in favor of the inductive method; his statements are generally based on historical facts. When he discusses with Tzŭ-yu the evolution of civilization, he takes up the economic development of the remotest time as the starting point. The discussion of the first stage is concerned only with primitive technique, such as the building of houses, the cooking of food, and the making of clothes. Indeed, technical invention is the basis of civilization.

Confucius begins his discussion with the so-called root-grubbing period which was supplemented by the hunting stage. Such an economic condition was before the age of Pao Hsi. His exact words are as follows:

Formerly the ancient kings had no houses. In winter they lived in caves which they had excavated, and in summer in nests which they had framed. They did not yet know the transforming power of fire, but ate the fruits of plants and trees, and the flesh of birds and beasts, drinking their blood, and swallowing also the hair and feathers. They did not yet know the use of flax and silk, but clothed themselves with feathers and furs.

The later sages then arose, and men learned to make use of fire. They molded the metals into articles and fashioned clay into pottery. By using fire, metals and earth, they built towers with structures on them, and houses with windows and doors; they toasted, grilled, boiled and roasted their foods; they produced must and sauces; they dealt with the flax and silk so as to form linen and silken fabrics. They were thus able to nourish the living and to give burial to the dead, to serve the ghosts, the spirits, and God. In all these things the people still follow the example of that early time.[1]

Food, clothes and housing are the three most important things in economic life. But they never can be made by the human hand until the development of technique. The utilization of fire is the most important of all, and the molding of metals and baking of earth come next. Then these crafts can be used for the purpose of getting food, clothes and houses. After the economic life has been satisfied, the religious life begins. This is the origin of civilization, based on economic development.

In the " Appendix " of the *Canon of Changes,* just after the first paragraph speaking about " administering wealth " which has been partly quoted above,[2] there are thirteen paragraphs pointing out the historical facts of " administering wealth " by the ancient emperors. The whole chapter is really an outline of the economic development of China. The order of paragraphs is chronological, and everything is traced back to the age of invention and discovery.

The first emperor the "Appendix " mentions is Pao Hsi. It says:

[1] *Li Ki,* bk. vii, pp. 369-370.

[2] See *supra,* p. 48.

> Anciently, when Pao Hsi had come to rule the world, looking up, he contemplated the brilliant forms exhibited in the sky; and looking down, he surveyed the patterns shown on the earth. He contemplated the ornamental appearances of birds and beasts, and the different possibilities of the soil. Near at hand, in his own person, he found things for consideration, and the same at a distance, in things in general. From this he devised the eight trigrams, in order to show fully the attributes of spiritual and intellectual life, and to classify the natures of the myriads of things. He invented the making of nets of various kinds by knitting strings, both for hunting and fishing.

By his name and inventions we may know that the age of Pao Hsi was in the hunting and fishing stage, and also in the pastoral stage.[1]

The Chinese really have no accurate knowledge about the earliest history of China, but it is said that the reign of Pao Hsi lasted one hundred and ten years, and that the fifteen reigns which followed all adopted the name of Pao Hsi. It is certain that the period between Pao Hsi and Shên Nung must have been very long. Since Shên Nung was a great inventor, the "Appendix" mentions him next. It says: "He fashioned wood to form the share, and bent

[1] The name of Pao Hsi has some significance. Pao means kitchen, and Hsi domestic animal. Such a name would mean that he was the inventor of kitchen and cookery. He is also called by the name of Fu Hsi. Fu means subjugating or domesticating, and such a name would mean that he was the inventor of the domestication of animals. At that time, both hunting and fishing were by means of different nets. The eight trigrams were the first invention of writing. For example: ☰ represents heaven; ☷, earth; ☳, thunder; ☴, wind; ☵, water; ☲, fire; ☶, mountain; and ☱, marsh. They are really eight characters. In the Chinese language, they are called *pa kua; pa* means eight, and *kua* means hanging. The latter means that the phenomena of things are hung in order to show them to the people. This was the first step toward civilization.

wood to make the plough-handle. The advantages of ploughing and weeding were then taught to the whole empire." The age of Shên Nung was thus the beginning of the agricultural stage.[1]

This age was also, however, the beginning of the primitive commercial stage. The "Appendix" says: "He caused markets to be held at midday, thus bringing together all the people, and assembling in one place all their commodities. They made their exchanges and retired, everyone having got what he wanted." This was a very important advance of civilization. Since the "Appendix" does not mention money, it would seem that the exchanges of this period were mostly in the form of barter.

According to the historians, the reign of Shên Nung lasted one hundred and twenty years. After seven subsequent reigns, Huang Ti arose. His reign lasted one hundred years (2147-2048 B. K. or 2698-2599 B. C.). After two hundred and forty-one years, came the Emperor Yao whose reign lasted ninety years, and the Emperor Shun whose reign lasted fifty years. Huang Ti, Yao and Shun were the three greatest emperors, and they were in the historical periods; hence, the "Appendix" mentions them as a whole. It says:

After the death of Shên Nung, there arose Huang Ti, Yao and Shun. They carried through the necessary changes of material things, so that the people would not get tired of them. They transformed the economic conditions miraculously in order to make them fit the people. They were harmonized with the principle of the *Canon of Changes:* when the course of any

[1] The name of Shên Nung also has some significance. Shên means divine, and Nung means farmer. As he was called Divine Farmer, it is very clear that he was the discoverer of agriculture. Especially from the word "fashioned", we know that there was the utilization of metal, although the share was made of wood.

thing comes to an end, it should be changed; when it is changed, it passes through freely; when it passes through freely, it can continue for a long time.

The principle of the *Canon of Changes* is the theory of evolution, but the "Appendix" illustrates it by the economic development of these three emperors.

Indeed, economic changes form the most powerful elements in evolution in the course of civilization. K'ung Ying-ta (1125-1199 A. K. or 574-648 A. D.), for the explanation of this point, gives this illustration:

Preceding the time of Huang Ti, the people wore the furs of animals. Later, the population grew larger, and the animals became fewer; hence the material for such a dress would be somewhat exhausted. Therefore, the adoption of silk and flax for the making of clothes was a miraculous transformation, in order to adapt them to the people.

This is quite an economic interpretation of history. In short, the age of Huang Ti, and that of Yao and Shun, marked an epoch-making advance in the history of civilization, and such an advance was chiefly based on economic development. Therefore, the "Appendix" does not mention anything but the material civilization.

Concerning the material civilization of these three emperors, the "Appendix" mentions only nine things. The nine things were all invented in the time of Huang Ti, and were completed or improved in the time of Yao and Shun. Therefore, the "Appendix" does not make any distinction among them. The nine things are in the following order.

(1) They made the new system of dress and established the social order by the means of it. Hence, the "Appendix" says: "Huang Ti, Yao and Shun simply wore their upper and lower garments, as patterns to the people, and good order was secured throughout the whole empire." It shows

the peaceful, graceful, orderly, and industrial society of that time, and it takes dress first as a sign to mark the distinction between this age and the ages previous.

(2) They discovered the means of navigation. The "Appendix" says: "They cut open trees to form boats, and cut others long and thin to make oars . . . . They could now reach the most distant parts, and the whole empire was benefited." In the making of the boats and oars, they made use of metal.

(3) They discovered the means of transportation. The "Appendix" says: "They used oxen in carts, and yoked horses to chariots, thus providing for the carriage of what was heavy, and for distant journeys, thereby benefiting the whole empire."

(4) After navigation and transportation had been developed, there was need of protection for the cities. Hence, the "Appendix" says: "They made the system of double gates, and the warning of the clapper, as a preparation against the approach of marauding visitors."

(5) For the refinement of the food, they made the pestle and mortar. The "Appendix" says: "They cut wood and fashioned it into pestles; they dug in the ground and formed mortars. Thus the myriads of the people received the benefit arising from the use of the pestle and mortar." As the "Appendix" takes them as a great invention among all other great things, we can see how much importance the Chinese ascribe to rice.

(6) Since society was now highly developed, and the double gates and clapper were not sufficient for protection, there was need of good weapons. The "Appendix" says: "They bent wood by means of string so as to form bows, and sharpened wood so as to make arrows. The utility of bows and arrows was to produce a feeling of awe over the empire." These things seem more military than economic,

but they really are for economic purposes, because they are for the protection of wealth.

(7) They changed the form of shelter. The "Appendix" says: "In the highest antiquity, they made their homes in winter in caves, and in summer dwelt in the open country. In subsequent ages, for these the sages substituted houses, with the ridgebeam above and the projecting roof below, as a provision against wind and rain."

(8) As we shall see, the Chinese always consider the funeral as a part of economic life;[1] the "Appendix" mentions the invention of coffins as follows:

When the ancients buried their dead, they covered the body thickly with pieces of wood, having laid it in the open country. They raised no mound over it, nor planted trees around it; nor had they any fixed period for mourning. In subsequent ages, the sages substituted for these practices the inner and outer coffins.

(9) So far as the physical needs had been satisfied, there should be mental and legal development, and the most important thing was the complete invention of writing. The "Appendix" says:

In the highest antiquity, government was carried on successfully by the use of knotted cords to preserve the memory of things. In subsequent ages, the sages substituted for these written characters and bonds. By means of these, the doings of all the officials could be regulated, and the affairs of all the people accurately examined.[2]

This was the last thing in the economic development of ancient China.

[1] See *infra.*

[2] *Yi King,* pp. 382-5.

The age of Huang Ti, Yao and Shun was in the agricultural stage. Through the improvements of navigation and transportation, it belonged also to the stage of primitive commerce. But what made this age a great advance was that it had reached the beginning of the primitive industrial stage. The ships and oars, the carts and chariots, the gates and clappers, the pestles and mortars, the bows and arrows, the ridgebeams and projecting roofs, the different coffins, and the tablets which were to be written, all these things required some kind of skilled labor. And above all, there was the silk industry. It changed the face of the whole society, and distinguished the social order by the system of dress. It marked a great advance not only in the economic development, but also in the social and political organization.

Looking at the whole chapter of the "Appendix," we can see it is really a historical treatise on Chinese economic development. Or, since the writer of the "Appendix" would be interested in the general development of Chinese civilization as a whole, and not in the economic development particularly, we may better say that it is certainly an economic interpretation of history. From its beginning to its end, it mentions thirteen things; and, except four things only—namely, the eight trigrams, the double gates and clappers, the bows and arrows, and the written characters and bonds—all of them are absolutely essential to economic civilization. Moreover, even among those four things, the double gates and clappers and the bows and arrows are mainly for the protection of economic life; and the different forms of writing, from the eight trigrams to the written characters and bonds, are partially for the development of economic life. In short, economic development is the principal factor of civilization, while writing is the most important tool to promote civilization.

The "Appendix" was written by the immediate pupils of Confucius, and its importance is equal to that of the "Great Learning" and the "Doctrine of the Mean." It was the basis of the philosophical schools of the Sung dynasty, and it gave a great impetus to thought. But the Schools of the Sung did not understand this chapter well, so that the economic development of China has been retarded since that time. The reason was simply that they did not know that technical invention and material welfare are the chief cause of civilization. If we read this chapter carefully, we see how important to the progress of civilization economic development is from the point of view of the Confucians.

Besides this chapter, we should like to quote four passages more from the "Appendix," in order to show that Confucianism is somewhat materialistic and praises technical invention very highly. It says: "The sages, fully understanding the way of Heaven, and having clearly ascertained the experience of the people, invented these divine things as a provision for the use of the people." [1] As the "Appendix" calls such material things "divine things" and the results of "the way of Heaven", we can see how materialistic is Confucianism; nay, we may even say that Confucianism is a religion of the economic world. It gives its explanation as follows:

> The first appearance of anything as a bud is what we call a semblance; when it has received its complete form we call it an article. How to make and how to use it is what we call a law. The utilities arising from it in external and internal matters, so that the people all use it, stamp it with a character which we call divine.[2]

Again, it says: "In preparing material things for the reali-

[1] *Yi King*, p. 372.

[2] *Ibid.*, p. 373.

zation of practical use, and inventing the complete articles for the benefit of the whole world, there are none greater than the sages."[1] Hence, the Confucians call all the great inventors by the name of sages. It says again:

> That which is antecedent to the material form exists, we say, as a principle, and that which is subsequent to the material form exists, we say, as an article. Transforming and shaping it is what we call change. Carrying it out and putting it in operation is what we call success. Taking the result and setting it forth for all the people of the whole world is what we call the business of life.[2]

This passage is simply an explanation of the process of invention. It traces back to the beginning when there is merely a principle without anything existing, and comes down to the end when the article is utilized in the business of life. By these four passages, we can understand perfectly that the Confucians take technical invention as the basis of economic development, and the economic development as the basis of all civilization.

What Confucius discusses in the "Evolution of Civilization" and what the "Appendix" narrates is the economic development of the earliest China. But we should like to say something about the economic progress made about the time of Confucius. The Chou dynasty, as we know, was the period of maturity of the Chinese civilization. In the beginning of this dynasty (about 571 B. K. or 1122 B. C.), there were two great statesmen; the Duke of Chou and T'ai Kung. They both were very efficient in developing Chinese economic civilization. But T'ai Kung, especially, after he withdrew from the imperial government and came to his feudal state, Ch'i, devoted all his attention to economic development, and made Ch'i the chief state for industry

[1] *Yi King*, p. 373. [2] *Ibid.*, p. 377.

and commerce in the Chinese world. This was the first time that China rose to the stage of national economy; and even began to reach that of international economy.

Later, Ch'i declined; but Kuan Chung, or Kuan Tzŭ (died 93 B. K. or 644 B. C.), minister of Ch'i, raised Ch'i again to the chief state of industry and commerce, and its prosperity lasted until the end of its political life (331 A. K. or 221 B. C.). In the period of Spring and Autumn (171 B. K.—71 A. K. or 722—481 B. C.), there were many industrial and commercial states besides Ch'i; hence, economic civilization in the time of Confucius was highly developed. This period was really in the stage of international economy or world economy. Of course, what the ancient Chinese called world was simply the Chinese world. But we must understand that the territory of the leading states of this period was really equal to that of the leading European states in modern times. Therefore, there is no reason why we should not call it world economy In the period of Warring States (149-331 A. K. or 403—221 B. C.), the whole Chinese world was divided up into only seven states, and economic development was still higher. This period was the most dynamic in the whole history of China, and it marked the sharp distinction between ancient and modern China. Such a dynamic condition was ended at the beginning of the Han dynasty (about 412 A. K. or 140 B. C.).

Taking Chinese history as a whole, we may divide the economic stages as follows: From the standpoint of the relation of production to consumption, the period from the beginning of Chinese history to the beginning of the Chou dynasty was the stage of self-sufficing or isolated economy; that from that period to the period of Spring and Autumn was the stage of local or village economy; and that from that period to the present day was and is, the stage of national economy. Of course, such a division is very rough.

If we want to get a finer division, we may say that the period preceding the age of Spring and Autumn was ancient economy, that the period covering the age of Spring and Autumn and that of Warring States was a transitional period; and that the period from the Ch'in dynasty (331, or 221 B. C.) to the present was modern economy. From the political point of view, the period preceding the Ch'in dynasty was feudalism, and that after that dynasty was absolute monarchy; and from the economic point of view, the former period was marked by the government ownership of land, and the latter period, by its private ownership. These are the only general statements we can make.

If we wish to make a general comparison between China and Europe, we may say that China passed through the pastoral stage in a short period, but has stayed in the agricultural stage for a very long time; and that Europe had stayed in the pastoral stage for a very long time, but passed through the agricultural stage in a short period. We do not wish to go into the details of history, but we may pick out some features of the present day in order to show some of the more striking contrasts between the Chinese and the European economic civilizations.

First, we may take up foods. In the western world, steaks and chops are the principal meats, but their cooking is quite simple, because they are merely burned by fire. Milk is a common drink, and butter is used as oil. These foods are quite similar to those consumed by the Huns described in the Han dynasty In China, the people have much more varied food, and their cutting, seasoning and cooking are much finer and more complex. Milk is not a common drink in China, and the Chinese do not use butter, but peanut oil.

Second, we may take up the subject of dress. In the western world, wool is the principal material for clothes and hats, and leather for shoes. The men's dress is simple in color; and the children in most countries wear only short trousers and short dresses, having their legs below the knees covered only by stockings. Furs and feathers are still used by women, not only for warmth, but also for fashion. In China, silk, linen and cotton are the principal materials for clothes, hats, or shoes. The men's dress has different colors, and the children do not purposely expose any part of their body. The people wear furs only as fur coats, but never use feathers. All these things show that Europe has passed the pastoral stage only a short time ago, and still has indications of the survival of that stage; and that China has long since come to the agricultural stage, and has the indications of the agricultural life.

It is fortunate for Europe and unfortunate for China, however, that Europe has come to the true industrial stage much earlier than China. The great difference is marked by machinery. Besides food and dress, moreover, the building of Europe is better than that of China. It is probably because in the ancient times, Greece and Rome had slaves for erecting their buildings, and in the medieval times, the church and the feudal princes had great power to build up the churches and castles. But in China, there was no slavery; the church had no such power; and the feudal princes were not so oppressive as those in Europe. Whatever the cause may have been, there can be no doubt that Chinese buildings are inferior to those of Europe. The chief defects of Chinese buildings are that the material of the walls is brick instead of stone, and that the inside structure is finished in wood, for the most part, that is, there are wooden beams and wooden pillars to support the roof, and wooden floors. Hence they do not endure very long. Moreover, the Chinese have not shown any great interest in preserving their old buildings. Therefore, even though there have been many good buildings, they have been destroyed during the revolutions of different dynasties.

II. THEORY OF PROGRESS

From different writings, we may infer the theory of progress of Confucius. There is no better example than the principle of The Three Stages, as pointed out above,[1] for proof that Confucius believed in progress. But the principle of The Three Stages is very general, and it can be applied to every case. If we wish to get a specific theory about economic progress, we may come to the *tsing tien* system, and see how Confucius expects that general progress of every kind will result from this system. On this specific point, his theory of progress is periodical, and can be measured by the length of one year, three years, nine years, eighteen years, twenty-seven years, and thirty years. According to his theory, progress can be realized within three years, and it can be completed within thirty years. It comes from the *tsing tien* system, and we shall take the interpretation of Pan Ku from his "Economic History."[2]

Under the *tsing tien* system, in the cultivation of three years, the people have a surplus of food sufficient for one year. Hence, the sense of pride and shame is developed, and quarrels and litigations do not exist. Therefore, every three years, an examination of merit is given to the officials. Confucius says: "If there were any of the princes who would employ me, in the course of twelve months, I should have done something considerable. In three years, the work would be accomplished."[3] In saying that the work would be accomplished in three years, he refers to the *tsing tien* system. From his point of view, *tsing tien* is not only a

[1] See *supra*, pp. 16-20.

[2] *History of Han*, ch. xxiv.

[3] *Classics*, vol. i, p. 267.

theoretical system, but a practical one; and the period of three years is the first step of progress. In nine years, after three examinations have been held, the undeserving officials are degraded, and the deserving promoted. There is a surplus of food sufficient for three years; and the improvement of the occupations of the people is called "advancement." In eighteen years, there are two periods of "advancement", and such a condition is called "peace"; the surplus of food is sufficient for six years. In twenty-seven years, there are three periods of "advancement", and this is called "extreme peace"; the surplus of food is sufficient for nine years. Then virtue prevails, and the government is perfected. Confucius says: "If a true king were to arise, it would still require a generation, and then the benevolent government would be complete." [1] He means that the completion of the *tsing tien* system requires thirty years. *Kung-yang's Commentary* says: "If the system of tithes, [the whole system of *tsing tien*], shall prevail, the praise of peace will arise."

Although the tendency of the *tsing tien* system is to level the whole society into a static condition, there is, at the same time, a dynamic principle. In every period of nine years, it requires a total improvement in all the different occupations;—that is, among all the agricultural and industrial occupations no stationary condition is allowed. Such an improvement is called by the name of advancement; two steps of advancement are called by the name of peace; three steps of advancement, extreme peace. It is peculiar enough that the name of peace or extreme peace is assigned for the advancement of the occupations of the people; it means that we can obtain the stage of peace only by the improvement of productive power. Therefore, for the in-

[1] *Classics,* vol. i, p. 267.

dividuals, the *tsing tien* system does not give anyone an advantage; it is a static model. But for society as a whole, advancements are necessary; and it is the dynamic principle. This is the theory of progress of Confucius.

His theory of progress, however, is based on many phases. Some of them have been discussed above, and the others will be discussed later. If we want to sum up his whole theory of progress in a few words, it will be:

I. The Abolition of War. A peaceful society is necessary for industrial development.[1]

II. Technical Invention. It is the basis of economic progress, and is also the basis of all other progress.[2]

III. The Control of Nature. It makes man the rival and the assistant of Heaven and Earth.[3]

IV. The *Tsing Tien* System. Everyone has an equal share of the most important part of the means of production.[4]

V. The Universally Free Education. It gives everyone equal opportunity for intellectual and moral development.[5]

VI. The Election System. It makes a representative government based on the educational system.[6]

VII. The Great Similarity. It abolishes such social institutions as state, family and private property.[7]

[1] See *infra.*

[2] See *supra*, pp. 119-128.

[3] See *infra.*

[4] See *infra.*

[5] See *supra*, pp. 82-84.

[6] See *supra*, pp. 87-93.

[7] See *supra*, pp. 18-20.

VIII. The Change of Human Nature. The end of the Confucian system is to make human nature perfect.

All other phases are discussed in other places, and we shall discuss here only the last one, the change of human nature. Since there are many different views regarding human nature, we must go back to Confucius first. He says: "By nature, men are nearly alike; by practice, they get to be wide apart." Again, he says: "There are only the wise of the highest class, and the stupid of the lowest class, who cannot be changed."[1] From this point of view, therefore, human nature is about the same everywhere and in everyone, but it generally can be greatly changed. What Confucius means by nature is the qualities received by birth, the same meaning that has been given by the *Adjunct to the Canon of Filial Piety* and by Kao Tzŭ. Mencius and Hsun Tzŭ both differ from Confucius in their views, and each opposes the other. Hsun Tzŭ holds that human nature is evil; hence education is the most important thing for the correction of human nature. Mencius holds that human nature is good; hence the only thing which is needed is to extend what man already has. They both are not quite correct, but each has established his doctrine. If we make a compromise, we may say that Hsun Tzŭ speaks of human nature in the stage of Small Tranquility, and that Mencius speaks of it in that of Great Similarity. If they have different stages in mind, their doctrines are both correct.

According to the theory of Confucius, in the stage of Great Similarity or Extreme Peace, human nature is good. As we have quoted before, in the Great Similarity selfish schemings are repressed and find no way to arise. This means that the selfishness of human nature is changed. In

[1] *Classics*, vol. i, p. 318.

the *Spring and Autumn*, the Extreme Peace Stage is that in which everyone in the world conducts himself like the superior man, and all the barbarians become civilized. Therefore, changing human nature so that it will be perfectly good is the final aim of Confucianism.

But how can we go about changing human nature? Simply by means of those seven things just mentioned above, but the chief thing is economic prosperity. Mencius is the chief representative of those who advocate that human nature is good, yet he still says that in good years the children of people are most of them good, while in bad years the most of them abandon themselves to evil.[1] Therefore, the human nature changes to either good or evil in accordance with the economic condition. If there is economic prosperity equally distributed to everyone, the nature of the people must be good. Mencius says: "When a sage governs the world, he will cause pulse and grain to be as abundant as water and fire. If pulse and grain are as abundant as water and fire, how shall the people be other than virtuous?"[2] Therefore, if we shall come to the highest development of the economic world, we shall come also to the highest development of the ethical world. The former is the cause, and the latter is the effect. Hence, Confucius regards economic progress as the means, and moral perfection as the end. If we understand this, we have the general view of his theory of progress.

Besides economic prosperity as a general condition, Confucius has a special device for changing human nature. As we have seen, Confucius makes universally free education a necessary institution; it is really a most important force for modifying human nature. But the educational system of Confucius begins not only in the school age of a child,

[1] *Classics*, vol. ii, p. 404.

[2] *Ibid.*, p. 463.

but even before his birth. This is a peculiar doctrine of Confucius, and it is known as gestatory education.

According to *Elder Tai's Record of Rites*, the first thing in gestatory education is the choice of the mother. Therefore, when the parents choose the wife of their son, they must select her from among those families which have had a high standard of morality for all generations. There are five women who are not to be taken in marriage: (1) the daughter of a rebellious house; (2) the daughter of a disorderly house; (3) the daughter of a house which has produced criminals for more than one generation; (4) the daughter of a leprous house; (5) the daughter who has lost her mother and has grown old.[1]

When a woman is pregnant, the rules are as follows: While sleeping, she should lie on her back; while sitting or standing, the body should be in an upright position, and the weight evenly distributed. She should not laugh too loudly; nor eat food of bad flavors, nor anything which is not cut properly; nor sit down on anything which is not placed properly. The eyes should not see bad colors, the ears should not hear bad sounds, and the mouth should not utter bad words. She should read good poetry, and tell good stories. By this means, the child will be physically, morally, and mentally excellent. Whenever a woman is pregnant, she must be very watchful in regard to the things by which the mind is affected. If she is affected by good things, the child will be good; if by bad things, he will be bad. These are the rules of gestatory education. The mothers of Wên Wang and of Ch'êng Wang are good examples of such educators.

When a child is born, moreover, he receives the family education for a long time before he goes to school. There-

[1] Bk lxxx.

fore, Confucius says: "When a child is trained completely, his education is just as strong as his nature; and when he practices anything perpetually, he will do it naturally as a permanent habit." [1]

This is Confucius' plan for changing human nature. If every generation of the world would put it in practice, human nature would soon be perfect. It is the same principle as that man should control nature in the economic world. Man must control nature not only without him, but also within him, so that progress will be complete and continuous.

[1] Bk. xlviii.

CHAPTER X

Economic Organization

I. THE WHOLE WORLD AS THE LARGEST ORGANIZATION

When we come to the topic of economic organization, we must say that according to the view of Confucius, there are two organizations. The one is the largest—the world; the other, the smallest—the family. As Chinese philosophy is mostly synthetical, going from the whole to the part, and as world economy is a special theme of Confucius, we shall take up the largest organization first, in order to show the economic thought of Confucius prominently and clearly.

How do we know that Confucius regards the world as an economic organization? It is found in the "Great Learning." The "Great Learning" may be called the catalogue of the teachings of Confucius. The objects of the principles of the "Great Learning" are three: to brighten the brilliant virtue, to renovate the people, and to rest in the highest excellence. The first object is to care for the individual himself; the second for the other people as a whole; the third is the perfect state which forms the goal for the other two objects. Having understood these three objects, we now come to its eight subjects: (1) the investigation of things; (2) the extension of knowledge; (3) sincerity of thought; (4) composing the mind; (5) the cultivation of the personality; (6) the regulation of the family; (7) the governing of the state; (8) the equalization of the whole world. These eight subjects are taken step by step, one following another; yet the student must have the whole world in view from the beginning. Among all the eight subjects, the cultivation of the personality is the root of everything. From this point, Confucius regards the individual as the unit. But sincerity of thought is, in turn, the root of cultivating the personality.

Having understood the whole outline of the "Great Learning," we come now to see how Confucius regards the whole world as an economic unit. We have already seen that Confucius ascribes very much importance to economic life. But, in the "Great Learning," he does not say a single word about economic life until the last chapter—namely, the equalization of the whole world. It is not for the cultivation of the personality, not for the regulation of the family, not for the governing of the state, but for the equalization of the whole world, that Confucius gives his economic principles. He feels that the whole world is the economic unit, and that the economic life can never be confined to any particular person, family or state. The student can never study economics completely unless he takes the world as a whole. And the world can never be equalized unless the economic life of the whole world is equal. This is a special concept of Confucius.

The economic principles given in the "Great Learning" are conspicuous above all the other economic principles given in other Confucian books. The reason is simply that the "Great Learning" simplifies the principles for equalizing the world into only two things—namely, employing the best men, and administering wealth. Hence, everyone knows that a part of the "Great Learning" is devoted to the principles of economics. What we wish to emphasize is, however, that Confucius has the world economy in his mind, and that he thinks about the world as an economic unit.

But we must understand that the economic principles of the "Great Learning" are very general. Although they are given in the chapter on the equalization of the world it does not mean that they are fitted only for world economy. Indeed, they can be applied to either a person, a family, or a state.

All other economic principles given in the "Great Learning" are quoted in other places, and we shall quote here only one, the fundamental principle of world economy;—namely, the principle of reciprocity. It is stated in a metaphorical sense as follows:

> What you do not like above, do not place below; what you do not like below, do not place above; what you do not like in front, do not shift to the back; what you do not like in back, do not turn to the front; what you do not like on the right, do not bestow on the left; what you do not like on the left, do not bestow on the right;—this is what is called the principle with which we are, as with a measuring-square, to establish the law of justice.[1]

The principle of reciprocity, as stated in the second chapter, is one of the fundamental concepts of Confucius But there it is discussed from the purely moral point of view. Here we must consider it from the economic and political point of view. The principle is the same, but its application is a little different. Taking this principle as the basis of world economy, it develops commercial policy and international law. It is the golden rule of the business world, and we cannot say that there is no moral standard for politics and diplomacy.

The economic system of Confucius is not nationalism, but cosmopolitanism. Before Confucius, economic theories were mostly like the doctrines of the mercantile school and took the nation as the unit. The chief representative was Kuan Tzŭ, who was the most successful minister for the

[1] *Classics*, vol. i, pp. 373-4.

realization of mercantilism and of state socialism. He was the first one to have a complete economic system which we can see to-day. But we have no room to deal with his economy, and the only reason we mention him is to contrast him with Confucius.

1. *Doctrine of Peace*

The most important principle for international relations is the doctrine of peace. This doctrine is based not only on the principle of humanity, but also on that of utility. Confucius says: "Talking about sincere agreement and cultivating universal peace are what are called the advantages of men. Fighting, plundering, and killing each other are what are called the calamities of men." [1] In the *Spring and Autumn*, Confucius records about four hundred wars within the period of two hundred and forty-two years, and condemns them all, for war is contrary to the principle of humanity. Therefore, Mencius says that in the *Spring and Autumn* there are no righteous wars. He holds that military force is used only as a punishment by the supreme authority to its subjects, but that the independent states have no right to engage in such punitive war against one another.[2]

For the condemnation of war, Mencius gives many passages in very strong language. He says:

> When contentions about territory are the ground on which they fight, they slaughter men till the fields are filled with them. When some struggle for a city is the ground on which they fight, they slaughter men till the city is filled with them. This is what is called "leading on the land to devour human flesh". Death is not enough for such a crime. Therefore, those who are skilful in fighting, should suffer the highest punishment.[3]

[1] *Li Ki,* bk. vii, p. 380.

[2] *Classics,* vol. ii, p. 478.

[3] *Ibid.*, p. 305.

He says again: "Those who say that we can, for our sovereign, form alliances with other states, so that our battles must be successful, are nowadays called good ministers, but anciently they were called pests of the people."[1] Mencius also calls such persons the destroyers of the people.[2] Moreover, he condemns not only the ministers, but also the rulers. When he speaks of King Hui of Liang, who to gain territory, tore and destroyed his people in battle, he condemns him as brutal.[3] Therefore, according to the principle of Confucius, there is no absolute justification for any war; it is only that some wars are relatively better than others. Hence, war should be abolished.

The doctrine of peace is harmonious with economic principles. First, it makes the life of man more valuable than the land. In the *Analects*, Confucius attaches the chief importance to the life of the people; even food ranks only second. In the *Spring and Autumn*, he condemns those who employ the people in a bad year for the reparation of an old house, because they exploit the people in hard labor. But how much more strongly would he condemn those who injure the people? And how much more strongly still would he condemn those who kill the people in war? Generally, the object of war is getting land. But, getting land by sacrificing numerous lives of the people is a most costly enterprise, and will not pay. This is what Mencius calls sacrificing what is really dear on account of what is not so dear.[4] This is also what he calls "leading on the land to devour human flesh."

Second, it makes the people's production continuous, and their consumption satisfactory. As a matter of fact, war is most injurious to the people, although it may give a use-

[1] *Classics*, vol. ii, p. 441.
[2] *Ibid.*, p. 439.
[3] *Ibid.*, pp. 477-8.
[4] *Ibid.*, p. 478.

less glory to the ruler. Mencius describes the suffering of the people on account of war as follows: "The rulers of those states rob their people of their time, so that they cannot plough and weed their fields in order to support their parents. Their parents suffer from cold and hunger. Brothers, wives, and children are separated and scattered abroad." [1] In fact, the evils of war are the interruption of production, the lessening of consumption and the destruction of the family. It is only peace that can cure these evils.

Third, it saves the economic waste in the preparation for war. Confucius condemns not only actual war, but also the preparation for it. Preparation for war is a great waste of wealth, and a heavy burden upon the people. Therefore, the doctrine of peace is based partially on economic principles.

Abolishing war and changing the military society into an industrial one is the common wish of Confucious and his best pupil, Yen Yüan. The *Park of Narratives* [2] tells us that when Confucius went up to the Nung Mountain, Tzŭ-lu, Tzŭ-kung and Yen Yüan accompanied him, and Confucius asked them each to tell his individual wishes. Tzŭ-lu said that he wished to raise an army and to attack the enemy, so that he was sure to take the territory for a thousand miles. Tzŭ-kung said that he wished to wear a white garment and a white cap to persuade the two armies under the white swords, in order to take away the calamity of the two nations. Yen Yüan said:

I wish to have a wise king or a sage ruler and to become his minister. I shall cause the city walls to have no need to be repaired, the ditches and moats to have no foe to cross over them, and the swords and spears to be melted for the making of agricultural implements. I shall cause the whole world to

[1] *Classics*, vol. ii, pp. 135-6.

[2] Bk. xv.

have no calamity of war for thousands of years. Under such a condition, how can Yu go to fight angrily? And how can Tz'ŭ go to make arbitration cheerfully?

Then Tzŭ-lu asked what the wish of Confucius was. He said: "What I wish to do, is the plan of the son of Yen. I wish to carry my clothes and hats and to follow him." This conversation shows clearly the common wish of Confucius and Yen Yüan. The aim of Tzŭ-lu is but that of a soldier; that of Tzŭ-kung is but that of a diplomatist; but that of Yen Yüan and Confucius is that of the highest statesmanship, and the plan of a sage. The most important sentence is "the swords and spears are melted for the making of agricultural implements." Thus one would turn the instruments for killing men into instruments for nourishing men, and change the soldiers to farmers; in short, the military society would be entirely destroyed, and an industrial society would be universally and permanently established. This is the ideal of Confucius.

The evils of feudalism, with its constant wars, impressed Confucius profoundly, and led him to the vision of a world-state and world-peace. Plato's ideal state, on the other hand, is a small city-state, ever ready for war. The spirit of the Chinese people, under the influence of Confucius' teachings, is such that they are more nearly ready than any western people for the realization of this lofty vision.[1]

II. THE FAMILY AS THE SMALLEST ORGANIZATION

While the whole world is the largest economic organization, the family is the smallest one, and the one having closest economic relation to the individual. As long as there is a family, the individual never can make his economic

[1] In the second book of Kang Yu-wei's *Book on the Great Similarity*, the details of how the world is to be united are given.

life absolutely independent. Therefore, the family life is very important in affecting the economic life. Whenever we use the term family we mean that there are at least two generations, although the principal factor of production is only of one generation. For example, a family means husband and wife. But it may have either old parents, or young children, or both. Hence, it may include three generations at the same time. But in any case it must have two generations, if it has children. Therefore, we may consider the family as an economic organization from two points of view,—namely, the relation of husband and wife, and that of father and son.

The happy life of the family in Confucius' mind is given in the "Doctrine of the Mean." It first quotes from the *Canon of Poetry*, as follows:

> Loving union with wife and children,
> Is like the music of lutes and harps;
> When there is concord among brothers,
> The harmony is delightful and enduring.
> Thus you make your family happy,
> And enjoy pleasure with your wife and children.

Then it quotes from Confucius, who gives to this poem the following appreciation: "In such a state of things, parents have entire complacence!"[1] The poem itself mentions only wife and children, and brothers. But Confucius adds to them the parents, in order to make the happy life of the family complete. This is what Confucius thinks a happy family.

1. *Relation of Husband and Wife*

According to the social system of Confucius, the relation of husband and wife is the starting-point. He always puts the matrimonial significance at the beginning of all his writ-

[1] *Classics*, vol. i, pp. 396-7.

ings. The "Doctrine of the Mean" says: "The way of the superior man, [Confucius], is beginning with its course from the relation of husband and wife. But in its utmost reaches it shines brightly through heaven and earth."[1]

(a) *Marriage*

It is well known to the Western world that marriage in China is a matter arranged primarily by the parents of the parties, and through the services of a go-between. This was an old custom, and it is in accordance with the teachings of Confucius. It has, of course, the disadvantage that the contracting parties cannot be sure in advance that they are perfectly suited to each other. It is not the practice, however, for parents to disregard the wishes of their children in these matters. These marriage customs are a necessary consequence of the Chinese custom which forbids social intercourse between the sexes prior to marriage—the obvious reason for which is, of course, to prevent not alone any improper relations, but even the suspicion of them. In China there is no marriage license and no church to take charge of the ceremony. The parents' order takes the place of the license, and the go-between takes the place of the minister or justice of the peace.

The ninth book of the *Record of Rites* says: "Once mated with her husband, all her life she will not change her feeling of duty to him; hence, when the husband dies she will not marry again."[2] This is the ideal of marriage. But, at the death of her husband, if her age is below fifty, and that of her son below fifteen, and he has no close relatives on his father's side to take the economic responsibility, the widow may marry again. Therefore, according to the *Canon of Rites*, a step-son should mourn for his step-father,

[1] *Classics*, vol. i, p. 393.

[2] *Li Ki*, bk. ix, p. 439.

who is the second husband of his mother.[1] The fact that Confucius allows the woman to marry a second husband under some circumstances shows the practicality of Confucianism. It is Ch'êng Yi (1584-1658 A. K. or 1033-1107 A. D.) who first says that a woman should not marry a second husband, even if she should die in hunger. But this is not the teaching of Confucius.

(b) *Divorce*

Having understood the proceeding of marriage, we now come to the subject of divorce. According to *Elder Tai's Record of Rites*, there are seven grounds for divorcing a wife: (1) disobedience to parents-in-law; (2) not giving birth to a son; (3) adultery; (4) jealousy of her husband's attentions, that is, to the other inmates of his harem; (5) leprosy; (6) talkativeness; (7) thieving. But there are three considerations which may overrule these grounds: (1) having no family for her return; (2) having passed through the three years' mourning for his parents; (3) his condition formerly poor and mean, and now rich and honorable.[2] But these rules are entirely applied only to the classes of the great officials, the students, and the common people. The prince can divorce his wife on six other grounds, but not because she has no son. And the emperor cannot divorce the empress on any ground, but simply separates from her. These rules are adopted even in the *Law Code of the Ts'ing Dynasty*, the present dynasty.

Because the emperor, the prince, and also the great officials, have not so much freedom of divorce as those below them, they do not consummate the marriage upon the date of marriage. When the wife comes in, she lives apart from the husband. After the period of three months, she is presented to the ancestral temple, and begins to be called wife.

[1] Ch. xxxi.

[2] Bk. lxxx.

This period is just long enough for the examination into her character and for her special training. If the parents-in-law and husband cannot get along with her, she can return to her family a virgin, and can marry another without any trouble. This is for the benefit of both sides, although the men get more advantage. But the student and the common people have more freedom of divorce, so that they consummate the marriage the same night. This was an old custom.

As to the third reason for the prohibition of divorce, that one should not divorce his wife if his condition formerly was poor and mean, and is now rich and honorable, this provision is very just. But, as a matter of fact, divorce is generally caused by economic conditions. In the *Canon of Poetry*, there is a poem against the corrupt custom of divorce. The people of Wei loved new wives and abandoned the old ones. Therefore, the poet, speaking for the divorced wives, made this a subject for satire. We should like to quote a few lines of this poem, which refer to the economic aspect of the affair.

Whether you had plenty or not,
I exerted myself to be getting.
* * * * * * *
Formerly, I was afraid our means might be exhausted during our old age,
And I worked hard with you in the struggle for existence.
Now when your means are abundant and you are old,
You compare me to poison.
* * * * * * *
Feasting with your new wife,
You think of me as a provision only against your poverty.[1]

Disapproving such a divorce, Confucius puts this poem in this Canon to serve as a warning.

[1] *Classics,* vol. iv, pt. i, pp. 55-8.

It is true that, in the Confucian writings, there is no statement about divorce issued to the woman. Though this is not wholly just, in a paternal society it must be so. In ancient time, the Disorderly Stage, if woman should be allowed to have the right to divorce her husband, the paternal family could not be established, and social life would be disorderly. This is the reason a woman cannot divorce her husband. Han Fei Tzŭ, however, speaks of T'ai Kung as a divorced husband of an old woman. This shows that in ancient times, even long before Confucius, a woman did have the right to divorce her husband. It might have been that a woman could divorce her husband if her husband agreed to it, but that there was no legal ground for her doing so. The *Law Code of the Ts'ing Dynasty* says that if the husband and wife are not harmonious and both wish to be separated, they may be allowed to do so.[1] Therefore, in the present day, the woman is legally allowed to divorce her husband, with his consent.

However, when we say that the Confucian writings have no statement about divorce issued to the woman, we are simply referring to the ordinary case. If in the unusual case, a woman shall have the absolute right to divorce her husband. The *General Discussion in the White Tiger Palace* says: "If the husband should either violate the social relations, or kill his parents-in-law, or break down the most important laws, it would be the greatest of disorder. In such cases, the ethical relation between husband and wife is cut off, and the wife may divorce her husband."[2] According to the *Law Code of the Ts'ing Dynasty*, whenever the ethical relation between husband and wife is cut off, they must be separated, and are not permitted to remain in union. From this point, we can see that the Chinese re-

[1] Ch. x.

[2] Bk. x.

gard the ethical relation as very important, and that the husband and wife cannot remain in union, even though they love each other.

The Chinese consider the marriage tie as very strong, and continue it through the whole life. Although their marriages are not directly arranged by themselves, husbands and wives love each other and do not get divorces. The fundamental reason is that they have a habit of bearing moral obligations for which they sacrifice their sentimental feelings. Second, they accept the philosophical doctrine of fate, and content themselves on the ground that their marriage had been predestined. Third, their social condition does not allow either husband or wife to have any sweetheart beside the other. These are the most important reasons why the Chinese have very few, practically no, divorces. And we must understand that the Chinese are not concerned with formal law at all, when they either marry or divorce, but merely with the rites prescribed by religion and custom. Yet they keep their marriages sacred, and make them even stronger than if they were fixed by law. At the present day, there is practically no divorce, unless in the case of adultery; and such cases are rare.

(c) *Economic Position of Woman*

Since we have discussed above the social position of woman, we should now discuss her economic position, in which we are especially interested. Inside the family, the housewife is the chief worker. First of all, she must care for the children. The "Great Learning" says: "There never has been a girl who learned to nourish a child, that she might afterwards marry."[1] This implies that every married woman must know how to nourish a child without special training, and that it is a duty of woman. The

[1] *Classics*, vol. i, p. 370.

"Pattern of the Family" says: "The son of the great official has a nurse. The wife of the student nourishes her child herself."[1] Therefore, the wives of students and common people must nourish their own children, although the empress, the princess, and the noble ladies may hire nurses. This is the chief work of woman.

Second, she must take charge of the food. The *Canon of Poetry* says: "It will be hers neither to do wrong nor to do good. Only about the spirits and the food will she have to discuss."[2] The *Canon of Changes* says: "She does nothing of her own initiative, but stays at home for the preparation of food."[3] These two passages are sufficient to indicate the principal work of the housewife.

Third, she must take charge of the clothes. According to the "Pattern of the Family," when a girl reaches the age of ten, she ceases to go out from the home. Her governess teaches her to handle the hempen fibres, to deal with the cocoons, to weave silks and form fillets, and to learn all woman's work in order to furnish garments.[4]

In ancient times, all, from the empress to the wives of the common people, had to make clothes for their husbands. The *Record of Rites* tells us that the emperor must be personally a farmer, and the empress a weaver. This has three significances: First, it indicates religious piety, because the emperor and empress personally furnish the materials for the food and clothes used for sacrifices. Second, it indicates political democracy, because it makes the emperor and empress not entirely different from the farmer and weaver. Third, it indicates economic productivity, because it makes even the emperor and empress produce material things.

[1] *Li Ki,* bk. x, p. 476.

[2] *Classics,* vol. iv, pt. ii, p. 307.

[3] *Yi King,* p. 137.

[4] *Li Ki,* bk. x, p. 479.

There is a silk-worm's house. From the washing of the seeds in the stream, gathering of the leaves from the mulberry trees, feeding the worms, to the presenting of the cocoons to the empress, all the processes of work are done by the honorable ladies. Then the empress rinses some of them thrice in a vessel, begins to unwind them, and distributes them to the honorable ladies to complete the unwinding. After the dyeing and embroidering have been finished, garments are made for use in sacrifices.[1] This custom still exists to-day. In the *Canon of Poetry*, there is a poem directed against the Emperor Yu and his wife. In criticism of his wife, it says that she leaves her silkworms and weaving.[2] Since even an empress must take up the work of silkworm culture and weaving, it goes without saying that the women in general must take charge of the clothes.

In order to show that woman is in an honorable position which is equal to that of her husband, here is a good example. Though we have seen that the preparation of food is the principal work of woman, still this does not mean that she is a slave in the kitchen. One chief function of food is for religious sacrifices, and in such sacrifices the wife participates in the ceremonies with her husband. Because they are both equal in the family, they both sacrifice to the ancestor. When a girl of ten, she watches the sacrifices, supplies the liquors and sauces, fills the various stands and dishes with pickles and brine, and assists in setting forth the appurtenances for the ceremonies.[3] Such an education is simply for the duty of a housewife. But, if a housewife is required to take part with her husband in sacrifice to his ancestor, how honorable is her position!

[1] *Li Ki*, bk. xxi, pp. 223-4.

[2] *Classics*, vol. iv, pt. ii, p. 562.

[3] *Li Ki*, bk. x, p. 479.

There is a Confucian principle giving respect to woman. This principle is clearly indicated, as we have seen, in the ceremony of the personal receiving of the bride. But there is another example which illustrates the respect for woman in regard to her economic position. According to Confucianism, although a woman should work for the family, she should be treated nicely, and should not be employed only for financial gain. Therefore, when a woman is married, she need not take up any household work until the end of three months. If her husband causes her to work within this period, it seems cruel to Confucius. In the *Canon of Poetry,* there is a poem directed against a man of the official family, who makes his wife sew within the period of three months. It reads as follows:

Shoes thinly woven of the dolichos fibre
May be used to walk on the hoarfrost.
The delicate fingers of a bride
May be used in making clothes.
Putting the waistband to his lower garment and the collar to his upper,
The beautiful woman fixes them.

The beautiful woman moved gracefully,
And politely stood aside to the left [when she just came into the family];
From her girdle hung her ivory comb-pin.
But it is the narrow-mindedness [of her husband],
Which makes the subject for satire.[1]

This poem describes the woman beautiful in every way, as a contrast to the work of making clothes, and it censures expressly the mean character of her husband. It serves as an example to indicate that Confucius regards the housewife as in a respected position.

Since the wife is equal to her husband, and husband and wife are considered to be one body, she shares all the various

[1] *Cf. Classics,* vol. iv, pt. i, pp. 163-4.

conditions with her husband. Even though she may have no title of her own, she holds the title of her husband. And, in all social positions, she takes her seat according to the rank of her husband.[1]

Regarding the ownership of property, the ownership of woman is included in the name of her husband. If her husband is dead and she has no son, she may succeed to the property of her husband, or may sell it for her support, if she is poor. If she marries a second husband, the property of her former husband and her dower should belong to the family of her former husband, and she cannot take them away. These are stated in the *Law Code of the Ts'ing Dynasty.*[2] But, according to the recent commercial law (2454 A. K. or 1903 A. D.), a wife, or a daughter above the age of sixteen, may be a merchant and may use her own name to own the business. A wife or a daughter, however, must register as a merchant either directly or indirectly in the Department of Commerce in Peking (now the Department of Agriculture, Industry and Commerce); and a wife must also get the written consent of her husband, while he still cannot relieve himself from liability.

2. *Relation of Father and Son*

(a) *The Love for the Same Kind*

The relation between father and son is the strongest tie of Chinese society, and it is the basis of Confucius' philosophy and religion. This relation is fixed by birth, so that the love between father and son is quite natural, without any other consideration. But there is one thing which causes such a love and which is independent of the blood relationship:—namely, " the love for the same kind." The *Record of Rites* says: "All living creatures between heaven

[1] *Li Ki,* bk. ix, p. 441.

[2] Ch. viii.

and earth, being endowed with blood and breath, have a certain amount of knowledge. Possessing that amount of knowledge, there is not one of them but knows to love its own kind." [1] The love for kind is a feeling common to all creatures,[2] and man especially develops such a feeling to a great extent. This is the foundation upon which human society is built. Of course, when parents give birth to a son, they love him. But why do they do so? It is not merely because he is their product, but also because he is of the same kind with them. Among different sons, the father will love the one most who is most similar to himself, and that one who is least similar he will love least. Indeed, the degree of his love given to his sons is according to the degree of similarity which they show to him. In the case of a step-son, although he is not the child of the father, the father will love him, if he is similar to him. In fact, the love for the same kind is the basis of the relation between father and son. And the one who can extend such a feeling and love all of mankind, is called a man of great filial piety. The *Canon of Poetry* says: "The love of a filial son can never be exhausted; it is given to your same kind for ever." [3]

(b) *Doctrine of Filial Piety*

Taking such a natural love as the basis, Confucius establishes the doctrine of filial piety, a doctrine that has much to do with economic life. In the *Canon of Filial Piety*, he thus sums up the duties of a son:

The service which a filial son renders his parents is as follows:

[1] *Li Ki,* bk. xxxv, p. 392.

[2] Confucius' conception is very closely kin to Professor Giddings' conception of "the consciousness of kind."

[3] *Cf. Classics,* vol. iv, pt. ii, p. 477.

In his general conduct to them, he manifests the utmost reverence; in his nourishing of them, his endeavor is to give them the utmost pleasure; when they are ill, he feels the greatest anxiety; in mourning for them dead, he exhibits every demonstration of grief; in sacrificing to them, he displays the utmost solemnity. When a son is complete in these five things, he may be pronounced able to serve his parents.[1]

In the *Canon of Filial Piety*, there are five chapters describing respectively the different duties among the five classes,—namely, the emperor, the princes, the great officials, the students, and the common people. It is the last chapter of the five that interests us especially. Although it is an ethical teaching of Confucius, it is really of great economic significance. He says: "They follow the course of heaven in the revolving seasons, they distinguish the advantages afforded by different soils, they are careful of their conduct, and they are economical in their expenditure, in order to support their parents: this is the filial piety of the common people."[2] It is very interesting to see that Confucius identifies the filial piety of the common people with economic efficiency. The first two phrases refer to production, and the last two to consumption. Although the third phrase is mixed with an ethical element, it is a provision for the control of personal expenditure, because to be careful for the conduct means a moral control of material wants. Therefore, if a man among the common people is diligent in production and frugal in consumption for the support of his parents, it suffices to make him a filial son. This is the type for the farmer.

Among all the pupils of Confucius, Ts'êng Tsŭ is the chief representative of filial piety. He says: "There are

[1] *Sacred Books of the East,* vol. iii, p. 480.

[2] *Ibid.,* pp. 471-2.

three degrees of filial piety. The highest is to honor our parents; the second is not to disgrace them; and the lowest is to be able to support them." Again he says: "To prepare the fragrant flesh and grain which he has cooked, tasting and then presenting them before his parents, is not filial piety, it is only nourishing them." Yet he says that the fundamental lesson for all is filial piety, and the practice of it is seen in the support of parents.[1] Therefore, although the support of parents is the lowest type of filial piety, it is a necessary step. There may be some who cannot be called filial sons, because they can only support their parents, but there never has been anyone who could be called a filial son without fulfilling the duty of supporting his parents. Based on such ethical and social teachings, the chief economic burden of the Chinese is the support of parents.

Since all these teachings are in the positive form, let us now consider the support of parents on the negative side. When Mencius enumerates the five things which are pronounced in common usage to be unfilial, the first four out of the five are economic. The first is laziness in the use of one's four limbs, without attending to the support of one's parents. The second is gambling and chess-playing, and being fond of wine, without attending to the support of one's parents. The third is being fond of commodities and money, and selfishly attached to wife and children, without attending to the support of one's parents. The fourth is following the desires of one's ears and eyes, so as to bring one's parents to disgrace. The fifth is being fond of bravery, fighting and quarreling, so as to endanger one's parents. Among the first four things which are economic, the first refers to production, the second and the fourth, to consumption; and the third, to distribution. To sum them

[1] *Li Ki*, bk. xxi, pp. 226-7.

up in a word, what the Chinese call unfilial is failure to attend to the support of parents on account of any one of these five causes.

The third of the five unfilial things has a great significance. In China, the son must support his parents first; and his wife and children are regarded as secondary, because the parents are much more to be respected. It is true that the parents never want to sacrifice their daughter-in-law or grandson for their own sake, and that they usually do sacrifice themselves for them. But the Chinese think they ought to care for parents first. In the first place, they cannot work very well; and even though they can work, they ought to be given a rest, because they have worked for a long time. In the second place, they cannot live very long, so that a son ought to discharge his filial duty as soon as possible, otherwise in no way can he pay off his moral debt.

The most conspicuous fact which marks the difference between China and the West is that the Chinese regard their parents above their wives and children, and the people of the West regard their wives above anything else. In a word, China emphasizes the relation between father and son, while the West emphasizes that between husband nad wife. This is the fundamental difference which causes many other differences in the social and economic life. Such a difference not only is found in modern times, but also existed in ancient times. It is the chief antagonistic point between Confucianism and Christianity. Although the fifth of the Ten Commandments say, " Honor thy father and thy mother,"[1] Genesis says, "A man shall leave his father and his mother, and shall cleave unto his wife."[2] Jesus[3] and Paul[4] repeat the same words, commending them. Hence, it has become

[1] *Exodus* 20:12.

[2] *Genesis* 2:24.

[3] *Matthew* 19:5.

[4] *Ephesians* 5:31.

the fundamental basis of western society. Whenever the son marries a wife, he leaves his parents and cleaves to her only. As soon as the relation between husband and wife begins, the relation between father and son becomes less important.

As human nature is everywhere about the same, the Chinese do not love their parents more than the western people, and the western people do not love their wives more than the Chinese. Mencius says:

> The desire of a child is towards his father and mother. When he becomes conscious of the attractions of beauty, his desire is towards young and beautiful women. When he comes to have a wife and children, his desire is towards them. . . . But the man of great filial piety, to the end of his life, has his desire towards his parents.[1]

Therefore, a man turns his heart away from his parents not only when he marries, but also when he becomes conscious of the attractions of beauty. There is no need to teach a man to leave his father and his mother, and to cleave unto his wife, because this is his strongest passion. Even in China, there is always a tendency this way. But, by the teachings of Confucius, this natural passion is controlled by the ethical doctrine. Hence, it has become the general spirit of the Chinese that they should support their parents first and above the support of their wives and children. This is the fundamental point, marking the differences between China and the West.

Accepting the teachings of Confucius, the Chinese embody them in their laws. In the *Law Code of the Ts'ing Dynasty,* there is a provision that those who purposely do not give sufficient support to their grandparents or parents shall be punished with one hundred blows with the long

[1] *Classics,* vol. ii, p. 345.

stick. For the infliction of this punishment, however, the complaint must be lodged by the grandparents or parents. If a son, who is poor, but who does not work for the making of a living and for the support of his parents, causes his parents to resort to suicide, he shall be punished with one hundred blows with the long stick, and shall be exiled for the distance of three thousand miles from home.[1] If the age of his grandparents or parents is above eighty, or they have severe sickness, and there is no other son attending to them, the son or grandson shall not leave them at home and go to take official employment in another place. If he does so, he shall be punished with eighty blows with the long stick, and compelled to go home for the support of his parents.[2] Even among criminals, under certain conditions, one may be saved from capital punishment or from exile, for the support of his grandparents or parents.[3] Therefore, the support of parents is a positive institution, which is established not only by the moral law, but also by the legal law.

According to the regulations of the present day, when a filial daughter whose parents have neither son nor grandson, serves them till their death, remaining unmarried for that purpose, she shall be honored as the filial sons; *e. g.*, an arch shall be built for her in her locality, and her name shall be dedicated in the "Temple of Faithfulness, Righteousness, Filiality and Fraternity," *etc.* Therefore, although a daughter is not compelled to support her parents by the punitive law, she is encouraged to do so by the honorary reward.

In the *Principle of Population*, the first edition, Malthus does not approve the Chinese law which requires that a son support his aged and helpless parents. He says: "It seems at any rate highly improper, by positive institutions, which render dependent poverty so general, to weaken that dis-

[1] Ch. xxx. [2] Ch. xvii. [3] Ch. iv.

grace, which for the best and most humane reasons ought to attach to it."[1] His argument is true. But he looks only at the side of parents, and not at the side of children. According to the view of the Chinese, they may say that, while the parents should maintain their economic independence, the sons should nevertheless support their parents in order to return something for their kindness. If the sons are not obliged to support their parents, although it may strengthen the economic motive of the parents and promote their desire of saving, it weakens the economic motive of the sons and their desire of working. For the economic society as a whole, it may have no gain. It simply makes the old and weak people live in a harder way, and the young and strong people in an easier way. Even though it should be of some advantage to society, it is unjust and unkind.

Moreover, according to human nature, at least Chinese nature, the old people are generally diligent and frugal to acquire and to accumulate wealth not only for their own sake, but mainly for the sake of their sons, grandsons, great-grandsons, great-great-grandsons, *etc.* Therefore, Confucius says that, when the superior man is old, and the animal powers are decayed, he guards against covetousness.[2] In fact, there are very few parents who like to be dependent upon their sons. If they are compelled to depend upon them, they have a sense of disgrace, because none will feel good if he falls into dependent poverty. The really fortunate parents are those who themselves are very prosperous and independent, while their sons are also very rich and dignified, and contribute their service and honor to their parents in order to please them. Therefore, the public has no fear that the parents will lower themselves to be a

[1] Ashley's *Economic Classics,* p. 33.

[2] *Classics,* vol. i, p. 313.

dependent class, and it ought not to deprive them of their claim upon their sons. We are afraid only that the sons will not support their parents when there is need of it, and not that the parents will not take care of themselves.

(c) *Holding of Property*

Since Confucius attaches much importance to the doctrine of filial piety, he gives the parents great power over the property of the whole family. He says: "When his parents are alive, a son should not dare to consider his body as his own, nor to hold his wealth as his private property. . . . . His gifts or presents should not extend to the carriage and horse."[1] The controllers of the property of a family are not the sons, but the parents.

The "Pattern of the Family" says:

> A son and his wife should have no private commodities, nor animals, nor vessels; they should not presume to borrow from, or give anything to, another person privately. If her relatives give the wife an article of food or dress, a piece of cloth or silk, a handkerchief for her girdle, an iris or an orchid, she should receive and offer it to her parents-in-law. If they accept it, she will be as glad as if she were receiving it afresh. If they return it to her, she should decline it; and if they do not allow her to do so, she will take it as if it were a second gift, and lay it by to wait till they may want it. If she wants to give it to some of her relatives, she must ask leave to do so, and that being granted, she will give it.[2]

When her father-in-law is dead, her mother-in-law retires from the open headship of the family, and hands her duties to the wife of her eldest son; but the latter, on all occasions of sacrificing and receiving guests, must ask her

[1] *Li Ki*, bk. xxvii, p. 295.

[2] *Li Ki*, bk. x, p. 458.

directions in everything, while the wives of the other sons must ask directions from her.[1]

In this type of family, wealth is acquired by the father, and it is owned in common by all the members of the family. Therefore, the father is the head of the family, and the mother is the head of the household. Or, the wealth is acquired by any one of the brothers, usually the eldest, but he is willing to give it up to the family as a whole, and regards his parents as the heads. In Chinese history, some families can hold their property under the common ownership for nine generations. But the management of this is very difficult. In the present day, the tendency is towards the limitation of family, basing it on the husband and wife only. But as long as the institution of family exists, the Chinese can never separate their parents from the family, just as they cannot separate their children from it.

Moreover, the marriage of a son is usually arranged by his parents, before he has become a producer. Under such circumstances, he has nothing to call his own, and he and his wife are economically dependent upon his parents. How can he be the real head of a family? During this period, his mother takes charge of the household, and his wife works merely as a student or an assistant to her. In reality, it is much better for his wife to work under his mother, because Chinese social life is very complex, and a young woman can never understand all the affairs of her new home. Of course she may own some private property, such as the dower; but, when she receives, or borrows, or gives anything beyond the limit of the family, it is polite for her to ask leave from her mother-in-law. Since her mother-in-law must treat her reasonably, the asking for leave is simply a formal ceremony, otherwise the Chinese could not

[1] *Li Ki,* bk. x, pp. 457-8.

have held such a family type for thousands of years. A few years later, when she has more experience, or more children, or when her husband becomes economically independent, she may be separated from her mother-in-law and manage a family of her own. But, even after such a separation, it is natural for her to seek direction from her mother-in-law, and to regard her at least as an honorary head of the family. If the new family is less prosperous than the old one, the son and his wife may still draw benefit from the latter; if the old family is less prosperous than the new one, the son must support his parents. In short, since the son and his wife owe a great debt to the parents and parents-in-law, they can never sever the economic relation between them. Even in a very poor family, when the son establishes himself, arranges his marriage himself, and maintains his family himself, he still must support his parents, and serve them as the honorary heads of the family. This is the type of Chinese family which still exists to-day. The difference between this and the type of family organization prevalent in the West is obvious, and will help to explain the Chinese emphasis on the duties of sons to parents, already discussed.

Basing them on the Confucian doctrine, the Chinese draw the following laws. According to the *Law Code of the Ts'ing Dynasty*,[1] if grandsons or sons whose paternal grandparent or parent is still alive, separate themselves from their homes to settle elsewhere, or detach parts of the family possessions, they shall be punished with one hundred blows with the long stick. For the infliction of this punishment, however, it is required that the complaint be lodged by a paternal grandparent or parent. During the life of their paternal grandparents or parents, no sons or grandsons shall

[1] Ch. viii.

be allowed to divide the family possessions or to dwell apart. But they may split up their possessions if their parents approve thereof, or order them to do so. If brothers, while in mourning for one of their parents, separate themselves from the home to fix their domicile in another locality, or detach parts of the patrimony, eighty blows with the long stick will be inflicted upon them. It is, however, required that a complaint be first lodged by a superior or senior from among the relations who are to be mourned for during one year or longer. Should such separation from the family or division of the patrimony have taken place in obedience to the testamentary dispositions of a paternal grandparent or parent, it does not fall under this law.

Within the family which holds a common possession, if a member of the lower generation or younger age, without asking the authority of the higher generation or older age, presumes to use the money or goods of the family privately, he shall be beaten with a small stick twenty times, when the money or goods used amount to ten taels. The number of blows shall be proportionately increased for every ten taels which he shall use privately. But the punishment is limited to one hundred blows. If a member of the higher generation or older age, who has the power to divide up the wealth of the family, does not divide it up proportionately and equally, the punishment is the same Although the junior must ask the permission from the senior, he has a right to the common possessions. Although the senior controls the affairs of the family, he has no right to divide up its wealth unequally among the members. In short, the head of a family is but a trustee.

When there is any title or office which is given to the descendant of a man, it shall be first received by the eldest son or grandson of his wife. But, when his property, personal and real, is divided, it shall be distributed equally according to the number of sons, without difference between the son of his wife and that of his concubine. If he has an illegitimate son, this son may have only half the portion of those sons who are the children of his wife or concubine. If he has no son but an illegitimate one, he shall adopt a step-son who has the proper relation with him, and the step-son shall divide his property equally with the illegitimate son. If he cannot adopt a proper step-son, the illegitimate son is allowed to inherit the whole portion of his property.

When a family is extinguished without any proper step-son, the daughter of the family may receive its property. If it has no daughter, the magistrate shall report it to the superior, and it may be taken by the public.

These are the laws of the present dynasty concerning the holding of property. In conclusion, the institution of family has been most highly developed in China, because of the doctrine of filial piety of Confucius. The rest of the world has no clan system so complete and highly developed as that of China. A clan which is composed of many families under a common remote ancestor, may occupy a whole town for over a thousand years, may number over one hundred thousand souls, and may hold its property as long as the clan exists. It has its own history, and it has its own law, not contrary to the national law, however. It is a very strong local government, taking charge of birth and death, marriage, religion, education, charity, election, arbitration, punishment, taxation, police, public work, *etc.* It is a Confucian system of the Disorderly Stage, but it has developed into a refined form. But we must understand that a family is an economic organization, while a clan is only a social organization, although holding common property for unlimited generations.

CHAPTER XI

Economic Policies and the Divisions of Economics

I. GOVERNMENT REGULATION

Since economic life is very important to man, everyone naturally considers first what he is to get, rather than what he ought to do. Each man is concerned primarily about his own interests. It is because of this fact that competition arises. According to the theory of the *laissez-faire* economists, if competition is absolutely free, everyone will get just what he ought to get, because everyone is careful for his own interest. Hence these economists advocate competition as necessary to economic life, and believe government interference should be reduced to a minimum. The Confucian doctrine is just the opposite; government interference is necessary for economic life, and competition should be reduced to the minimum. In order to explain this doctrine, we shall indicate first why competition should not be absolutely free, even if it could be so.

First, let us consider the principle of natural selection. In the Chinese language, the word *tien* has three meanings: the first is God; the second, Heaven; and the third, nature. We now use this word only in the second and third senses. Confucius is an evolutionist. He says, " In its production of things, Heaven is sure to give addition to them, according to their own qualities. Hence, when the things or men are flourishing, Heaven nourishes them; when they are ready to fall, it overthrows them." [1] This statement suggests the principle of natural selection.

[1] *Cf. Classics,* vol. i, p. 399.

Mencius, also, says:

> When the good principle prevails over the world, men of little virtue are submissive to those of great, and those of little worth to those of great. When the good principle does not prevail over the world, men of small power are submissive to those of great, and the weak to the strong. Both these cases are the rule of Heaven. They who accord with Heaven are preserved, and they who rebel against Heaven perish.[1]

Therefore, Heaven does not help anyone in competition; it simply stands on the side of the few who can help themselves, and eliminates the many who cannot help themselves.

What Heaven is, is a problem transcending the question of good or evil, because Heaven is neither good nor evil. The "Appendix" says, "The cosmic processes give their stimulus to all things, but have not the same anxiety as the sage."[2] On the natural side, Heaven represents cosmic processes; while on the social side, the sage represents ethical processes. These two can never be harmonized, because the one has purpose, and the other has not. In a religious sense, we may say that God helps the virtuous; but in reality, we are bound to admit that God does not help anyone but the strongest. If we should follow closely the *laissez-faire* policy, and should let competition be absolutely free, the world would be left to the few strongest only. Although we cannot do very much against nature, how can we bear to see the sufferings of the weak, who constitute the greatest part of mankind? Therefore, no great religious teachers, nor great moralists, nor great statesmen, let nature alone without some sort of regulation. Since natural selection is good, not for the weak, but for the strong only, artificial adjustment for society as a whole is necessary. The *Canan of Changes* says: "The sage sov-

[1] *Cf. Classics*, vol. ii, p. 296.

[2] *Yi King*, p. 356.

ereign regulates the natural course of heaven and earth, and assists the application of the adaptations furnished by them. —in order to help the people." [1]

Second, let us consider the nature of man. The strong are never satisfied unless they take all from the weak. Ho Hsiu says: "When the rich compete with the poor, even though the law were made by Kao Yao, [the judge of Emperor Shun], no way can prevent the strong from pressing upon the weak." When anyone has a little power over others, he usually employs that power without any hesitation to sacrifice the interest of others for his own sake, if it be allowed. Everyone is looking after his own interest indeed; but some can protect themselves, and prosper, and some cannot, although they may know the need of it perfectly. Therefore, human nature being as it is, competition should not be unlimited. For, although the minority may profit by absolute freedom of competition, the majority have no free hand to take part in competition with the minority, and must be overcome by them. Hence, self-interest cannot be the regulator of economic life, and government regulation is necessary.

Confucius does not abolish competition, but proposes instead many governmental regulations to control consumption, production and distribution. We shall mention them below under these different headings. What we shall discuss here is the general policy of Confucius. On this point, it is best to refer to the "Great Model." According to the "Great Model," the final end of a government is to enable the people to enjoy the five blessings and to escape the six calamities. The five blessings are: (1) abundance of wealth, (2) long life, (3) good health, (4) love of virtue, (5) good looks. Contrasted with these are the six calamities: (1) premature death, (2) sickness, (3) sorrow, (4)

[1] *Yi King*, p. 281.

poverty, (5) ugliness, (6) weakness. It is to be noticed that, among these eleven things which sum up Confucius' conception of human happiness, only three, love of virtue, sorrow, and weakness, pertain to man's moral and mental condition, while all the others refer to physical and material enjoyment.

Having stated what is the final end of government, let us now see what are the duties of a sovereign. The central point of the "Great Model" is the standard of royal perfection: "The sovereign must establish a perfect standard first. Then he concentrates in his own hand the sources of the five blessings, in order to diffuse and to confer them on all the people." In fact, his most important duties are only two, namely, distribution of wealth and selection of men. It admonishes him specially by saying, "Do not insult the widowers and widows; do not fear the high and honorable." In short, the sovereign should establish universal and equal laws in order to help the weak and to curb the strong. Then it points out: "Even among all the right men, they have begun to be good only after they had been enriched." Therefore, the distribution of wealth should be very just; and the condition of the whole society should be as follows:

> Without deflection, without unevenness,
> Pursue the royal righteousness;
> Without any selfish likings,
> Pursue the royal way;
> Without any selfish dislikings,
> Pursue the royal path.
> Without deflection, without partiality,
> The royal way is broad and long;
> Without partiality, without deflection,
> The royal way is level and easy;
> Without perversity, without onesidedness,
> The royal way is right and straight.
> All concentrates to the perfect standard;
> All comes to the perfect standard.

This form of government is the ideal of Confucius. The emperor is the parent of the people.[1]

Such a government regulates not only the economic life of the people, but also many other things. Yet their economic life is the most important and the chief source of all the five blessings. The reason why the "Great Model" puts wealth first among the five blessings is told by the *Park of Narratives.* It says that wealth is the cause that makes the state prosperous, men and women beautiful, morality prevailing, and the mind satisfied.[2] Therefore, when the sovereign concentrates in his own hand the sources of the five blessings in order to diffuse and to confer them on all the people, he controls all the means of production, and distributes equally the benefits of them to the people. This resembles the principle of state socialism. The only difference is that, in state socialism, there is no personal sovereign, while in Confucius' mind, there is an unselfish, wise, just, and benevolent sovereign of perfect character. Since wealth is the first thing among the five blessings, and the fountain of the other four blessings, the government must control the economic life of the people above anything else.

The *Great Commentary of the Canon of History* says:

> The mothers can give life to the people and can feed them; the fathers can instruct and can teach them; but the sage king includes the two functions of father and mother together with all the details. . . . He makes the city walls for their settlement; builds the houses for their dwelling; establishes the different schools for their education; and divides the lands and fixes the number of acres for their nourishment. . . . The emperor is the parent of the people, to whom the people of the world will go.

From this statement, we can see that the emperor takes

[1] *Classics,* vol. iii, pt. ii, pp. 328-333, 343. [2] Bk. iii.

charge of the economic life of the people even more than do their parents.

Concerning government interference with the economic life of the people, the *Canon of History* gives the words of the Emperor Yao as follows: "I wish to help the people on the left and the right."[1] K'ung Yin-ta thus explains this: "To establish a sovereign is for the shepherding of the people. Therefore, when the people are working for the production of wealth, the sovereign should assist and help them." Such a conception is general among the Confucians.

To describe the evils which spring from the absence of regulations, Pan Ku gives an example. His statement refers to the age of Spring and Autumn and to that of Warring States, but it is also a picture of the capitalistic stage of the present day. He says:

Under the influence of luxury and extravagance, the students and the common people all disregarded the regulations and neglected the primary occupation. The number of farmers decreased, and that of merchants increased. Grain was insufficient, but luxurious goods were plenty. After the age of Duke Huan of Ch'i and Duke Wên of Tsin, moral character was greatly corrupted, and social order was confused. Each state had a different political system, and each family had different customs. The physical desires were uncontrolled, and extravagant consumption and social usurpation had no end. Therefore, the merchant transported goods which were difficult to obtain; the artisans produced articles which had no practical use; and the student practised ways which were contrary to orthodoxy; all of them pursued the temporary fashion for the getting of money. The hypocritical people turned away from truth in order to make fame, and the guilty men ran risks in order to secure profit. While those who took the

[1] *Classics*, vol. iii, pt. i, p. 79.

states by the deed of usurpation or regicide became kings or dukes, the men who founded their rich families by robbery, became heroes. Morality could not control the gentlemen, and punishment could not make the common people afraid. Among the rich, the wood and earth wore embroidery, and the dog and horse had a superabundance of meat and grain. But, among the poor, even the coarsest clothes could not be completed; beans made their food, and water was their drink. Although they were all in the same rank, of common people, the rich, by the power of wealth, raised themselves to kings, while the others, although their actual condition was slavery and imprisonment, had no angry appearance. Therefore, those who were deceitful and criminal were comfortable and proud in the world, but those who held principles and followed reason could not escape hunger and cold. Such an influence came from the government, because there was no regulation to control the economic life.[1]

This statement represents the general theory of the Confucians. They always have the socialistic idea in mind. The best thing is the equal distribution of wealth, while the worst thing is the division of people into the rich and the poor. Such a theory is not communism, but rather state socialism.

In practice, however, the Chinese government very seldom takes up a positive policy of interference with the economic life of the people. According to history, whenever the government adopted any minute measure, it failed, with few exceptions. The territory of the empire is large, the term of the magistrate is short, and the people by nature do not like to have anything to do with the government. Therefore, since the Ch'in dynasty, the government of modern China has not controlled the economic life of the people as did the government of ancient China.

[1] *History of Han,* ch. xci.

On account of the teachings of Confucius, however, the people respect social order and public interest. Hence, their competition is not very sharp, and moral influences still control their economic motives. Therefore, although their production is not very great, their distribution is comparatively equal. It is not the result of government regulation, but the outcome of Confucius' teachings.

II. LAISSEZ-FAIRE POLICY

By the word *laissez-faire*, we do not mean to imply that Confucianism leaves every thing wholly unregulated. It simply indicates that the Confucian socialism depends not upon any revolutionary force, but upon the development of the natural course of things; that human nature can be developed to perfection, and that there is no need of too many artificial laws to restrain it and to retard its progress, except in special cases. Universal equality, universal opportunity, and economic freedom are the most important doctrines of Confucius. The class system, monopoly, and the tariff, are the objects of his condemnation. According to the true Confucian theory, a full chance is given to the people for their natural development. This is the way to realize Confucian socialism. On the one hand, we find that Confucianism is in favor of social legislation; on the other, we find also that it is in favor of the *laissez-faire* policy They are both advantageous. Confucianism is the golden mean, and it never goes to extremes. What is fitted to the time or condition is the best. In a word, the Confucian social legislation is by means of moral, rather than governmental laws.

For the exact statement of the *laissez-faire* policy, we find a general economic principle given by Confucius himself When Tzŭ-chang, his pupil, asks Confucius about the art of government, he enumerates for him the five excellent things. The first of them is "bounteousness without any cost." Tzŭ-chang asks again: "What is meant by bounteousness without any cost?" "Follow what is the profit of the people, and profit them," answers Confucius; "is this not bounteousness without any cost?"[1] This statement is most general and comprehensive, and needs no particular explanation.

In the *Many Dewdrops of the Spring and Autumn,* Tung Chung-shu also expresses the principle of the *laissez-faire* policy as follows: "If a sage governs a state, he must follow the nature of heaven and earth, and the personal interest of the senses of man."[2] This is the general policy of leading the economic life of the people in the natural way.

Among all the Confucians, Ssŭ-ma Chien is the one who advocates the *laissez-faire* policy most strongly. His theory is based on human wants. He says:

Before the time of Shên Nung (2287 B. K. or 2838 B. C.), I do not know; but since the dynasties of Yü and Hsia, told of by the Canons of *Poetry* and *History,* the ear and eye want to exhaust the fineness of sound and beauty; the mouth wants to exhaust the taste of meat; the body wants to be easy and pleasant; and the mind wants to be proud of the glory of power and ability. These economic wants have produced a general habit and have fixed the nature of the people for a very long time. Even though we should persuade them from door after door with a fine speech, we cannot change their habits. Therefore, the best policy is to follow the economic activities of man; the second is to lead them on profitably; the third is to teach them; the fourth is to regulate them; and the worst is to fight with them.

This is the basis of his theory. In a word, economic wants.

[1] *Classics,* vol. i, pp. 352-3.

[2] Bk. xx.

or self-interest, is the foundation upon which economic policy is based.

Then he comes to the process of production and says:

> Society depends upon the farmer for the supply of food; upon the miner for the development of the mine; upon the artisan for the manufacturing of goods; and upon the merchant for the exchange of them. Has this natural process anything to do with either political action, or religious teaching, or special order and meeting? It is simply that everyone respectively employs his own ability, and exhausts his own energy, in order to get what he wants. Therefore, when the commodity is cheap, it calls forth demand, and raises its price; and when it is dear, it calls forth supply, and lowers its price. Everyone respectively encourages his own occupation, and enjoys his own work. Such a natural thing is like the water drifting to the low place through day and night without any cessation. There is no one to call for it especially, but it comes itself; there is no one to demand it especially, but the people offer it themselves. Is it not the result of the natural law and the proof of the natural course?

The reason he is in favor of the *laissez-faire* policy is because he is afraid that the natural process of production would be interrupted if it were interfered with by the government. He quotes the four following sentences from the *Book of Chou*: "If there were no farmer, society would be in want of food; no artisan, it would be in want of business; no merchant, the three kinds of money [copper, silver and gold] would disappear; no miner, wealth would be exhausted and insufficient."

He emphasizes the last sentence by saying that, if wealth were exhausted and insufficient, the natural resources of the mountains and marshes could not be developed. By this he points out the importance of capital. Then he concludes this quotation with the following remarks:

These four branches of production are the sources of the economic life of the people. When the sources are great, the people are rich; and when the sources are small, they are poor. Such sources are the causes for the enrichment, both of the state and of private families.

Here he means that there should be large production. If production be large, the sources of wealth are great, and it is good not only for the private families, but for the public as a whole. Therefore, the natural process of production should be left free, because it will bring great sources of wealth to society.

In regard to distribution, he says: "The reason why there are the rich and the poor is not by reason of taking something from the one and giving it to the other. It is simply that the clever get more than sufficient, and the stupid get less than they need." Thus, the division of the people into rich and poor is merely the result of free competition.

After describing the different lives of rich men, and the various economic conditions of great cities, he continues as follows:

Among the common people generally, if a man's wealth is tenfold, the people respect him; if one hundredfold, they fear him; if one thousandfold, they serve him; and if ten thousandfold, they enslave themselves to him. It is the nature of things. Generally, if one wishes to acquire wealth from a poor condition, to be a farmer is not so good as to be an artisan; to be an artisan is not so good as to be a merchant; and to make embroidery is not so good as to speculate in the market. This means that the commercial and industrial occupations are the resorts of the poor.

According to this statement, Ssŭ-ma Chien admits that there is an inequality of wealth on account of free competition, yet he points out that the employment of the poor depends upon the rich.

Through the ages of Spring and Autumn and of Warring States to the beginning of the Han dynasty, the economic condition of China was very dynamic, and great capitalists were numerous. Great capitalists would control whole provinces; smaller ones, whole districts; and still smaller ones, whole towns. Their wealth was accumulated by different occupations, such as agriculture, animal-breeding, mining, manufacture, trade and commerce. Since there had been a great amount of production and of accumulation, Ssŭ-ma Chien believed in the *laissez-faire* policy.

However, he does not go to the extreme. In conclusion, he says:

> When wealth is not confined to any certain occupation, goods have no permanent owners. They go to the efficient as all the trains come to the central station, and dissolve from the grasp of the inefficient as the tiles fall from the roof to the ground. A millionaire is equal to the prince of a feudal state, and a billionaire even enjoys the same pleasure as a king. Are they not the so-called titleless lords? No.[1]

At the very end of the whole chapter, he puts this negative answer for the withdrawal of his former statements. In fact, on the one hand, he likes large production, so that he thinks free competition is worth while; on the other hand, he hates unequal distribution, so that he employs sarcasm against the rich. To enlarge production and to equalize distribution is his final aim. Therefore, in his conclusion, he comes to the common point of the Confucians.

Taking Chinese history as a whole, we may say that the Chinese have enjoyed a great deal of economic freedom.

[1] *Historical Record,* ch. cxxix. It is interesting to compare this theory of Ssŭ-ma Chien with that of Pan Ku in the last section, since they wrote on the same subject.

Except for a few laws regulating consumption for social reasons, the people really do what they please. The fundamental cause is that, since the Chinese Empire is very large and its government is monarchical in form, it is impossible for the government to interfere closely with the economic life of the people. Therefore, although there are some laws respecting economic life, the people need not come in touch with them at all. In fact, the commercial community of the Chinese is governed by custom rather than by law.

III. DIVISIONS OF ECONOMICS

For the divisions of economics in the Confucian school, there is no passage more comprehensive than that in the "Great Learning." It reads: "There is a great principle for the increase of wealth: those who produce it should be many; and those who consume it, few. Those who create it should be rapid; and those who use it, slow. Then wealth will always be sufficient."[1] According to this great principle, there are only two things, namely, production and consumption. While the terms many and few refer to the number of men, the terms rapid and slow refer to the process of production and consumption. This is a most comprehensive principle covering the whole field of economics.

This great principle makes production and consumption equal in rank, but recommends that production should be over and above consumption. This is quite correct. If production were just equal to consumption, there could be not only no increase of production, but also no increase of consumption. The only means of extending consumption, is to produce wealth over and above the limit of consumption. This is the way to accumulate capital, and to make wealth always sufficient. Such terms as many and few, rapid and slow, are only comparative expressions. They

[1] *Classics*, vol. i, p. 379.

mean that the consumers should be fewer than the producers, and the using of wealth slower than the creation of it. This does not mean that the consumers should be so few as to check the producers, and the using of wealth so slow as to block its creation. Should it mean this, it would be not only inadvisable, but also impossible.

This great principle holds true not only in ancient times, but also to-day. As the words many and few refer to the number of men, their meaning is self-evident, and needs no explanation. The word rapid, however, has great significance. It includes all the improvements in economic life. In short, all those things which can quicken the process of creating wealth are embraced. Therefore, time-saving machines, transportation and communication, the money and banking system, business organizations, *etc.*, all are included in the principle that those who create wealth should be rapid. Hence, this sentence covers not only production, but also exchange and distribution.

According to Professor J. B. Clark, exchange is only a part of production, because it produces either form utility, or place utility, or time utility. Distribution is intimately linked with production, because distribution to each member is according to the amount he has contributed to the product. Indeed, production continues up to the time when consumption begins. Therefore, the "Great Learning" in dividing economics into two parts, instead of four, covers the whole ground.

Following the statement of the "Great Learning," we shall divide our treatise on the same basis,—that is, we shall divide the economic principles of Confucius and his school into only two parts, namely, production and consumption. Within the part of production, we shall include the principles of exchange and distribution. In the natural order, production precedes consumption. For the convenience of our arrangement, however, we shall take up consumption first. In the first place, human wants are the basis of economic life and the object of production. In the second place, the part dealing with production needs to be much fuller than that dealing with consumption, so that it seems best to discuss the more simple subject first and then the more complex one.

PART II
CONSUMPTION

BOOK IV. CONSUMPTION

CHAPTER XII

General Principles of Consumption

I. HUMAN WANTS

All founders of religions turn their attention to God, but Confucius turns his to man. In the "Evolution of Civilization," he says: "Man is the product of the attributes of Heaven and Earth, by the interaction of the dual forces of nature, the union of the animal and intelligent souls, and the finest subtle matter of the five elements."[1] By this statement he means that man is a spiritual being. Again, he says: "Man is the heart and mind of Heaven and Earth, and the visible embodiment of the five elements. He lives in the enjoyment of all flavors, the discriminating of all notes of harmony, and the enrobing of all colors."[2] By this passage, Confucius means that man is also a material being. He takes the feelings of man as the basis of his philosophy. Or, as Confucius himself puts it: "The sage cultivates the feelings of man as the fields, so that man regards the sage as the landlord."[3]

Now, what are the feelings of man? According to Confucius, man has seven feelings which are given to him by nature and not by learning, namely, joy, anger, sadness, fear, love, hatred and desire.[4] The last one, desire or want,

[1] *Li Ki,* bk. vii, p. 380.
[2] *Ibid.,* p. 382.
[3] *Ibid.,* p. 384.
[4] *Ibid.,* p. 379.

is the strongest of all. Confucius says: "For food and drink and sexual pleasure, there is the greatest desire of man; against death and poverty, there is the greatest hatred of man. Thus desire and hatred are the two great elements in the mind of man." [1]

In fact, Confucianism is more human than any other religion. Mankind is the object of its teaching. Human feeling is the field of its work. Since desire is the strongest feeling of man, no matter how spiritual he may be, the economic wants for food, drink and sexual pleasure, are the corner stones of human society. Therefore, human desire is the starting point both of ethics and of economics.

Kao Tzŭ, a Confucian living in the time of Mencius, says: "The appetite of food and of sex is the nature of man." [2] Mencius says: "A beautiful woman is what man desires . . . Wealth is what man desires . . . Political dignity is what man desires." [3] Of course, Confucius and his followers do not mean that man should be enslaved by his desires. Yet they recognize that the human wants are necessary to man. Therefore, the Confucians, since Confucius, never advocated the doctrine of extinguishing desires until the time of Chou Tun-yi (1568-1614, or 1017-1073 A. D.). The true doctrine of Confucius is not that man should have no desires, but that the fewer he has, the better. The "Details of Rites" says: "Desires should not be indulged; . . . pleasure should not be carried to excess." [4] This is the true teaching of Confucius in regard to human wants.

It should be noticed that the theory of Malthus is formulated upon the same basis as that of Confucius. The two postulata made by Malthus are: "First, that food is necessary to the existence of man. Secondly, that the pas-

[1] *Li Ki*, bk. vii, p. 380.

[2] *Classics*, vol. ii, p. 397.

[3] *Ibid.*, p. 344.

[4] *Li Ki*, bk. i, p. 62.

sion between the sexes is necessary, and will remain nearly in its present state."[1] These two postulata are similar to those of Confucius. However, Malthus develops from these wants his famous doctrine of population, while Confucius works out a general system of philosophy. This is because Malthus is a specialized economist, while Confucius is a great teacher, in the broadest sense. Taking parts of his general system, however, Confucius, too, shows himself an economist.

Human wants, however, are progressive and unlimited. Such characteristics are described by Hsun Tzŭ, as follows:

> In the nature of man, in his eating, he wants flesh of grass- and grain-fed animals; in his dressing, he wants silk of beautiful dye, and embroidery; in his traveling, he wants carriages and horses. Besides these, he wants the riches of accumulated surplus. But, year after year, and generation after generation, man still does not know what "enough" is; this is the characteristic of human nature.[2]

II. THE DOCTRINE OF RITES

Although Confucius recognizes human wants, and sanctions their gratification, he does not allow the human wants to be uncontrolled. Therefore, he sets forth rules for their regulation, known as rites. This means what is proper, in every way. The scope of this word is too broad; it has no real equivalent in English, except that the word civilization might cover its whole sense.[3] As we are considering the principles of consumption, however, we shall confine ourselves to those rites which are connected with consumption. We shall divide the functions of rites into two heads:

[1] *Principle of Population.* Ashley's edition, p. 6.

[2] Bk. iii.

[3] *Cf.* Montesquieu's *Spirit of Laws*, vol. i, pp. 324-5.

the one for the satisfaction of wants, and the other for their regulation. These are the chief aspects of rites. There are many other details, but we shall study them under other sections.

1. *Satisfaction of Wants*

The first function of rites is the satisfying of human wants. This is pointed out most clearly by Tsun Tzŭ:

> Where do the rites come from? Man is born with wants. When he wants something and cannot get it, he must try to acquire it with all his effort. When people acquire things without measure or limitation, they must fight with one another. When they fight with one another, society becomes disordered. If society became disordered, it would come to an end. The ancient kings hated social disorder, so they established rites and justice to mark the social distinctions, in order to satisfy the wants of man and to supply his demands. Preventing the wants from exhausting the commodities, and not allowing the commodities ever to fail the wants, two elements that help each other and keep society going—this is the point from which the rites arose.
>
> Therefore, the rites are made for the satisfying of wants. The flesh of grass- and grain-fed animals, the rice and millet, made savory with the five flavors, are used to satisfy the sense of taste. The scents of the spice-plants and orchids satisfy the sense of smell. Sculptures, embroideries and the different colors satisfy the eyes. The bell, drum, flute, sounding-stone, lute, harp, reed-pipes and reed-organ satisfy the ears. And the pleasant room, magnificent buildings, rush mat, bed, chair and table satisfy the body. Therefore, the rites are necessary for satisfaction.[1]

From what Hsun Tzŭ has indicated we know that the fundamental purpose of rites is to satisfy wants. Rites have not grown out of the religious or ethical sense, but out of

[1] Bk. xix.

economic wants.[1] Therefore, economic wants are at the basis of civilization.

A particular characteristic of Confucius' system is that he takes human wants as the foundation of his philosophy, and combines the economic and ethical elements into one single principle. He says:

> The rites have their origin in Heaven; their movement reaches to the earth; their distribution extends to all the business of the world; they change with the times; they agree with the variations of condition and skill of man. When they come down to man, they serve to satisfy the human wants. They are practiced by means of wealth, efforts of labor, words and postures of courtesy, eating and drinking, in the observances of capping, marriage, funeral, sacrificing, games of archery, district-drinkings, princely visiting to the emperor, and diplomatic intercourse.
>
> Therefore, rites and justice are great elements of man. They are the instruments to express truth and to promote harmony in dealing with others; and to strengthen the union of the cuticle and cutis, the binding together of the muscles and bones, in dealing with one's self. They are the great systems to nourish the living, to give funeral to the dead, and to serve the spirits and gods. They are the great channels through which we carry out the principles of Heaven and satisfy the feelings of man.[2]

This is the most wonderful system of Confucius. He brings his principles from Heaven, and establishes his real kingdom upon the earth. His system is not unhuman, but human; not theoretical, but practical; somewhat spiritual,

[1] What the Confucians call rites are simply rules of consumption for the satisfaction of wants. The reason Confucius uses the word rites, instead of an economic term, is merely because he is not a pure economist.

[2] *Li Ki*, bk. vii, p. 388-9.

but very material; ethical, but at the same time economic. He especially emphasizes that, when the rites come down to man, they serve to satisfy the human wants. He takes care of not only the heart and mind, but also the body; he regards not only the individual, but also society and the diplomatic world. Indeed, he takes the economic needs as the basis of his ethical teachings, and prescribes social systems for the satisfaction of economic wants. The principles of Heaven are included in the desires of man, and the social and spiritual duties are discharged by the physical and material means: without economics there would be no ethics. Hence, he makes economics and ethics one system, and the satisfaction of human wants the first function of rites.

It is at this point that Confucius establishes his religion differently from that of Lao Tzŭ and that of Mo Tzŭ. They were the two great rivals of Confucius; but they were surpassed by him. It is because their religions, Taoism and Moism, do not satisfy the human wants. Lao Tzŭ says:

> The five colors make the eyes of man blind. The five notes of music make the ears of man deaf. The five tastes make the mouth of man lose its sense. Riding and hunting make the mind of man insane. The articles which are hard to be obtained make the conduct of man harmful.[1]

This is exactly opposite to the doctrine of Confucius. On this point, Lao Tzŭ is similar to Mo Tzŭ. The economic doctrine of Mo Tzŭ depends entirely upon parsimony. He reduces the consumption of man to a bare living. He opposes the practice of rites and the use of music, and makes life as uncomfortable as possible. Taoism and Moism are

[1] *Tao Tê King,* ch. xii. The five colors are green, red, yellow, white, black. The five notes correspond to c, d, e, g, a. The five tastes are sour, bitter, acrid, salt, sweet.

very unnatural and impracticable, because they do not satisfy human wants. But Yang Chu changed Taoism to resemble Epicureanism.

Basing it on economic principles, Confucius makes his religion not only different from Taoism and Moism, two religions native to China, but also from the foreign religion that had been introduced into China, that is, Buddhism.

In the *Canon of History*, there is the "Announcement About Drunkenness," in which Chang Shih (1684-1731 A. K. or 1133-1180 A. D.) gives a famous interpretation to show the differences between Confucianism and Buddhism. We shall quote it as follows:

Strong drink is a thing intended to be used in offering sacrifices and in entertaining guests; such employment of it is what Heaven has prescribed. But men by their abuse of such drink come to lose their virtue and destroy their persons; to such employment of it Heaven has annexed its terrors. The Buddhists, hating the use of things where Heaven sends down its terrors, put away as well the use of them which Heaven has prescribed. It is not so with our Confucians;—we only put away the use of things to which Heaven has annexed its terrors; and the use of them of which it approves remains as a matter of course.

For instance, in the use of meats and drinks, there is such a thing as wildly abusing and destroying the creatures of Heaven. The Buddhists, disliking this, confine themselves to a vegetable diet, while our Confucians only keep away from the wild abuse and destruction. In the use of clothes, again, there is such a thing as wasteful extravagance. The Buddhists, disliking this, will have no clothes but those of a dark and sad color, while our Confucians only condemn the extravagance. They, further, through dislike of criminal connection between the sexes, would abolish the relation between husband and wife, while our Confucians only denounce the criminal connection.

The Buddhists, disliking the excesses to which the evil desires of men lead, would put away, along with them, the actions which are in accordance with the justice of heavenly principles, while our Confucians put away the evil desires of men, and what are called heavenly principles are the more brightly seen. Suppose the case of a stream of water. The Buddhists, through dislike of its being foul with mud, proceed to dam it up with earth. They do not consider that when the earth has dammed up the stream, the supply of water will be entirely cut off. It is not so with our Confucians. We seek only to cleanse away the mud and sand, so that the pure, clear water may be available for use. This is the difference between Buddhism and Confucianism.[1]

Along this line, we may make a comparison between Confucianism and Christianity. The position of St. Paul in Christianity is more important even than that of Mencius in Confucianism, because Paul is the real founder of Christianity. When we study his first epistle to Timothy, he speaks of "forbidding to marry and commanding to abstain from meats which God created to be received with thanksgiving" as the doctrine of demons.[2] This seems quite similar to Confucianism, but there is a difference. In regard to marriage, Confucius not only does not forbid it, but recommends it as a necessary thing. Among all great Confucians, none has spoken of celibacy, although anyone might practice it from personal choice. But Jesus regards the unmarried men as those who "have made themselves eunuchs for the kingdom of heaven's sake."[3] And Paul says also: "It is good for a man not to touch a woman."[4] This is really the orthodoxy of Christianity; hence, apostles and fathers of the church alike have ever looked upon

[1] *Classics,* vol. iii, pt. ii, p. 402.

[2] *I Timothy* 4:3.

[3] *Matthew* 19:12.

[4] *I Corinthians* 7:1.

marriage as a necessary evil, and even to-day the Catholic Church still clings to the orthodox view. This is similar to Buddhism, but entirely different from Confucianism.

Concerning marriage, Christianity goes further than Confucianism, but concerning the eating of meat, it is a little behind it. Paul says that God has created meats "to be received with thanksgiving by them that believe and know the truth. For every creature of God is good, and nothing is to be rejected." Comparing such a theory with that of Confucius, it seems narrow-minded, and not very humane. Man is also a creature of God; but how can we say that we may eat his flesh with thanksgiving? To say that every creature of God is not to be rejected is not very good reasoning. Of course, we may, and ought to, eat meat now; but we should not base the eating of it on such a theory.

Confucius, although not abstaining from meat entirely, has a tendency to such abstinence. In the "Royal Regulations," there is a rule that no one should kill animals without sufficient cause.[1] Confucius says: "To fell a single tree, or kill a single animal, not at the proper season, is contrary to filial piety." [2] And there is a suggestion that the tendency of Confucianism is toward abstaining from meat, because there is the principle of "keeping away from the kitchen" where the victims are both killed and cooked. Mencius says: "For the relation of the superior man to animals, having seen them alive, he cannot bear to see them die; having heard their dying cries, he cannot bear to eat their flesh. Therefore, the superior man keeps away from the kitchen." [3] This is the way to develop the spirit of humanity. The *Record of Rites* says: "A superior man

[1] *Li Ki*, bk. iii, p. 227.

[2] *Ibid.*, bk. xxi, p. 228.

[3] *Classics*, vol. ii, p. 141.

keeps away from the kitchen, and does not tread wherever there is such a thing as blood or tainted air." [1] The *Many Dewdrops of the Spring and Autumn* says: "Sincerely love the people; and love also even the animals and insects. If we do not love them all, how can it be called humanity?" [2] The reason the Confucians extend their love to animals is exactly because they are the creatures of God. But, since Confucianism is very practical, it does not insist on abstinence from meat under existing conditions. Mencius says: "The superior man is affectionate to his relatives, and lovingly disposed to people generally. He is lovingly disposed to people generally, and kind to creatures." [3] This is the standard of giving love, and it is harmonious with the principle of the Three Stages. According to Kang Yu-wei, when we shall have a suitable substitute for meat, we shall abstain from meat entirely. This will be the Extreme Peace Stage of Confucius.

In short, concerning abstinence from meat, from the point of view of love, Buddhism is the highest, but it is impracticable. The theory of Paul is somewhat cruel, although it is an unavoidable fact. Confucianism here takes the middle ground between Buddhism and Christianity. It embraces the whole principle of love, but practices it step by step. It is the golden mean.

All these discussions are introduced not as a comparative study of religions, but merely to indicate the fact that Confucius combines the economic and ethical elements into one system, and that this is a characteristic peculiar to his religion.

[1] *Li Ki,* bk. xi, p. 4.

[2] Bk. xxix.

[3] *Classics,* vol. ii, p. 476.

2. *The Regulation of Wants*

(a) *Moral Control*

Although the primary function of rites is for the satisfaction of wants, a secondary function is for their regulation. There are many bases according to which the regulation of consumption is made. But the ethical basis is the first one, that is, self-control. The "Record of Music" says:

The ancient kings, in their institution of rites and music, did not seek to extend the wants of the appetite and of the ears and eyes to an extreme; but they intended to teach the people to regulate their passions of liking and disliking, and to bring them back to the normal course of humanity.

When man is born, he is still; it is the nature given by God. When he is affected by external things, he is active; it is the wants coming out from his nature. When things come to him more and more, his knowledge is increased. Then arise the passions of liking and disliking. If these are not regulated by anything within, growing knowledge leads him more astray without, and he is unable to come back to himself: his principle given by God will be extinguished.

Now, the moving power of things upon man is ceaseless; and if his passions of liking and disliking are not subjected to regulation from within, he is changed into the nature of things as they come before him; that is, he destroys the principles of God and gives utmost indulgence to the wants of man. From this we have the rebellious and deceitful heart, together with licentious and violent disorder. Therefore, the strong oppress the weak; the many are cruel to the few; the intelligent impose upon the ignorant; the bold make it bitter for the timid; the diseased are not nursed; the old and young, orphans and those who are solitary are neglected: such is the great disorder that ensues.[1]

[1] *Cf. Li Ki,* bk. xvii, p. 96.

From this passage, we can understand why the ethical element comes into the economic field. First, man by nature has wants. Second, his wants become more active when he is affected by external things. Third, his wants increase as his knowledge increases, and the latter is the result of the coming of things. Fourth, things that affect man are ceaseless, and the wants of man are limitless. With all these four reasons, if man were driven only by economic wants without any ethical consideration, society would surely become disordered, and the majority of the human race would be unable to satify their wants.

In order to make everyone able to satisfy his wants to some degree, it is necessary to make everyone able to regulate his wants. And such regulation is best made by each for himself. Everyone has a good nature given by God; if he can come back to himself, he will make his own mind the master of his body, and his passions will be controlled within. This is an ethical regulation upon the human wants, but it has two objects. On the one hand, it prevents the existence of the rebellious and deceitful heart, and of licentious and violent disorder. This is the ethical result. On the other hand, it helps to supply the material needs for the weak, the few, the ignorant, the timid, the diseased, the old and young, the orphans and the solitary. This is the economic result. Therefore, we may ethically control our consumption, but its effect will help the consumption of others, and the distribution of wealth throughout the whole society.

(b) *Social Control*

The second basis for the regulation of economic wants is the social order. In Confucian literature, society is divided into five orders; namely, emperor, princes, great officials, students, and common people. Each class has its own standard, and regulates its own consumption. For all food, clothes, dwellings, furniture, decorations, *etc.*, there are certain rules prescribed by law. For example, the emperor has seven ancestral temples; each prince five; each of the great officials three; each student one; the common people have none, but worship their ancestors in their houses.[1] Again, when a son is three days old, there is a ceremony of receiving him. If he is the eldest son of the emperor or of a prince, three animals are killed for the occasion; of a great official, two small animals; of a student, a single pig; of the common people, a sucking pig. If he is not the eldest son, the provision is diminished in every case one degree.[2]

The *Many Dewdrops of the Spring and Autumn* says:

> The ordinary people do not dare to wear different colors; the artisans and merchants do not dare to wear the thick furs of fox and badger; those criminal people who have been punished by bodily penalty do not dare to wear silk, or deep azure and purple colors, nor do they dare to ride on horses. This is called the system of dress.[3]

All these regulations are ancient customs, and they are recognized by Confucius. Of course, they prevent the economic development a good deal, but they have three essential purposes.

First, they have the ethical reason. *Han's External Commentary of the Canon of Poetry*[4] says:

> The ancients have the "appointed people." When those people, who are able to respect the old, to help the orphan,

[1] *Li Ki*, bk. iii, p. 223.

[2] *Ibid.*, bk. x, p. 472.

[3] Bk. xxvi.

[4] Written by Han Ying, one of the three oldest and greatest authorities on the *Canon of Poetry*. He was professor during the reign of Han Wên Ti (373-395 A. K., or 179-157 B. C.). Bk. vi.

to be moderate in their getting and diligent in their working, are commended to their ruler, the ruler appoints them to have the right to ride with decorated carriage and two horses. Those who have no such appointment cannot have the right; if they do ride with decorated carriage and two horses, they shall pay a penalty. Therefore, if the people had no rites, justice, merit, and virtue, even though they have superfluous wealth and luxurious things, they could not use them. Therefore, the people rise for love and justice, and look down on wealth. Looking down on wealth, they do not struggle for money. Not struggling for money, the strong do not oppress the weak and the many do not hurt the few.

Similar statements are given by the *Great Commentary of the Canon of History*, and the *Park of Narratives, etc.* This is an important principle of Confucius, to raise the standard of morality above the standard of living. You cannot raise the standard of living, unless you raise the standard of morality. The moralist can get all the material enjoyments, but the financier can get nothing. Therefore, the people will struggle for virtue rather than for wealth, and the two standards will be identified.

Second, they have the social reason. That all are born equal is a theory, but that all are not equal is a fact. Therefore, the superior man should occupy the high position, and the common man the low position. Again, those who occupy the high position should enjoy high living, and those who stay in the low position should content themselves with low living. If the common people can use everything which is used by the ruling class, they will have no respect for their authority, and fight for usurpation. Then society will become disordered, and depend only upon force. This is especially true under a monarchical government. Therefore, the social scale should have order, and the dress should have system. The *Canon of History* says: "The carriage and the clothes are according to service. Who will dare not to cultivate a humble virtue? Who will dare not to respond to this rule with reverence?"[1]

The significance of social distinction is also indicated by N. W. Senior as follows:

> We do not, of course, mean it to be inferred that all personal expenditure beyond mere necessaries is necessarily unproductive. The duties of those who fill the higher ranks in society can seldom be well performed unless they conciliate the respect of the vulgar by a certain display of opulence.[2]

This is a theory similar to that of Confucius.

Third and last, they have an economic reason, and this is the most important. If wealth were always unlimited for the satisfaction of human wants, even though there were no regulation of consumption, there would be neither moral corruption nor social disorder. But the great trouble is that wealth is limited, and that it cannot satisfy the wants of everybody. Hence the principles of distribution come in. Before the wealth is distributed, the Confucians believe that standards of consumption according to the social standing should first be set forth. If consumption had no legal standard, and were regulated only by the law of final utility, no one would feel quite satisfied, even though the distribution were very just. This is because human wants are unlimited. The *Many Dewdrops of the Spring and Autumn* says: "The objects of wants are limitless; their quantity never can be enough. Hence, there is the suffering of poverty."[3]

The modern economic theory is to increase consumption in order to increase production. But the theory of Con-

[1] *Classics,* vol. iii, pt. i, pp. 83-4.

[2] *Political Economy,* pp. 56-7.

Bk. xxvii.

fucius is to limit consumption. Why so? In ancient China, there was no machinery; there was no slavery; agriculture was the principal occupation; and every kind of work depended upon the two hands. Under such conditions, how could the existing production be increased? Of course, Confucius appreciates invention and improvement. But, before the modern machine came to exist, there was no epoch-making advance in the increase of production. At that age, when everyone was afraid that production would fall short of consumption, who should dare to advise the people to extend consumption in order to stimulate the increase of production? Therefore, the regulation of consumption, although not a happy thing, was, nevertheless, at that time, a necessary measure for economic society.

Furthermore, the limitation of consumption had the effect of encouraging production. By production, we mean both the material and immaterial production of value. If the higher class can consume more than the lower, and the lower are jealous of the higher, the lower class will endeavor to raise themselves to the higher scale, and will enjoy the same. According to the principles of Confucius, there is no fixed social order, but every one can find his own place by his contribution to society. The higher classes are open to everybody; or anyhow a man can become one of the "appointed people" very easily. If he wants to consume more, he has to raise himself higher. If he raises himself higher, he produces more value to society; and if he consumes more, the aggregate of material production must be larger. Therefore, the regulation of consumption does not prevent the progress of society, but helps it along.

(c) *Financial Condition*

The third basis for the regulation of human wants is the financial condition of individuals. One day Tzŭ-lu says:

"Alas, for the poor! While their parents are alive they have not the means to nourish them; and when they are dead, they have not the means to perform the mourning rites for them." Confucius gives him the lesson as follows:

> Bean soup, and water to drink,[1] while the parents are made happy, may be pronounced filial piety. If a son can only wrap the body round from head to foot, and inter it immediately, without a shell, that being all which his means allow, he may be said to discharge all the rites of mourning.[2]

Again, when Tzŭ-yu asks about the articles to be provided for the mourning rites, Confucius says: "They should be according to the means of the family." Tzŭ-yu urges: "How can one family that has means and another that has not have things done in the same way?" "Where there are means," replies Confucius, "let there be no exceeding of the prescribed rites. If there be a want of means, let the body be lightly covered from head to foot, and forthwith buried, the coffin being simply let down by means of ropes. Who in such a case will blame the procedure?"[3] Moreover, the "Details of Rites" gives a general princple that the poor need not use goods and wealth to discharge the rites.[4]

Everyone knows that Confucius has given very many details of rites. When he comes to economic questions, however, he describes them most simply and convincingly. Confucius, indeed, is a very practical man. The principles of life are summed up by him thus:

> The superior man does what is proper to the position in which he is; he does not desire anything outside of it. In a position

[1] Even at the time of Confucius, drinking water was considered a mark of poverty. But, at present, America uses water as a national drink.

[2] *Li Ki,* bk. ii, p. 182.

[3] *Ibid.,* pp. 153-4.

[4] *Ibid.,* bk. i, p. 78.

of wealth and honor, he does what is proper to a position of wealth and honor. In a poor and low position, he does what is proper to a poor and low position. Situated among barbarous tribes, he does what is proper to a situation among barbarous tribes. In a position of sorrow and difficulty, he does what is proper to a position of sorrow and difficulty. The superior man can find himself in no situation in which he is not himself.[1]

One may say that consumption according to means is a very common thing, and needs no special teaching from Confucius. This might be true. When we study the human wants, however, we find that those who have means will spend more than is proper for them, and that those who have no means will spend more than they can bear. In the former case, it disturbs the social order, or at least it must be an economic waste. In the latter case, it makes the poor poorer. Although the poor cannot spend beyond a certain limit, they may still use up all they have, or borrow money in the expectation of future income, or come to the worst, corruption and robbery. That is an economic and social evil. Furthermore, even if a man spends what his means allow, but is not satisfied with his poor condition, his mind still suffers great pain. By the teaching of Confucius, he will not only maintain his financial condition, but also enjoy a good deal of happiness in life. The "Details of Rites" says: "When the rich and noble know to love rites, they do not become proud nor dissolute. When the poor and mean know to love rites, their minds do not become cowardly."[2]

(d) *Time Element*

The fourth basis for the regulation of wants is the time element. Tzŭ-ssŭ says: "I have heard that when there are

[1] *Classics*, vol. i, p. 395.

[2] *Li Ki*, bk. i, p. 65.

certain rites to be observed, and he has not the necessary wealth, a superior man does not observe them, and that neither does he do so, when there are the rites, and he has the wealth, but the time is not suitable." [1] When he speaks of the rites, he refers to the ethical considerations, the social orders, and all the other proper rules. These principles have been discussed above. We shall discuss the time element now.

The principle of the time element is very broad; it takes into consideration all the things that are related to the period when the wealth is spent. Above all, however, the national spirit is a most important consideration. Ts'êng Tzŭ says: "When a nation is not well governed, the superior man is ashamed to observe all rites to the full. When a nation is extravagant, he shows an example of frugality. When a nation is frugal, he shows an example of the strict observance of all rites." [2] Therefore, the national spirit is the chief barometer of the time, and determines the scale of spending. But we must understand that the superior man does not bend himself to follow the national spirit, but raises himself as a guide for the correction of his nation. This is the principle of the golden mean, that is to say, not adding anything to the prevailing habit, or tending toward either extreme, but drawing the nation of that age back and keeping it in the middle way.

Confucius says: "When good order does not prevail in the state, one should not use the full dress as prescribed." [3] And "Small Rules of Demeanor" also says: "When a state is at the time of luxury and decay, the carriages are not carved and painted; the buff-coats are not adorned with ribbons and cords; and the dishes are not carved; the super-

[1] *Li Ki,* bk. ii, p. 152.

[2] *Cf. ibid.*, p. 175.

[3] *Ibid.*, bk. xi, p. 11.

ior man does not wear shoes of silk; and horses are not regularly supplied with grain."[1] These five things are given as examples of showing frugality during times of national extravagance.

As China is an agricultural country, the condition of the crops is very important in judging of the time element. If the crop fails, consumption ought to be cut down. The eleventh book of the *Record of Rites* says: "If the year is not good and fruitful, the emperor wears white and plain robes, rides in the plain and unadorned carriage, and has no music at his meals." It says again: "If the year is not good and fruitful, the ruler wears linen, and sticks in his girdle a tablet made of bamboo instead of ivory . . . No earthworks are undertaken. The great officials do not make any new carriage for themselves."[2] Its first book says:

In bad years, when the grain of the season does not come to maturity, the ruler at his meals will not make the usual offering of the lungs [that is, he will not take more than one kind of meat]; nor will his horses be fed on grain. His special road will not be kept clean and swept, nor even at sacrifices will his musical instruments be suspended on their stands. Great officials will not eat the large-grained millet; and the students will not have music, even at their drinkings.[3]

In the *Spring and Autumn*, there is a principle that the construction of any public work should not be performed during a bad year. The fundamental idea is that, in a bad year, all expenditures should be cut down to the minimum. Since the work of construction is most expensive, the *Spring and Autumn* takes it as an example. But we must understand that, in ancient times, the public work was done by

[1] *Li Ki,* bk. xv, p. 81.
[2] *Ibid.*, bk. xi, pp. 2, 4.
[3] *Ibid.*, bk. i, p. 106.

forced labor; hence, if the people were employed in a bad year, they would suffer more severely than usual. Since hired labor was established in the Sung dynasty,[1] public work is now advisable for the help of the poor in a bad year. This scheme is carried out in order to give the people public employment instead of alms, because thus they can receive wages.

When a crop is bad, not only should human beings cut down their consumption, but the gods also should suffer for it. The ninth book of *Record of Rites* says:

> The *Cha* with its eight sacrifices serves to record the condition of the people throughout all the quarters of the empire. If in any quarter the year has not been good, the gods of that quarter are excluded from such sacrifices held in the imperial state, in order to notify these people that they should be very careful in the use of their wealth. If those quarters have had a good year, such sacrifices are opened to their gods, in order to please those people, that they should have enjoyment.[2]

By this rule, the gods share sorrow and joy with the people. In fact, in a bad year, religious expense must be cut down. Confucius says that "victims lower than a man's standard requires should be used."[3]

Supplementing the time element, is a consideration for the place. The *Canon of History* says: "Loving the products of your land only, the heart will be good."[4] This means that you will not fall into temptation, if you have no desire for the luxurious things from other lands. This seems more ethical than economic.

[1] See *infra.*

[2] *Cf. Li Ki,* bk. ix, p. 434.

[3] *Ibid.,* bk. xviii, p. 166.

[4] *Cf. Classics,* vol. iii, pt. ii, p. 403.

But there is also a real economic teaching on this point. The *Record of Rites* says:

> What the land does not produce will not be used by a superior man in performing the rites. . . . If mountaineers were to seek to use fish and turtles in their rites, or the dwellers near lakes, deer and pigs, the superior man would say of them that they did not know the nature of those usages.[1]

This is both economic and economical. On the one hand, the rites are easily performed, because they do not require certain things from another land. But on the other hand, money is saved, because it spares the unnecessary expense of getting something away from their own land.

[1] *Li Ki,* bk. viii, pp. 395-6.

CHAPTER XIII

Happiness for Both Rich and Poor

When we study the proposition that consumption should accord with one's financial condition, we see that Confucius would make everyone contented with his own lot. But we shall inquire further to see how Confucius creates happiness for both the rich and the poor. For, if we say that one's consumption should be according to his means, the consumer might still feel economic pressure because he cannot do otherwise. But, if we say that one always finds pleasure in whatever he consumes, independent of the amount, then the consumer is really a happy man; and this is especially true when he is poor. In the former case, the consumer adapts himself to his condition, and needs some effort to regulate his wants. In the latter case, the consumer raises himself above his condition, and pays no attention to his wants. It is the highest ideal in economic life, and it is nevertheless very practicable for everyone This is the value of the teachings of Confucius.

I. HAPPINESS OF THE RICH

1. *Contentment with Means Possessed*

For the consumption of the rich, the principle is contentment with means possessed. Wealth does not make the rich happy, but contentment does. Confucius sometimes said of Prince Ching of Wei that he knew the economy of a family well. When he began to have means, he said, "Ha! here is a collection!" When they were a little increased, he said, "Ha! this is complete." When he had become rich, he said, "Ha! this is admirable!"[1] These utterances are not the exact expressions of Prince Ching, but they represent his feelings as described by Confucius. He sets forth Prince Ching as a good example of managing the household. The essential thing is that Ching did not care much for getting wealth, because his wants were few and were easily satisfied. He was contented with what he had, so that he was very cheerful through all the three periods of his economic life.

Everyone ought to be contented with what he possesses; then he may find himself rich. If he is not contented, even if he be an emperor, he will still find himself poor, and his hunting for wealth will never cease. But how can he be contented? He should accept his economic condition as it is, and not extend his wants beyond his means.[2] In modern times, if the millionaire followed the teaching of Confucius, there would be no suicide on account of economic troubles.

II. HAPPINESS OF THE POOR

1. *Personal Pride*

For the consumption of the poor, the primitive principle is that personal pride should not be affected by one's economic condition,—that is, personality is worthier than any material thing outside of oneself. Confucius says: "A student, whose mind is set on truth, and who is ashamed of bad clothes and bad food, is not fit to be discoursed with."[3] To respect oneself as the most valuable object in the world, and to pay no attention to whatever one consumes, this is

[1] *Classics,* vol. i, p. 266.

[2] *Han's External Commentary of the Canon of Poetry,* bk. v.

[3] *Classics,* vol. i, p. 168.

the first step to obtain the truth of Confucius. And it is a very simple, but very effective, way to make the poor happy.

Confucius speaks of Tzŭ-lu, whose personal name is Yu. He says:

Dressed himself in a tattered robe quilted with hemp, yet standing by the side of men dressed in furs of fox or badger, and not ashamed;—ah! it is Yu who is like this!

> "He has no jealousy and no entreaty;—
> What is not good when he does anything?"[1]

The last two sentences are quoted from the *Canon of Poetry* in admiration of Tzŭ-lu. When anyone is ashamed because he is poor, he may either be jealous of the rich, or entreat them for something. But neither is good. The best thing is to maintain personal dignity and disregard material welfare.

When Confucius describes the different types of the conducts of the Ju, the Confucian, he gives one type as this:

The Ju may have a house in only one acre of ground; its apartment is ten feet in width and height; the outer door is made of thorns and bamboos, and its side door is simply an opening of the wall, long and pointed; the inner door is stopped up by brushwood, and the little round window is like a jar's mouth. The members of the family may have to exchange alternately the same clothes when they go out. They may have to make one day's food serve for two days. Despite such a condition, if the ruler responds to him, he does not lose his confidence; and if the ruler does not respond, he does not offer any flattery. This is the type when the Ju take the small office for the relief of poverty.[2]

[1] *Classics,* vol. i, p. 225.

[2] *Li Ki,* bk. xxxviii, pp. 405-6.

From this passage, we can see how strong is the character of a Confucian. No matter how poor may be his shelter, clothing and food, he is confident of his principles, and is honorable because of his personality. This law is given by Confucius to dignify his followers.

The poor feel unhappy about their consumption not only because it is difficult for them to satisfy their physical needs, but mainly because they cannot reach a higher social standard, and so they fear to have no standing in society. To cure such a feeling, and to raise oneself above petty social ambitions, it is well to read the passage of Mencius. He says:

To desire to be honored is the common feeling of men. But all men have in themselves that which is truly honorable. Only they do not think of it. The honor which some men confer on others is not good honor. Those whom Chao the Great[1] ennobles he can make mean again. It is said in the *Canon of Poetry:* "He has filled us with wine; he has satiated us with virtue." "Satiated us with virtue" means satiated us with love and justice, and he who is so satiated, consequently does not wish for fat meat and fine millet of men. When a good reputation and far-reaching praise fall to him, he does not desire the elegant embroidered garments of men.[2]

When one reads this chapter, he will certainly find himself very worthy, and he will get from himself real satisfaction, even truer and better than that from material things. Such a theory is not based upon an ideal imagination, but upon real facts. As Mencius points out, "those whom Chao the Great ennobles he can make mean again". How can such a temporary and uncertain honor be worth while

[1] This title was borne by four ministers of the family of Chao, who at different times held the chief sway in the state of Tsin.

[2] *Classics,* vol. ii, pp. 419-20.

to a man who is really noble in himself? One can make no comparison between the virtue and reputation which a worthy man enjoys and the food and clothes which a rich man consumes, because the satisfaction in the former case is too great to be compared with that in the latter. As soon as one understands this truth, he will occupy the most honorable position in society, no matter how poor he may be.

Mencius has a great deal of pride and expresses this most frankly. He says:

> Those who give counsel to the great should despise them, and not look at their pomp and display. Halls several times eight cubits high, with beams projecting several cubits,—these, if my wishes were to be realized, I would not have. Food spread before me over ten cubits square, and attendants and concubines to the number of hundreds,—these, though my wishes were realized, I would not have. Excessive pleasure in drinking, and the dash of hunting, with a thousand chariots following after me,—these, though my wishes were realized, I would not have. What they esteem are what I would have nothing to do with; what I esteem are the rules of the ancients. Why should I be afraid of them?[1]

In fact, if we maintain our high moral standard, although our standard of living be low, we are never afraid of the rich.

The superiority of virtue over wealth is a principle of Confucius, and it has become the national spirit of the Chinese. Adam Smith points out four causes of subordination, namely, (1) the superiority of personal qualifications—strength, beauty, and agility of body, wisdom and virtue, prudence, justice, fortitude, and moderation of mind; (2) the superiority of age; (3) the superiority of fortune; and (4) the superiority of birth. Mencius enumerates only three things worthy of honor; he sums up the personal quali-

[1] *Classics,* vol. ii, p. 496.

fications in the word virtue, combines the two elements, fortune and birth, in the word nobility, and counts age as a separate one.[1]

The classification of Mencius is essentially the same as that of Adam Smith. But their theories are entirely different. The theory of Smith is based on general facts, so that he thinks fortune is the most important of all the four causes in getting authority. The theory of Mencius is an ideal, though also based on facts, so that he puts virtue as the most honorable thing. Smith's theory may be true when he refers to the western world, but Mencius' theory also is true when he speaks of China. China has honored virtue above anything else, and this is a peculiar product of Confucius. Smith says: "There never was, I believe, a great family in the world whose illustration was entirely derived from the inheritance of wisdom and virtue."[2] But, in China, besides the family of Confucius, there still are many families of his disciples, and of the greatest Confucians of the Sung dynasty, whose illustriousness is derived entirely from the inheritance of wisdom and virtue. Although their descendants do not possess virtue equal to that of their ancestors, the Chinese confer upon them special nobility in honor of the virtue of their ancestors. Creating the real nobility in honor of virtue, leaving the descendants of the great princes, great kings and great emperors in the background, and giving no honor at all to the millionaires, —this is the influence of Confucius. Under his influence, the poor really do not lose social standing on account of their low standard of life, if they in themselves are worth anything.

Confucius first teaches the poor how to maintain personal

[1] *Classics,* vol. ii, pp. 213-4.

[2] *Wealth of Nations,* vol. ii, pp. 204-6. Cannan's edition.

dignity over and against material wealth, and second, he teaches society how to appreciate the honor of virtue over and above the power of fortune. Following his teaching, virtue really holds the place of honor in the Chinese social life. Such a national spirit, during the Latter Han dynasty, and the Sung and the Ming dynasties, flourished at its best times; even at the present day, it still prevails over the whole empire. It is the flower of China, and the fruit of Confucius. Although it may retard material development to some extent, it has brought a large sum of happiness to society. Indeed, Confucius makes man far nobler than wealth.

2. *Pleasure in Truth*

The highest principle for the consumption of the poor is that the pleasure in truth should not be affected by the economic condition; that is, pleasure in truth is the most enjoyable thing, and there is nothing else able to attract the mind. This is the highest type of living for the poor. It is an advance over the primitive principle. For, if we maintain personal pride against material wealth, we still feel that we are poor in something, and that the wealth is there, in our minds. We must make a comparison between our immaterial riches and the material riches of others. Hence, we hold our honor with some purpose, and struggle for social standing with some effort. But, if we enjoy the pleasure of truth, and have no concern whatever when we consume anything, we really forget our own condition, and ignore the wealth of others. Hence, we live naturally with great pleasure, and raise our minds far above the economic world. This is the happiest type of the living of Confucians.

To illustrate this principle, Confucius gives his own case. He says: " With coarse rice to eat, with water to drink, and my bended arm for a pillow, I still have pleasure in the midst of these things. Riches and political position acquired by unrighteousness are to me as a floating cloud."[1] He takes great pleasure in truth; even in great poverty, he does not suffer any pain, nor is his pleasure affected. We must understand that he does not regard those things as his pleasure, but simply that those things have no influence upon his pleasure.

Confucius gives also the case of Yen Yüan, whose personal name is Hui. He says:

> Admirable indeed is the virtue of Hui! With a single bamboo dish of rice, a single gourd dish of drink, and living in his mean, narrow lane, while others could not have endured the distress, he does not allow his pleasure to be affected by it. Admirable indeed is the virtue of Hui![2]

This is an extreme case showing that happiness can be independent of poverty. Yen Yüan did not take his poverty as a pleasure, but enjoyed his own pleasure, which was not affected by poverty.

Confucius does not forbid the people to make a living; he simply teaches them that they should not let their happiness depend upon material wealth. The creating of true happiness beyond the material world, and the elevating of the mind to be independent of physical needs, are the essentials of his teaching. Moreover, the type of Confucius and Yen Yüan is the highest standard, especially for those who devote themselves to the study of truth. Hence, they should find great pleasure in truth, and should not disturb their minds with material things. But, for the common people in general, to make a living is their duty. Even though their happiness is affected by their economic condition, Confucius excuses them. Therefore, while Confucius is anxious

[1] *Classics,* vol. i, p. 200.

[2] *Ibid.,* p. 188.

to provide a good condition for the common people, he gives the highest standard to inspire the superior man. But, although the common people are not expected to realize this highest principle, they may still know that happiness is independent of the mode of living, when they study the teachings of Confucius. Hence, they may enjoy their life better, even though they are poor.

CHAPTER XIV

Different Ways of Getting Pleasure

When we consume anything, we get pleasure; hence, whenever we get pleasure out of material things, it is consumption. According to Confucius, there are many ways to get pleasure. But we may study a few things which particularly belong to Confucius, and serve as means of obtaining pleasure.

There is a general principle of enjoying pleasure, which is given by Mencius. To enjoy pleasure by one's self alone, is not so pleasurable as to enjoy it with others. To enjoy pleasure with a few is not so pleasurable as to enjoy it with many.[1] Bearing this general principle in mind, we shall know that the ways of getting pleasure are really good ways.

I. MUSIC

First, Confucius was very fond of music. When he was in Ch'i, he heard the Shao, the music of Emperor Shun, and he did not know the taste of flesh for three months. "I did not think", he said, "that music could have been made so excellent as this!"[2] Again, he said: "From the beginning of singing of Music-master Chih, to the end of the six pieces[3] of which Kuan Chü is the first one,—how magnificently it fills the ears!"[4] These two expressions

[1] *Cf. Classics,* vol. ii, p. 151.

[2] *Ibid.,* vol. i, p. 199.

[3] They are the first three poems in the first and second books of the *Canon of Poetry.*

[4] *Classics,* vol. i, p. 213.

show how Confucius delights in the enjoyment of music. In fact, his liking for music was much greater than that for flesh, and its pleasure, appealing to his ears, was much greater than that which appealed to his appetite.

Confucius regards music as necessary to daily life. The "Details of Rites" says: "Without some sad cause, a great official should not remove his music-stand away, nor a student his lutes."[1] We learn from the *Analects*, that Confucius sang every day, except after he had wept for a mourning on the same day. When Confucius was singing together with some one, if the one sang well, he usually made him repeat it, and then he followed it with his own voice.[2] The word sing in the old sense of the Chinese always means that there is an accompaniment of musical instruments. Therefore, Confucius got pleasure from music, not only as a listener, but mostly as a player and a singer.

Confucius taught music not only to his pupils, but also to the officials. He gave instruction to the Grand Music-master of Lu as follows:

The spirit of music may be known. At the commencement of music [ringing out the bells for the playing of the piece of Ssŭ Hsia], there is a movement in the hearts of men. A little later [when the men sing together], there is a harmony. [When the organ is played only with tunes to which there are no words], there is a distinction among the different tunes. [When the singing of men and the playing of organ take place alternately], there is a continuation. [After the music is closed with the six pieces of which Kuan Chü is the first], it is complete.[3]

[1] *Li Ki*, bk. i, p. 106.

[2] *Classics*, vol. i, pp. 197, 205.

[3] *Cf. ibid.*, p. 163.

This was the arrangement of music by Confucius himself, and he described his appreciation of it.

A great achievement of Confucius was the reformation of music. He said: " Since I have returned from Wei to Lu, the music is reformed and the tunes of *ya* and *sung* find their proper places." [1] Confucius loved music, but he hated vulgar music. He said: " I hate the tunes of Chêng which confound the music of the *ya*." [2] Chêng was a commercial state during the Eastern Chou dynasty; its influence was immoral, and its music was licentious; hence all kinds of vulgar music were called the tunes of Chêng. Therefore, the reformation of music of Confucius was the reformation of tunes. The tunes of *ya* and *sung* found their proper places, and they were not confounded by those of Chêng. Confucius made music an object of pleasure, but did not allow it to be licentious. He said: " Kuan Chü [and the two following pieces] [3] are expressions of pleasure without being licentious, and of grief without hurtful excess." This is the principle of the music of Confucius.

The theory of music is given in the " Record of Music," and we may select a few passages from it, and rearrange them.

For the origin of music, the " Record of Music " says:

All the modulations of the voice arise from the mind, and the various affections of the mind are produced by things external to it. The affections thus produced are manifested in the sounds that are uttered. Changes are produced by the way in which those sounds respond to one another; and those

[1] *Cf. Classics,* vol. i, p. 221.

[2] *Ibid.,* p. 326.

[3] They are the first three poems in the first book of the *Canon of Poetry.*

[4] *Classics,* vol. i, p. 151.

changes constitute what we call the modulations of the voice. The combination of those modulated sounds, so as to give pleasure, and the direction in harmony with them of the shields and axes, the plumes and ox-tails, constitute what we call music.[1]

This is the definition of music which includes the movement of dance or pantomime. In short, music is the product of the human mind.

Anything arising from the mind of man, however, is not artificial, but natural. The "Record of Music" says: "The influences of heaven and earth and all the various things flow forth and never cease; and they join together to form one great harmony, and then produce the changes:—in accordance with this, there is music."[2] Indeed, music is a natural product of the universe, and man is but an imitator of nature.

Concerning the reasons why music was made an institution, the "Record of Music" says:

Music is an object of pleasure, that which the nature of man cannot be without. Pleasure must be expressed in the modulations of the voice and manifested in the movements of the body; such is the rule of humanity. These modulations and movements are the changes required by human nature, and they are found complete in music. Thus men will not live without pleasure, and pleasure will not exist without its embodiment; but if that embodiment be not conducted according to principle, it is impossible to prevent disorder. The ancient kings, feeling that they would be ashamed in the event of such disorder, appointed the tunes and words of the *ya* and the *sung* to guide the pleasure. They made the notes give sufficient pleasure without any intermixture of what was bad, the words afford sufficient for discussion without ex-

[1] *Li Ki*, bk. xvii, p. 92.

[2] *Ibid.*, p. 102.

hausting their senses. And they directed the voice in singing, whether tortuous or straight, the sounds of musical instruments, whether increasing or diminishing, whether small or great, and the process of playing, whether pausing or starting; all sufficient to stir up in the minds of the hearers what was good in them, without inducing any looseness of thought, or depraved air. Such was the way of framing music of the ancient kings.[1]

Music has two functions: the one is for the administration of pleasure, and the other is for the guidance of it, in order to keep it in the right way.

The relation between music and society is very close. First, society has its influence upon music as the "Record of Music" says:

The airs of an age of good order are peaceful and pleasant; they indicate the harmony of the government. The airs of an age of disorder are dissatisfied and angry; they indicate the confusion of the government. The airs of a state going to ruin are grievous and gloomy; they indicate the suffering of the people. The spirit of the airs is connected with the government.[2]

In turn, music has its influence upon society. The "Record of Music" says:

When the airs are quick, small, dry and short, the people are gloomy and sad. When the airs are gentle, harmonious, slow, and easy, having various styles, but in a simple way, the people are comfortable and pleasant. When the airs are coarse and violent, so as to excite the body and cause anger, the people are resolute and daring. When the airs are pure, straightforward, strong, correct, grave, and true, the people are sober and respectful. When the airs are liberal and graceful, as a re-

[1] *Li Ki,* bk. xvii, p. 127.

[2] *Ibid.,* pp. 93-4.

sult of orderly performance and harmonious action, the people are kind and loving. When the airs are uncontrolled, perverse, immoral, dissipated, barbarous, and irregular, the people are licentious and disordered.[1]

Therefore, at first, music is a product of the mind of man; whenever his mind is affected by either a good or a bad thing, his music will be either good or bad. But, at the last, man is a subject under the influence of music; whenever the music is either good or bad, he will be moved either way. Man and music interact upon each other. Hence, man should be very careful about the affections, which come to his mind from external things and then express themselves through music; but man should be also careful about music, which in turn influences him.

As to the usefulness of music, we may divide it up into four categories. First, music has ethical value. The "Record of Music" says:

Rites and music should not for a moment be neglected by anyone. When one has mastered completely the principles of music, and regulated his heart and mind accordingly, the natural, honest, loving, and sincere heart is easily developed, and with this development of the heart comes a great pleasure. . . . If the heart be for a moment without the feeling of harmony and pleasure, meanness and deceitfulness enter it.[2]

Second, music has physical value. The "Record of Music" says:

From the manner in which the shields and axes are held and brandished, and from the movements of the body in the practice with them, now turned up, now bent down, now retiring, now stretching forward, the carriage of the person receives

[1] *Li Ki*, bk. xvii, p. 108. [2] *Ibid.*, p. 125.

gravity. From the way in which the pantomimes move to their several places, and adapt themselves to the several parts of the performance, the arrangement of their ranks is made correct, and their order in advancing and retiring is secured.[1]

In fact, in this way, music is something like a gymnasium, a theater, or a dancing school. It gives physical training to the body.

Third, music has social and political value. The "Record of Music" says:

When rulers and ministers, high and low, listen together to the music in the ancestral temple, all is harmonious and reverent. When old and young together listen to it at the clan, village and district, all is harmonious and deferential. When the fathers and sons, brothers and cousins, together listen to it within the gate of the family, all is harmonious and affectionate. . . . In this way, fathers and sons, rulers and subjects, are united in harmony, and the people of the myriad states are associated in love.[2]

Fourth, music has economic value. The "Record of Music" says:

Music is an object of pleasure. The superior man finds his pleasure in it because it satisfies his principles, and the common man finds his pleasure in it because it satisfies his wants. . . . When one enjoys alone the pleasure of music in his mind, he will not tire of his principles. When he keeps his principles fully, he will not satisfy his wants in a selfish way. . . . Hence it is said, "Of the principles of political economy, music is the greatest one."[3]

It is very interesting, this fact that the Record regards music as the greatest principle of political economy. It

[1] *Li Ki*, bk. xvii, p. 128. [2] *Ibid.*, p. 128. [3] *Ibid.*, pp. 112-3.

gives this quotation which may come from an old saying, from Confucius himself, or from his disciples. However it may come, it is certainly a principle of Confucius. It is because music can satisfy the economic wants without danger to the ethical principles. This is the characteristic of Confucius' economy.

The component parts of music are four, namely, musical instruments, poetry, singing and the dance. The "Record of Music" says: "Poetry gives expression to the thought; singing prolongs the notes of the voice; dance puts the body into action in harmony with the sentiments. These three things originate in the mind, and the musical instruments accompany them." [1]

Let us consider only singing and the dance. As to the beauty of singing, the "Record of Music" gives the following description:

> In singing, the high notes rise as if they were borne aloft; the low descend as if they were falling to the ground; the turns resemble a thing bending itself and then turning around; the stops resemble a dead tree without motion; emphatic notes seem to be made by the square, quavers are like the hook of a spear; and those prolonged on the same key are like pearls strung togther.[2]

From this description, we may get some idea about the singing of Confucius' time.

The dance of the ancient Chinese was something like a play. There were two kinds of dance; civil and military. In a civil dance, the plumes and ox-tails were waved, and in a military one, the shields and axes were brandished. Their general style is indicated by the "Record of Music" as follows:

[1] *Li Ki,* bk. xvii, p. 112. [2] *Ibid.*, pp. 130-1.

At first, there are three strokes on the drum to warn the performers to be in readiness, and then there are three steps to show the gradual start of the dance. On the second beginning, the dance really takes its place, and it is going on. At the end, they return to their position in good order.[1]

It is said that the wheelings and revolutions of the dance are like the wind and rain.

The ancient dance was the origin of the Chinese drama. Let us take the military dance for our example, as we cannot get the civil one. Confucius said:

Regarding the music of Wu, in the first scene, the pantomimes proceed towards the north to imitate the marching of Wu Wang against Shang, [or the Yin dynasty]. In the second scene, they show the extinction of Shang. In the third scene, they exhibit the victorious return to the south. In the fourth scene, they play the annexation of the southern states. In the fifth scene, they manifest the division of labor of the dukes of Chou and Shao, one on the left and the other on the right, in charge of the empire. In the sixth scene, they return to the point of starting to show that the work of the emperor is complete and that the whole empire recognizes him as the supreme ruler.[2]

These are the outlines of the music of Wu. Because it was a military dance, Confucius said, "It is perfectly beautiful, but not perfectly good."[3]

In ancient times, singing and the dance were taken by different persons and at different places. The singers were on the higher stage, and the dancers below it. But they worked together in harmony, and all the characteristics of the play were made intelligible. In modern times, the actors are both singing and acting at the same time, in harmony with music.

[1] *Li Ki*, bk. xvii, p. 113. [2] *Ibid.*, pp. 122-3.

[3] *Classics*, vol. i, p. 165.

We must understand that, according to Confucius, women should not take part in the dance at all. It was only in the vulgar music that women came on the stage. Ssŭ-ma Chien tells us that the tunes of Chêng arose from the feudal princes who competed with each other for fame and honor in such things.[1] This kind of music was composed either only of girls or of a mixture of both boys and girls.[2] But Confucius condemned it. Under his influence, China had no actresses in the theater. Very recently, however, Shanghai has plays performed entirely by girls, and Tientsin has plays performed by both sexes together. This is merely the beginning of the foreign influence.

Confucius generally does not approve of the social mixture of the two sexes; hence he does not approve of the dance between them. The ancient Chinese, however, had such a custom as the European or American dance, participated in by both boys and girls. In the *Canon of Poetry*, there is a poem indicating that in the morning the son of Tzŭ-chung and the daughter of Yüan danced at the market-place.[3] This is the only example we can find; it means that such a dance was a local custom only. Confucius puts this poem in this Canon only to condemn such a dance. Under his influence, China never has the social dance between men and women.

Confucius says: "For changing the influence of the people and altering their customs, there is nothing better than music."[4] Hence, his principle is to develop the taste for music among the people. To attack the principle of Confucius and establish his own, Mo Tzŭ has written three

[1] *Historical Record*, ch. xxiv.

[2] *Li Ki*, bk. xvii, p. 117.

[3] *Classics*, vol. iv, pt. i, p. 206.

[4] *Sacred Books*, vol. iii, p. 482.

books entitled "Condemnation of Music". His theory is based entirely upon the economic argument; for the player of music and the listener are wasting their time and checking their production of wealth. This is a very good example to illustrate the difference between Confucius and Mo Tzŭ, the one an advocate of music, and the other against it. Both defend their views with economic reasons. As Confucius looks at it from the point of view of consumption, he thinks music necessary. Mo Tzŭ looks at it only from the point of view of production, ignoring the principles of consumption entirely, so he thinks music a waste. This is the weakest point of Mo Tzŭ.

Since Confucius lays so much importance on music, why is the Chinese music so poor? To explain briefly, it is the fault of the Chinese scholars. In the Han dynasty, the *Canon of Music* of Confucius had been lost. Hence the tunes of the *ya* and the *sung* were unknown. Moreover, the pitch-tubes were also lost, so that the musical instruments of the classical music were also unknown. Whatever had remained was called vulgar music. The scholars found it impossible to trace back to the notes of Confucius; but they did not pay attention to the so-called vulgar music, and left it to the poor musician whose only object was money-making. They were much too conservative, and did not know the evolution and progress of music. Or it is better to say that they were influenced by Confucius too much on the ethical side, and forgot his most important principle, that music is an object of pleasure. Therefore, on the one hand, they tried to reproduce the old instruments, but did not get any result. On the other hand, they regarded the prevailing music as the tunes of Chêng, and would have nothing to do with it. Hence, the so-called classical music did not produce any pleasure, and the so-called vulgar music has necessarily become popular.

Since the vulgar music did not secure any help from the scholars, and lost their moral support, too, it was retarded in its development. As a matter of fact, although the vulgar music cannot be classical, it is by no means entirely licentious. If the scholars would accept it as a base and then reform it, China would have a natural development of music. Unfortunately, they made the great mistake of not dealing with the popular music, and it became a great loss to China. Indeed, they were not good followers of Confucius. Confucius says: "'It is music', they say; 'it is music', they say. Are bells and drums all that is meant by music?"[1] According to the principle of Confucius, the essentials of music are harmony and pleasure. If any music can produce these essentials without excess, it is good music. But most of the old scholars did not understand this principle. Even the few who did understand it had no influence.

II. DISTRICT-DRINKING

The second way of getting pleasure is the rite of district-drinking. It is one of the eight rites of Confucius. There are four occasions on which this rite is performed. First, when the best students are elected and sent to the ruler; second, when the ministers and great officials give entertainment to the best men of that state; third, when the head of the county collects the people to practice archery; fourth, when the president of the town observes the *Cha* sacrifice; —all these occasions have the rite of district-drinking. But we shall discuss the fourth only, as it is the most democratic one.

Before we go into the rites of drinking, we must explain what the *Cha* means. The word *Cha* expresses the idea of searching out. In the twelfth month of the year, they

[1] *Classics,* vol. i, p. 324.

brought together some of all the products of the harvest, and sought out the authors of them to present these products to them as offerings. There were eight objects to which the sacrifices were offered;—namely, the Father of Husbandry, the Oldest Minister of Agriculture, the discoverers of the various grains, the ancient overseers of husbandmen, the spirit of the buildings marking out the boundaries of the fields, the spirits of cats and tigers, the spirit of dykes, and the spirit of water-channels. These sacrifices were expressions of thanks. The principle was that when anything renders you service, you must give it a return. As the cats devoured the rats and mice of the field, the tiger devoured the wild boars, and the dykes and water-channels performed their business, they should receive return. Such a custom was originated in legendary times. In fact, it is a festival day of thanksgiving.

After these eight sacrifices, they proceeded to sacrifice to their ancestors and the five spirits of the house. They wore yellow robes and yellow caps for the performance of sacrifice, in order to indicate that the farmers should take a rest. The yellow-caps were the dress of the country, and they were the signs of the farmers. The harvest time being past, the people had nothing to do but to rest. Therefore, after the *Cha,* the ruler did not commence any public work for the employment of the people.[1]

On such an occasion, the rite of district-drinking takes place. There must be a great gathering of the people in the school house, and the president of the town is the host. Many details are given in the *Canon of Rites,* but we shall omit them, picking out three following passages from the "Principles of District-Drinking."

First, this rite has an ethical significance. The "Principles of District-Drinking" says:

[1] *Li Ki,* bk. ix, pp. 431-434.

The host bows to the coming guest as he receives him outside the door of the school. They enter and three salute one another, till they come to the steps. There each three yields the precedence to the other, and then they ascend. In this way they carry to the utmost their mutual demonstrations of honor and humility. The host washes his hands, rinses the cup, and raises it,—to give the highest idea of purity. The host bows when the guest arrives in the hall; the guest bows when the host washes the cup, and bows again when the cup is received; the host bows after the cup has been sent away; and the guest bows when the drinking is over,—in this way carrying to the utmost their mutual respect.[1]

Honor, humility, purity and respect are the manners of social intercourse. They will keep men away from quarrels and disputations, and prevent the evils of violence and disorder.

Second, it has a social significance. The "Principles of District-Drinking" says:

Those who are sixty years old sit down, and those who are only fifty stand up and wait for any order of service;—thus illustrating the honor which is paid to elders. Before those who are sixty, three additional dishes are placed; before those of seventy, four; before those of eighty, five; and before those of ninety, six:—thus illustrating how the aged are cherished and nourished. When the people know how to honor their elders and nourish their aged, they will be able to practice filial piety and fraternal duty in their own homes. Filial and fraternal at home, and honoring the elders and nourishing the aged outside of their family, the religion is complete, and this leads to the peace and tranquillity of the state.[2]

Third, it contains an economic lesson. The "Principles of District-Drinking" says:

[1] *Li Ki*, bk. xlii, p. 435.

[2] *Ibid.*, pp. 439-440.

When the guest sips some of the liquor . . . at the end of the table, it means that the middle of the table is not only for the purpose of eating and drinking, but also for the performance of rites. It shows that the rites are made valuable, while wealth is made of little account. When the guest drains the liquor of the cup at the top of the western steps, it means that the table is not merely for the purpose of eating and drinking, and shows the principle that rites stand at the first place and wealth at the last. When rites have the first place and wealth the last, the people become respectful and yielding, and are not contentious with one another.[1]

From this point of view, the district-drinking combines economic and ethical elements into one principle.

The "Miscellaneous Records," however, tells that this drinking harmonizes with a purely economic principle, that is, the balance between working and enjoying. Tzŭ-kung, having gone to see the festival of *Cha,* found all the people drunk. Confucius asked him, "T'zŭ, does it give you pleasure?" The answer was, "The people of the whole state appear to be mad; I do not know in what I could find pleasure." Confucius said:

For their hundred days' labor in the field, the husbandmen receive this one day's enjoyment from the state;—this is what you do not understand. Even Wên and Wu could not keep a bow in good condition, if it were always drawn and never relaxed; nor did they leave it always relaxed and never drawn. To keep it now strung and now unstrung is the principle of Wên and Wu.[2]

This dialogue shows the difference between Confucius and his pupil. Tzŭ-kung was too strict and thought that the people should not have the pleasure of drinking. Confucius was sympathetic with the laborers, and thought that

[1] *Li Ki,* bk. xlii, p. 439.

[2] *Ibid.*, bk. xviii, p. 167.

the festival day was necessary for them. "Now strung and now unstrung" is a good rule for keeping the physical strength of the people in good condition, and it suggests the principle of labor legislation.

Confucius says: "When I observe the district-drinking, I know that the principles of a royal government are very easy to carry out." There is a distinction between the honorable guest and the common guests: this exhibits the principle of social order between the noble and the mean. There is a difference in the number of ceremonies paid to the different guests: this illustrates the proper degree of using ceremonies. After the formal music is finished, a superintendent is appointed to look over the ceremonies: this means that they get harmony and pleasure without disorder. They pledge one another according to age, and even the keepers of the vases and the cup-washers enjoy the same: this is a practice of fraternity, without omitting anyone. Finally, taking off their shoes below the hall, and sitting in the hall for the feast, they drink as much as they can stand, and play music as much as they please; but the ceremonies are nevertheless observed: this shows that they are able to enjoy the feast without any confusion. These five qualities form the reason why Confucius says that the principles of a royal government are very easy to carry out.[1]

This rite still exists to-day, but only in a very aristocratic form. Its essentials are found in the country life when there is a social drinking; but it does not use its name, and has no so much ceremonies.

III. GAME OF ARCHERY

The third way of getting pleasure is by the game of archery. It is also one of the eight rites of Confucius. Its beginning and its end are the same as the rite of district-

[1] *Li Ki*, bk. xlii, pp. 440-442.

drinking, and the game takes place at the middle part. After the formal music is finished, and before the general pledging begins, there is the game of archery. We shall describe the game as simply as possible according to the *Canon of Rites*. There are one host, one guest, and the common guests, sometimes with great officials. The game is presided over by the master of archery and the superintendent, and has many curators. Two men make up one pair;—the one is called upper archer, standing on the right; and the other, lower archer, standing on the left. The distance between the two is about the length of a bow. Each one shoots four arrows; the lower archer follows the upper archer in each shooting, and the arrow of the winner must pierce the target which is made of cloth.

The game is divided into three parts. In the first part, there is the game of the three pairs who are made up of young students for the practice of archery. At first, the master of archery himself gives an example. Then he directs the three pairs in the game. But the score is counted later.

In the second part, there is the game of all the members. At first, they arrange the pairs; the host is with the guest; the great officials, even though their number may be many, are coupled with the students; and the common guests are coupled with one another; the host and the great officials act as the lower archers. After taking their arrows and coming to their positions, the score of the first game is counted. Then the three pairs take the first part of this second game; the guest and host follow them; the great officials come in third, and the common guests at the end. The score is counted in two ways. First, all the pairs are generally divided into right and left, the upper and the lower archers, and the accountant finds which set wins more than the other. Then he reports which is the better set;

if two sides are equal, he says that the left and right are equal. Secondly, the game is counted according to each individual in each pair. The master of archery gives an order that all the winners should show their left arms, their bowstring thimbles and armlets, and should hold the bows strung; that all those who are defeated should cover their left arms, take off their thimbles and armlets, leave their bows unstrung and hold the strip of bamboo by both hands. The victorious partner ascends to the hall a little earlier than the defeated partner; the latter drinks a cup of liquor as a fine, and then comes down a little earlier than the former.

In the third part, there is the principal game. Every part of it is the same as that of the second part; the only difference is the using of music for the regulation of the discharging of arrows. The same notes of music are repeated five times without any variation, the first note for the preparation of the archer, and the others for the discharging of the four arrows. If any arrow is not in harmony with the music, although it pierce the target, it is not counted as a point.

After the game is all over, the ceremonies are like those of district-drinking. The guest first pledges the host, and then comes the general pledging. Then the feast takes place; there is no limit as to the number of cups to be drunk, nor to the amount of music to be played. When the guests are about to go out, music is being played, and the host escorts them out of the door and bows.

The game of archery was the national game of ancient China. It was practiced by every man, from the emperor to the common people. When a boy was born, a bow was placed on the left of the door; and when he was only three days old, he began to be carried for the shooting of six arrows.[1] This showed that archery was a necessary pro-

[1] *Li Ki*, bk. x, pp. 471-2.

fession for any boy. Hence it is one of the six arts of Confucius. If a man was unable to take part in this game, it was a very shameful thing. In the *Canon of Rites,* there is a book entitled the "Ceremonies of Great Archery," which describes the game participated in by the feudal princes and their officials. What we have mentioned above is district-archery. It was practiced twice a year, in the spring and autumn; and it was held at the school-house of a county. But it might be practiced at any time. If it was at a social gathering, it was called social archery. District-archery and great archery were quite similar to each other, with only a little modification. For our purpose, district-archery should be given because it was much more popular than the other.

There is a description of an archery meeting that Confucius directed. When he takes part in the game in a vegetable garden at Kuo-hsiang, the lookers-on surround it like a wall. He appoints Tzŭ-lu as the master of archery, and orders him to go out with his bow and arrows to introduce those who wish to shoot and to see. Tzŭ-lu says to the crowd: "The general of a defeated army, the great official of a fallen state, and anyone who has schemed to be the successor and heir of another, will not be allowed to enter, but the rest may all enter." Owing to this, one half goes away, and the other half enters.[1] From this description, we know that the game of archery can be held at any place, and that it may be participated in by any stranger. This is true of both district-archery and social archery. Indeed, it was the most favored and popular game.

The game of archery is very useful. First, it has educational value, and this value may be divided into two parts. In the first place, it is a moral education. The "Principles of Archery" says:

[1] *Li Ki,* bk. xliii, pp. 449-450.

The archers, in advancing, retiring, and in all their movements, are required to observe the rules. Internally, the mind is correct; and externally the carriage of the body is straight; then they hold their bows and arrows skilfully and firmly. When they do so, they may be expected to hit the mark. In this way, their moral characters can be seen from their archery.[1]

Confucius says: " In archery we have something like the way of the superior man. When the archer misses the center of the target, he turns around and seeks for the cause of his failure in himself." [2] He says again: " To shoot exactly in harmony with the note given by the music, and to shoot without missing the center of the target:—it is only the archer of superior virtue who can do this! How shall a man of inferior character be able to hit the mark?" [3] In the second place, it is a military education. In ancient times, archery was the chief art of war; hence it was necessary for the national defence. Archery was a great ceremony, and required men of great vigor and strength to go through with it. The *Record of Rites* says:

[When men of great vigor and strength are about to engage in archery], though the liquor is clear and they are thirsty, they do not venture to drink it; though the stalks of flesh are dry and ready to their hand, and they are hungry, they do not venture to eat them; at the close of the day, when they are tired, they continue to maintain a grave and correct deportment. . . . Therefore, such men, bold and daring, full of vigor and strength, when the empire is at peace, employ their gifts in the exercise of propriety and righteousness; and, when there is trouble in the empire, employ them in the battlefield and in the gaining of victory.[4]

[1] *Li Ki*, bk. xliii, p. 446.

[2] *Classics*, vol. i, p. 396.

[3] *Li Ki*, bk. xliii, p. 453.

[4] *Ibid.*, bk. xlv, pp. 462-3.

From this point of view, this part of the educational system of Confucius is very wonderful. It trains the body as well as the mind and the character, and it can stand in time of war as well as in time of peace.

Second, it has a political value. In ancient times, the emperor used archery as an additional test for selecting the feudal princes, the ministers, the great officials, and the students.[1] And the princes, ministers, and great officials all selected the students for their employment in the same way. In fact, archery was one kind of civil examination throughout the whole political life, and one qualification for election.

Third, it has social value. District-archery includes the rite of district-drinking, hence gets all its benefits. It fixes the relation between seniors and juniors in good order, and makes society harmonious.

Fourth, it has economic value. In the first place, it gives immaterial pleasure. (a) There is the social pleasure in the gathering of different classes and different ages of men. (b) There is the physical pleasure in the exercise of the whole body for the whole day. (c) There is the pleasure in winning the game, by showing personal qualities. In the second place, it gives material pleasure. (a) There is the pleasure of drinking, both before and after the archery. (b) There is the pleasure of listening to music, before, during, and after the game. (c) There is the great pleasure of the feast.

Similar to the game of archery, there is the rite of pitch-pot. It takes place in the middle of a feast for the pleasure of the guests. In the *Record of Rites*, there is a book describing the game,[2] but we shall give only a little of it. The neck of the pot is seven inches long; its belly, five inches long; and its mouth is two and a half inches in

[1] *Li Ki*, bk. xliii, p. 448. [2] *Ibid.*, bk. xxxvii, pp. 397-401.

diameter. It is filled with small beans to prevent the arrows from leaping out. Regarding the length of the arrows, if the game is held in the chamber, it is two cubits; in the hall, two cubits and eight inches; in the courtyard, three cubits and six inches. The size of the arrows is one-seventh of an inch. This game can be practiced anywhere according to the sunlight; if at noon, it is held in the chamber; if in the afternoon, in the hall; if in the evening, in the courtyard. In all three places, the distance of the pot from the players is equivalent to the length of two and a half arrows; that is, in the chamber, five cubits; in the hall, seven; and in the courtyard, nine.

The partners of the game are two; and there are as many sets of partners as there are players. The party of the guests is in the right, and that of the host in the left. Each partner throws four arrows in each part of the game. Its rules are: when the arrow goes straight in, it is reckoned an entry; when it is not thrown according to the alternation, it is not reckoned. During the game, the pitching is in harmony with music. After the result of the game is announced, the cup-bearers of the successful side give drink to the unsuccessful side as a fine. When the three parts of the game are all over, the superintendent begs to set up figures of horses in honor of the victorious party. There are three horses, one for each part of the game. If the side wins only one part of it, it should give up its one horse to the stronger side to unite the three horses for the celebration of victory. Then the defeated partner personally offers drink to the winning partner for congratulation. After it is over, the horses are removed, and the feast is in order, with unlimited drinking.

IV. PUBLIC PARK AND HUNTING

The fourth way of getting pleasure is by the public park

system. According to the principle of the *Spring and Autumn*, the proportion of the ground of the public park to the total territory is one to ten. Based on the theory of Confucius, the territory of the imperial state is a thousand miles square; that of the states of a duke or a marquis, one hundred miles square; that of the state of an earl, seventy miles square; that of the states of viscount or baron, fifty miles square. Therefore, the area of the park of the emperor is one hundred miles square; that of a duke or a marquis, ten; that of an earl, seven; that of a viscount or a baron, five.[1] This proportion of public parks is quite sufficient for the pleasure both of the rulers and of the people.

When Mencius visits King Hui of Liang, the king leads him into the park, and stands with him by a pond. Looking round at the geese and deer, he asks Mencius, " Do wise and good rulers also find pleasure in these things?" Mencius replies: " Being wise and good, they may have pleasure in these things. If they are not wise and good, although they have these things, they may have no pleasure." To illustrate the two cases, Mencius first quotes the words from the *Canon of Poetry* which tell about the park of Wên Wang. Part of the quotation is as follows:

> When the king is in the Good Park,
> The does are lying down,
> The does are so sleek and fat,
> And the white birds shine glistening.
> When the king is by the Good Pond,
> How full is it of fishes leaping about!

Mencius remarks: " The ancients took the people with them for participation in their pleasure, and therefore they were enabled to have pleasure." Contrary to this, Mencius points out, that, if the people wish their ruler to die, although the ruler may have towers, ponds, birds, and animals,

[1] Eighteenth year of Duke Ch'êng.

how will he be able to have pleasure alone?[1] Taking people for the participation of pleasure is the fundamental principle of Confucianism, and it determines whether or no the ruler can have his pleasure. This is the principle of the public park system.

Wên Wang had a park of seventy miles square, and yet his people looked on it as small; King Hsüan of Ch'i had a park only of forty miles square, and yet his people looked on it as large. This difference is explained by Mencius, who says that the park of Wên Wang was open to the people, and that of King Hsüan was kept for his own interest. Mencius describes the system of the park of Wên Wang as follows: The grass-cutters and fuel-gatherers have the privilege of entrance into it, and so also have the catchers of pheasants and hares. Then Mencius says: "He shared it with the people, and was it not with reason that they looked on it as small?" The park of Wên Wang is an example of the public park system.[2] In a word, a park should be shared with the people.

Included with the park system, is the system of hunting, and this is also a source of pleasure. The public park is very large, outside of the city, and it has forests and wild animals; hence it can be used as a hunting ground. According to the *Spring and Autumn*[3] and the "Royal Regulations,"[4] the emperor and the princes have three huntings in every year, when they have no special business in hand. The three huntings are in spring, in autumn, and in winter. The game of the first grade furnishes dried flesh for the sacrificial dishes; that of the second grade is for the entertainment of guests and visitors; and that of the third grade is to supply the kitchen of the rulers. These

[1] *Classics*, vol. ii, pp. 127-9.
[2] *Ibid.*, pp. 153-4.
[3] Fourth year of Duke Huan.
[4] *Li Ki*, bk. iii, p. 220.

are not for the purpose of acquiring wealth, but serve only as regulations of the hunt. Besides the three grades of games, a hunting can also kill wild animals for the benefit of the farms, and it can practice the art of war. These are the grounds on which Confucius approves hunting.

In primitive life, hunting is production; but in civilized life, hunting is often consumption, because it gives a psychic pleasure, greater than that given by the game killed. When Mencius talks about pleasure with King Hsüan of Ch'i, he mentions only two things,—music and hunting. So he considers hunting a great source of pleasure. But, when a ruler does not share his pleasure with the people, they feel his hunting bad; and when he shares his pleasure with them, they feel his hunting good. The conclusion again is that a ruler must share his pleasure with the people.[1]

According to the system of Confucius, the common people have hunting as well as the emperor, the prince and the great officials. There were catchers of pheasants and hares in the park of Wên Wang. By the "Royal Regulations," the hunting of the common people is held during the winter. In the *Canon of Poetry*, two of the poems of Ch'i tell about the hunting of the common people.[2] In fact, the people just as their rulers, ought to have pleasure.

Though Confucius allows the rulers and people to have their pleasure in hunting, he does not allow them to have excessive pleasure. The second and the eighth of the poems of Ch'i just referred to are directed against the inordinate love of hunting. The *Canon of History* says: "Wên Wang did not dare to go to any excess in his excursions or his hunting."[3] Mencius quotes the words from An Tzŭ that

[1] *Classics*, vol. ii, pp. 150-153.

[2] *Ibid.*, vol. iv, pt. i, pp. 131-2, 158.

[3] *Ibid.*, vol. iii, pt. ii, p. 469.

pursuing the chase without satiety is called being wild.[1] Therefore, Confucius forbids hunting in summer time, and gives many rules in the "Royal Regulations." In short, Confucius prescribes always the happy medium; he approves social institutions as safety-valves for human passions, but he establishes regulations to control them. This is the doctrine of the golden mean.

[1] *Classics*, vol. ii, p. 160.

CHAPTER XV

General Standard of Expenditure

I. HAPPY MEDIUM BETWEEN PARSIMONY AND EXTRAVAGANCE

THE principles of Confucius always seek the golden mean, and this is especially true as regards consumption. There is only one proper way, neither parsimony nor extravagance. Confucius says:

Kuan Chung had carving on the square vessels for holding the grain of his offerings, and red ornaments for his cap; he set up a screen where he lodged on the way, and had a stand of earth on which the cups he had used in giving a feast were replaced; he had hills carved on the capitals of his pillars, and pondweed on the lower pillars supporting the rafters. He was a worthy great official, but made it difficult for his superiors to distinguish themselves from him. An Ping-chung, in sacrificing to his father and other progenitors, used a sucking-pig, even with its shoulders not large enough to cover the dish. He was a worthy great official, but made it difficult for his inferiors to distinguish themselves from him. A superior man will not encroach on the observances of those above him, nor put difficulties in the way of those below him.[1]

Kuan Chung is the representative of extravagance, and An Ping-chung of parsimony. They both depart from the rule of moderation, and both are condemned by Confucius.

Confucius says: " The rites should be most carefully con-

[1] *Li Ki*, bk. xviii, p. 165.

sidered. Rites are different; they are the standards above which it is too much and below which it is too little." [1] Hence, consumption should not be too great; if so, it is extravagant. Nor should it be too little; if so, it is parsimonious. Both are against the principle of rites.

Confucius gives an example to represent the proper way of spending. He says:

> I can find no flaw in the character of Yü. He himself used coarse food and drink, but displayed the utmost filial piety toward the spirits. His ordinary garments were poor, but he displayed the utmost elegance in his sacrificial cap and apron. He lived in low, mean houses, but expended all his strength on ditches and water-channels. I can find nothing like a flaw in Yü.[2]

Food, clothes, shelter, are the three necessities of life. Confucius takes them to test the character of Yü, and their standard is low. Yet Confucius applauds it. However, when he judges Yü from the viewpoint of social expenditure, such as religious sacrifices and public works, he praises his liberal spending. From this example, we see that when one spends money for his individual interest, he should be frugal, and that when it is for the social interest, he should be liberal.

II. EVILS OF LUXURY AND EXTRAVAGANCE

Speaking generally of the evils of luxury and extravagance, Confucius sums them up in a single word—injurious. He says: "There are three things that men find enjoyment in which are injurious . . . To find enjoyment in extravagant pleasure; to find enjoyment in luxurious excursions; to find enjoyment in the pleasure of disorderly feasting:—these are injurious." [3]

[1] *Cf. Li Ki*, bk. viii, p. 401.

[2] *Classics*, vol. i, p. 215.

[3] *Ibid.*, pp. 311-2.

In the *Canon of History*, there is a book entitled "Against Luxury." It thus pictures luxurious people: "When the parents have diligently labored in sowing and reaping, their sons often do not understand this painful toil, and abandon themselves to luxury and pleasure, and become quite disorderly, without any rule. They cast contempt on their parents, saying, 'Those old people have heard nothing and know nothing.'" Then it criticizes the emperors of the later generations of the Yin dynasty, and says: "From their birth enjoying luxury, they did not understand the painful toil of sowing and reaping, nor hear of the hard labors of the inferior people. They only sought after excessive pleasures, and so not one of them enjoyed the throne for a long period." It gives many good emperors as examples, who were all diligent and did not dare to indulge in luxurious ease. The most conspicuous example is Wên Wang. It says:

> Wên Wang dressed meanly and gave himself to the work of settlement and to that of husbandry. . . . From morning to mid-day and from mid-day to sundown, he did not allow himself time to eat; thus seeking to secure the universal harmony of the myriads of the people. Wên Wang did not dare to go to any excess in his excursions or his hunting, but carefully devoted his attention to the work of government only.

The conclusion is that all the succeeding emperors shall not indulge themselves to excess in drinking and in the luxury of excursions and hunting.

This book is directed against luxury; but it does not go to the extreme, and allows a reasonable luxury. In the very beginning of the book, it says: "The officials shall not live the life of luxury. But, after they have first understood the painful toil of sowing and reaping, they may then be allowed luxury; and thus they can understand the suffering of the inferior people."[1] Wang Chung (578-648, or 27-97 A. D.) explains this principle by saying that the muscle and bones of a man are not like wood and stone, and that they cannot get along without some reasonable indulgence. This is the principle of Confucius, when he talks about the drinking in the festival of *Cha.*[2]

The evils of luxury and extravagance are frequently condemned in the *Spring and Autumn.* The chief object of condemnation is the work of building, because it is expensive and lays the heaviest burden upon the people. For instance, in the twenty-third year of Duke Chuang, it records that the pillars of Duke Huan's temple were painted red. This was a usurpation of the right of the emperor, because the legitimate color of the pillars of a prince is black. In the following year, it records the carving of the rafters of Duke Huan's temple. This is worse than before, because it requires more labor than painting.

The reason Confucius always takes the work of building to illustrate his condemnations of extravagance is because it hurt the people to a great extent, besides taking much money. In ancient times, there was no slavery, and all constructive works were done by forced labor. When the princes were extravagant, the people were compelled to give painful labor in order to satisfy the wants of the princes. Or, at least, the people must have paid more taxes. Of course, Confucius does not want to sacrifice the labor and money of the people for the personal gratification of the princes. This is the reason he condemns extravagance in buildings. However, after forced labor was abolished, the condition of the people was quite different. But the Chinese did not understand the idea of Confucius very well, and clung to the old custom concerning buildings, because they

[1] *Classics*, vol. iii, pt. ii, pp. 464-470. [2] *Cf.* *supra*, p. 230.

were afraid of being condemned as extravagant. This explains why the Chinese buildings are, in general, inferior.

Besides the extravagance of building, the *Spring and Autumn* condemns all other extravagance. For the condemnation of extravagance in general, the *Spring and Autumn* records the fire of the altar of Poh in the fourth year of Duke Ai. The altar of Poh represented the ruined dynasty of Yin, and it was placed outside the gate leading to the ancestral temple in all the feudal states to serve as a warning to the princes to guard against the calamity of losing their states. According to the *Many Dewdrops of the Spring and Autumn,*[1] Chou, the last emperor of the Yin dynasty, is the strongest example of extravagance. His foods, drinks, clothes, buildings, parks, animals, different kinds of art, colors, forms, music and women, were all of the most luxurious and extravagant. But his empire was lost, and his head was cut off. This was the punishment of extravagance. Recording the fire of the altar of Poh, Confucius gives a warning against the danger of luxury and extravagance. Since it can ruin even an emperor and an empire, how much more easily will it ruin an ordinary man or an ordinary family?

However, Confucius condemns the evils of luxury and extravagance on social, as well as economic, grounds. In the third book of the *Analects,* there are many chapters about this point. Picking out the most conspicuous chapters, we may classify them into two parts. First, we may take up the usurpation of the class of great officials. In the first chapter, Confucius condemned the head of the Chi family, because he usurped the right of emperor and had eight rows of pantomimes in his area. Confucius said: "If this be allowed, whatever else may not be allowed?" In

[1] Bk. vi.

the sixth chapter, Confucius condemned him again, because he usurped the right of princes and sacrificed to the Tai Mountain. In the second chapter, Confucius censured the three families—the Chi family, the Chungsun, and the Shusun—because they used the song of the emperor at the conclusion of sacrifice. In the twenty-second chapter, Confucius censured Kuan Chung on the ground that he married three girls and had many officers performing separate duties, and that he had a screen at his gate and had a stand for the returning of cups. Those things belong to the class of princes, but Kuan Chung usurped them. Second, we may take up the usurpation of the class of princes. In the tenth chapter, Confucius condemned the prince of Lu who performed the great sacrifice which belongs to the emperor only.

In all cases, Confucius regards this from the social point of view. But, at the same time, it is an economic principle. Since Confucius regulates consumption according to the social order, if any class usurps the right of a higher one, it is a social usurpation on the one hand, but it is also an economic extravagance on the other. Usurpation and extravagance are the same thing, and the difference comes only from the differing view-points.

1. *Principles of Simplicity and Moderation*

Preventing the tendency to luxury and extravagance there is the principle of simplicity, which is illustrated in the ceremonies of sacrifices. The *Record of Rites* says:

> Admirable as are the spirits and sweet spirits, a higher value is attached to the dark spirit and the bright water,[1]—in order to honor that which is the source of the five flavors. Beautiful as is the elegant embroidery of robes, a higher value is

[1] Dark spirit and bright water both are simply the pure spring water.

set on plain, coarse cloth,—going back to the commencement of woman's work. Inviting as is the rest afforded by the mats of fine rushes and bamboos, the preference is given to the coarse ones of reeds and straw,—distinguishing the sacrifice to God. The "grand soup" is unseasoned,—in honor of its simplicity. The "grand symbols of jade" have no engraving on them,—in admiration of their simple plainness. There is the beauty of the red varnish and carved border of a carriage, but a plain one is used for riding,—doing honor to its plainness.[1]

All these things, of course, are for some religious reason. But, fundamentally, there is an economic reason. As pointed out by Ssŭ-ma Chien, they are used for the prevention of luxury, and for the remedy of decay.[2]

In the *Canon of Changes,* there is a book entitled "Diminution", which illustrates the principle of moderation. It says: "If there be sincerity in the method of diminution, . . . even in sacrifice, only two baskets of grain may be presented. But these two baskets ought to be offered at the fitting time. . . . Diminution and increase, overflowing and emptiness:—these take place in harmony with the conditions of the time." This means the cutting down of expenditure at the proper time, and the two baskets stand only as an illustration. Sincerity is worthier than material things; and yet material things should not be diminished at all times. This is the principle of moderation, and it is not parsimony. But, how can we be moderate? Bearing on this question, this Canon suggests the term, "repressing wants".[3] If we have ethical control over economic wants, we shall be moderate in a proper way.

[1] *Li Ki,* bk. ix, pp. 435-6.

[2] *Historical Record,* ch. xxiii.

[3] *Yi King,* pp. 246, 317.

III. EVILS OF PARSIMONY

Confucius' system is an advanced civilization, and not a primitive doctrine. Therefore, in his theory of economics, he does not put too much emphasis on frugality. On the contrary, he sets a check against the excess of frugality. In the *Canon of Poetry,* he gives the first poem of the nation of Wei for the condemnation of extreme parsimony in the higher class.[1]

Once again, Confucius sets forth the first two poems of the nation of Tang for the condemnation of extreme parsimony. The first one has three stanzas, all of which express practically the same thing, though in a rising scale. The first is as follows:

> The cricket is in the hall,
> And the year is drawing to a close.
> If we do not enjoy ourselves now,
> The days and months will be leaving us.
> But let us not go to great excess;
> Let us first think of the duties of our position.
> Let us not be wild in our love of enjoyment.
> The good man is anxiously thoughtful.[2]

The second one also has three stanzas, one of which we here quote:

> On the mountains are the thorny elms,
> In the low wet grounds are the white elms.
> You have suits of robes,
> But you will not wear them;
> You have carriages and horses,
> But you will not drive them.
> You will drop off in death,
> And another person will enjoy them.[3]

[1] This poem is given *supra*, p. 154.

[2] *Classics,* vol. iv, pt. i, p. 174.

[3] *Ibid.*, p. 176.

All these poems emphasize the same principle, and are arranged by Confucius in a most conspicuous place, as representing the spirit of the two nations. The poem of Wei is expressly against narrow-mindedness. The two poems of Tang are in encouragement of the enjoyment of things. When the first of these two considers the passing away of time, it looks only at the present day; but when the last one assumes the taking away of ownership by another person, it shares in the sadness of the future. The first one thinks of duty, but the last one only of pleasure. Yet Confucius takes them all for the indication of his economic principle against niggardliness. In fact, consumption is the end of economics, and production is only its means; if man does not consume in a moderate way what he produces, he will destroy the object of production, and there can be no economic progress.

Moreover, if extreme parsimoniousness is the general spirit of a nation, besides these economic defects there will be many defects of an ethical and social nature. When the people are stingy, their minds are narrow, their natures cruel, their characters mean; their ambition amounts to nothing; their lives are unhappy; they have no generosity in social relations, and social conditions are unpleasant.

1. *Principles of Aesthetics*

Confucius lays much emphasis on moral duties, and yet he does not entirely leave out material enjoyments. He has a sense of beauty, and suggests aesthetic principles for consumption. Unfortunately, since the Sung dynasty, the Confucians pay too much attention to internal character, and neglect almost entirely external well-being. They care only for the mind or heart, and not for the body; only for what is good, and not for what is beautiful. They narrow Confucianism into a sect like Puritanism. Hence, Chinese material development has been retarded. But we must go back to Confucius himself, and see how he cared for the aesthetic. For this purpose we may distinguish three forms of consumption: (1) food; (2) clothes, and (3) dwellings.

First, let us consider the foods which were consumed by Confucius. The *Analects* tells us:

He does not dislike to have his rice finely cleaned, nor to have his minced meat cut quite small. He does not eat rice which has been injured by heat or damp and turned sour, nor fish or flesh which has been spoiled. He does not eat what is discolored, or what is of a bad flavor, nor anything which is ill-cooked, or is not in season. He does not eat meat which is not cut properly, nor that which is served without its proper sauce. Though there might be a large quantity of meat, he does not allow what he takes to exceed the due proportion for the rice. It is only in wine that he lays down no limit for himself, but he does not allow himself to be confused by it. He does not partake of wine and dried meat brought in the market. He is never without ginger when he eats. He does not eat too much.[1]

From this description, we can imagine how careful Confucius was about the consumption of his food.

In the *Record of Rites,* there is a book entitled the "Pattern of the Family"; and we may say that it is a sort of domestic science, or economy of the household. It gives many details about the foods and the art of cooking. We may take a few passages from it as examples:

Of grain food, there are millet, the glutinous rice, rice, maize, the white millet, and the yellow maize, which are cut when ripe, or when green.

Of prepared meats, there are beef soup, mutton soup, pork

[1] *Classics,* vol. i, pp. 232-3.

soup, and roast beef; pickle, slices of beef, pickle and minced beef; roast mutton, slices of mutton, pickle, and roast pork; pickle, slices of pork, mustard sauce, and minced fish; pheasant, hare, quail, and partridge.

Of drinks, there is must in two vessels, one strained, the other unstrained, made of rice, of millet, or of maize. In some cases, either the gruel is fermented for one night, as the must, or simply as millet gruel. There are four more kinds of drink—soup of rice, pure water, syrup of prunes, and cold broth mixed with different grains and fruits.

Of wines, there are clear wine and white wines.

Of confections, there are dried cakes, and rice-flour scones.

For relishes, snail-juice and a condiment of the broad-leaved water-squash are used with pheasant soup; a condiment of wheat with soups of dried slices and of fowl; broken glutinous rice with dog soup and hare soup; the rice-balls mixed with these soups have no smart-weed in them. A sucking-pig is stewed, wrapped up in sonchus leaves and stuffed with smart-weed; a fowl, with the same stuffing, and along with pickle sauce; a fish, with the same stuffing and egg sauce; a tortoise, with the same stuffing and pickle sauce. For meat spiced and dried, the brine of ants is placed; for soup made of sliced meat, that of hare; for a ragout of elk, that of fish; for minced fish, mustard sauce; for raw elk flesh, pickle sauce; for preserved peaches and plums, egg-like suet.[1]

It is not necessary for the common people to possess all these articles of food. It is simply that, if they have such things, they ought to use them according to these rules. For religious worship, social entertainment, and the nourishment of parents, these are domestic arts for the women to learn. There are many rules, but we shall quote only one more:

For the art of baking, take a sucking-pig or a young ram.

[1] *Li Ki*, bk. x, pp. 459-60.

Having cut it open and removed the entrails, fill the belly with dates. Wrap it round with straw and reeds, which are plastered with clay; and then bake it. When the clay becomes all dry, break it off. Having washed the hands for the manipulation, the crackling is removed, and it is macerated with rice-flour, so as to form a kind of gruel which is added to the pig. Then the whole is fried in such a quantity of melted fat as to cover it. In the middle of a large pan of hot water, place a small tripod, which is filled with fragrant herbs and the slices of the creature which is being prepared. Care must be taken that the hot water does not cover this tripod, and that the fire has no intermission for three days and nights. After this, the whole is served with the addition of pickled meat and vinegar.[1]

From these passages, we can see how beautiful and intricate Chinese cooking was, even at the time of Confucius. It is no wonder that Chinese food is the best in the world.

Second, let us consider the clothes of Confucius. The *Analects* tells us:

The superior man [Confucius] does not use a deep purple, or a puce color, in the ornaments of his dress. Even in his négligée, he does not wear anything of a red or reddish color. In warm weather, he has a single garment of either coarse or fine texture, but he wears it displayed over an inner garment. Over lamb's fur he wears a garment of black; over fawn's fur, one of white; and over fox's fur, one of yellow. The fur robe of his négligée is long, with the right sleeve short. He requires his sleeping dress to be half again as long as his trunk. Staying at home, he uses thick furs of the fox or the badger. When he puts off mourning, he wears all the appendages of the girdle. His lower garment, except when it is required to be of the curtain shape, is made of silk cut narrow above and wide below. He does not wear lamb's fur or a

[1] *Li Ki*, bk. x, pp. 468-9.

black cap, on a visit of condolence. On the first day of a month, he puts on his court robes and presents himself at court. When fasting, he requires his underwear to be brightly clean and made of linen cloth.[1]

Here we get some idea about the dress of Confucius. It is timely, and most suitable in color, style and combination.

The theory of dress of Confucius is to make the clothes the symbols of personality. Hence they must have colors for distinction, and the colors must be classified according to the social orders. The *Canon of History* says: "God graciously appoints the virtuous;—are there not the five habiliments, and the five decorations belonging to them?"[2] According to Confucius' theory, all the officers should be virtuous, and should be awarded decorations according to their virtue. Thus, the decorations of the emperor are of yellow fowl, white tigers, red flames, and green dragons, all upon a black background. Those of a marquis are the same as those of the emperor, leaving out the yellow fowl. The viscount or baron has only the white tigers, the red flames, and the green dragons. The decorations of the great officials consist of only the red flames and the green dragons, while the decoration of the student is only the green dragons.

According to the *Canon of History,* the dress of the emperor is something like this: All his upper and lower garments are made of fine embroidered cloth. They all have the embroidery of (1) the drawing lines, (2) the grains of rice, (3) the combination of white and black, and (4) the combination of black and green. But, while the lower garment has only these four kinds of embroidery, the upper one has five kinds more, namely, as mentioned above, the

[1] *Classics,* vol. i, pp. 230-232.

[2] *Ibid.,* vol. iii, pt. i, p. 74.

green dragons, the yellow fowl, the white tigers, the red flames, and the black color of the garment itself. The *Canon of History* says: "Take the five colored silk threads, and apply them brilliantly to the five colors which are drawn for the base of embroidery, in order to make clothes." [1]

One sees that the costume of Confucius' system is by no means simple. On the contrary, it is intricate and very beautiful, and has social value. It is the mark of personal distinction, hence it inspires the people to do good and guards them against falling into disgrace. It is used as a means of reward and punishment of society. There is no plain dress, except at the time of mourning, during a bad year, and for receiving punishment. For example, a cap of white silk with edging of silk rough and plain, and with strings hanging down five inches, serves to mark the idle and listless student; a dark-colored cap with a roll of white silk marks exclusion from society.[2]

In civilized society, human wants go beyond the bare necessities; hence clothes are required not only for warmth, but also for display and beauty. Confucius is not like Buddha, whose system of dress is like that of a mourner. Nor does Confucius resemble Jesus, under whose church the dress of monk and nun is also very simple. The religion of Confucius is in the world, and does not seclude itself; this is the explanation of the whole thing.

Under the system of Confucius, even for the dress of a boy under twenty years old, there are regulations. The *Record of Rites* tells us: "His upper garment is of black linen, with an embroidered edging. His sash is embroidered, and also the strings for the button-loops of his girdle. With such a string he binds up his hair. All the embroid-

[1] *Cf. Classics*, vol. iii, pt. i, p. 80.

[2] *Li Ki*, bk. xi, pp. 9-10.

ered border and strings are red."[1] This is for his decoration. But he should not wear furs, nor should he wear jacket or trousers of silk, because both are too warm for children.[2] For the convenience of doing service, he should not wear the lower garment.[3] And because he has not come to maturity, he should not wear the ornamental points on his shoes.[4]

There are many details about dress in the *Record of Rites*, but we shall not go into them. The only other thing we care to mention is the "long dress." It is the most simple and most common dress of the Confucian system. It can be worn on all occasions, by both sexes, and by all classes, from the emperor to the common people. It is next only to the court and sacrificial robes. It is lasting and not expensive, and yet it has an ornamental border. Its details are given in a small book entitled the "Long Dress."[5] In fact, Confucius has given a complete system about the dress of the head, the feet, and the whole body. So far as their dress is concerned, the Chinese all say that their costume is most genteel and comfortable.

Third, let us consider dwellings. Unfortunately, we cannot find any description of the house of Confucius. The only thing we know is that the present temple of Confucius is his old house, which was also occupied by his pupils. As his house was at the same time a school-building, and his pupils were very numerous, such a house must have been very large. His school-house has been called by the name of Apricot Arena, so it must have presented a very beautiful scene with the apricot flowers. Its situation was good, as we can see at the present day.

[1] *Li Ki*, bk. xi, pp. 19-20.
[2] *Ibid.*, p. 20.
[3] *Ibid.*, bk. x, p. 478.
[4] *Ibid.*, bk. xi, p. 20.
[5] *Ibid.*, bk. xxxvi, pp. 395-6.

While we have no description of his own house, we still can get his ideas about buildings from his writings. In the *Canon of Poetry*, there is a poem praising Hsüan Wang (276-231 B. K. or 827-782 B. C.), who built a new palace according to the principle of frugality. Frugality is the essential of this poem, and yet it gives the sense of beauty. We shall quote a few lines about this palace.

> Like a man on tip-toe, in reverent expectation,
> Like an arrow, flying rapidly,
> Like a bird which has changed its feathers,
> Like a pheasant on flying wings,
> Is the hall which our noble lord will ascend.
>
> Level and smooth is the court-yard,
> And lofty are the pillars around it.
> Pleasant is the exposure of the chamber to the light,
> And deep and wide are its recesses.
> Here will our noble lord repose.[1]

This poem about the palace shows in the first stanza how magnificent and conspicuous is the hall, and in the second, how grand and lovely the private apartment.

Scattered throughout the *Canon of Rites* is the description of a house which is about the same as the ancestral temple. It was an old custom, adopted by Confucius. The Chinese house to-day still seems somewhat similar to this. Such a system was common to all classes, from the emperor to the student, the difference being only in size and details. Let us now consider the house of the student.

Imagine an oblong space enclosed by four brick walls. In the front, or southern wall, (a house must always face the south), is the "external entrance." Some distance behind it is a second wall, in the center of which is the "main entrance." Both entrances are roofed over, with oblong

[1] *Classics*, vol. iv, pt. ii, p. 305.

buildings, running east and west, on each side, each building divided into two lobbies, one within, one without, the entrance. The house proper, about square in outline, is situated well toward the back of this enclosed space. It consists of a great hall and behind it three apartments.

The great hall stretches clear across the front of the house, its front open, having two pillars instead of a dividing wall, one at the east, one at the west. This great hall is approached by two flights of steps, one toward the east, one toward the west. At the center of the northern wall of the hall, between a door on the east leading into the apartment behind and a window on the west, is the honorable place for guests. The east and west ends of the hall are partitioned off into long, narrow "assistant apartments."

Behind the great hall is the "principal apartment," used as a business office. At each side of this is a chamber. The northern half of the "eastern chamber" is called the "northern hall." It has an open front in the north, and it is for the exercising of ceremony by the ladies. The "western chamber" stores the valuable things. The whole house proper is covered by a peaked roof made of tile, sloping to back and front.

Behind the house proper are the "private apartment" for eating and sleeping, and several small buildings for the children, or perhaps for a son and his family. In the homes of those of higher rank, this third and back part may be expanded indefinitely.

The open space in front of the house proper is the court, which is usually three times the length of the hall.

The house of the common people is similar to that of the student. The only great differences are that it has only one entrance, without lobbies in its two sides, and that the court is only as long as the hall. It has not the "private apartment", and the principal apartment is used for eating, sleeping, *etc.* Besides these, there is no great difference in the house proper. In fact, according to the economic principles of Confucius, there is no pauper; and even the lowest people must have for their houses plenty of sunlight and good air.

The most beautiful building in the Confucian system is the "Brilliant Hall." The *Many Dewdrops of the Spring and Autumn* says: "The Brilliant Hall is round; its building is high, imposing, magnificent and round."[1] According to *Elder Tai's Record of Rites*, the Brilliant Hall has nine apartments in all. Each apartment has four doors and eight windows; in the whole hall, there are thirty-six doors and seventy-two windows. The roof is covered with grass, to symbolize cleanliness. The upper part is round, the lower part square. It is surrounded by a round body of water.[2] This is the most important building for all great exercises of the emperor: to worship God together with the founder of the dynasty, and to observe many other important ceremonies.

IV. CHOICE BETWEEN PARSIMONY AND EXTRAVAGANCE

If we are obliged to choose either extravagance or parsimony, however, which one is preferable? When Lin Fang asks Confucius what the essential of rites is, Confucius replies: "In festive rites, it is better to be sparing than extravagant."[3] This statement is clear enough to show his opinion in favor of parsimony. Again, Confucius says: "Extravagance leads to insubordination, and parsimony to meanness. It is better to be mean than to be insubordinate."[4] Therefore, we are sure that, if one cannot act in the proper way, Confucius would prefer parsimony rather than extravagance.

[1] Bk. xxiii.
[2] Bk. lxvi.
[3] *Classics*, vol. i, p. 155.
[4] *Ibid.*, p. 207.

V. SOCIAL STANDARD OF LIVING

1. *General Survey*

We have discussed above the doctrine of rites, and have seen how the standard of living enters into the Confucian system. We must now study it especially and definitely. In every age and every place, there must be different standards among different classes, and this holds in the teachings of Confucius. Since there are five classes, as we know, there are five standards,—that is, those of the emperor, the princes, the great officials, the students and the common people. But, on some occasions, the standard of the prince may be the same as that of the emperor, that of the great official as that of the prince, and so on down.

We must keep in mind that social standards have a great influence upon the economic life, in addition to marking social distinctions. They make everyone satisfy his wants according to the standard of his class. They help to make the wealth that is produced suffice for the needs of consumers. They stimulate everyone to do his best in production for the sake of raising himself to a higher class. Therefore, Confucius prescribes the different standards for the different classes.

Take religious expense, for example. The " Royal Regulations " says:

In sacrificing at the altars to the spirits of the land and grain, the emperor uses in each case a bull, a ram and a boar; the princes, only a ram and a boar. The great officials and students, at the sacrifices in their ancestral temples, if they have land, observe the full ceremonies of regular sacrifice; and, if they have no land, they simply present their offering, [that is, the great official offers a lamb, and the student a sucking-pig]. The common people, in the spring, offer scallions; in summer, wheat; in autumn, millet; and in winter, rice. The scallions are set forth with eggs; the wheat with fish; the millet with a sucking-pig; and the rice with a goose.[1]

This represents the standards of their worship; and it is somewhat according to their means.

Let us take their foods for another example. When there is any occasion, the emperor and prince may kill an ox; the great official, a sheep; the student, a dog or a pig; and the common people may eat delicate food. But, among all of them, nobody should do so simply to satisfy his appetite and without any other reason.[2]

The "Pattern of the Family" says:

The cupboards of the emperor are five in the assistant apartment to the left, and another five in that to the right; those of dukes, marquises, and earls are also five, but all in one chamber; those of great officials are three in the assistant apartment; and the students have only one on their buffet.[3]

It does not speak about the number of cupboards of the common people, but it may be understood that it is equal to that of the students.

The ancient Chinese liked to have a large area for a house, rather than many stories. Hence the standard of a house is generally measured by its size instead of its height. And yet there is a rule to regulate the height of a house. Such a rule is illustrated in the steps of a hall. According to the *Record of Rites*, the hall of the emperor has nine steps, each of one cubit, that is, it is nine cubits higher than the ground; that of the prince, seven; that of the great official, five; and that of the student, three.[4] The text does not say

[1] *Cf. Li Ki*, bk. iii, p. 226.

[2] *Ibid.*, p. 227, and bk. xi, p. 4.

[3] *Ibid.*, bk. x, p. 464.

[4] *Ibid.*, bk. viii, p. 400.

how high the hall of common people should be; but, judging from what has been described above, and drawing authority from Chia Yi and modern scholars, the hall of the common people must have one step, that is, be one cubit higher than the ground. Here we get some idea about the standard for their dwelling.

The Chinese have a peculiar index of social status; that is, the use of jade. The reason the Chinese set a high value on jade is explained by Confucius. His full explanation is given in the *Record of Rites*,[1] but it can be summed up in one line—jade has all the qualities which are similar to the virtues of a gentleman. The same book tells us:

> All the girdles must have the pendant of jade, except during the mourning only. At the end of the middle string is the tooth-like piece, colliding with the others. Without some sad cause, a gentleman will never let the jade leave his person; he regards the pieces of jade as emblematic of the virtues which he should cultivate.
>
> The pendant of the emperor is composed of beads of white jade, hung on dark-colored strings; that of a duke or marquis, of jade-beads of hill-azure, on vermilion strings; that of a great official, of beads of aqua-marine, on black strings; that of an heir-son, of beads of *yü* jade, on variegated strings; that of a student, of beads of jade-like quartz, on orange-colored strings. As for Confucius, he sometimes wears at his pendant an ivory ring, five inches round, on variegated strings.[2]

These are the different standards in connection with the use of jade for pendants, and this is a good example of the significance ascribed to ornaments.

[1] *Li Ki*, bk. xlv, pp. 463-4.

[2] *Ibid.*, bk. xi, p. 19.

2. *Standard of the Class of the Great Officials*

We are not much interested in the standard of living of the emperor and princes, but we are interested in that of the great officials, because they are of the middle class. In the *Record of Rites*, there is a passage telling about the daily life of great officials, which may be taken as a description of the higher standard of living. It says:

> A gentleman washes his hands five times a day. He uses millet-water in washing his head, and maize-water in washing his face. For his hair, when wet he uses a comb of white-grained wood, and an ivory comb for it when dry. After his toilet, there are brought to him the usual sup of wine and some delicacy; and the musicians come up the raised hall and sing. In bathing he uses two towels; a fine one for the upper part of his body, and a coarser one for the lower part. When he gets out of the tub, he steps on a straw mat; and having washed his feet again with hot water, he steps on the rush one. Then in his bathing robe of cloth, he dries his body again, and puts on his shoes; and a drink is then brought to him.[1]

Confucius once belonged to the class of great officials, and, when he lost his position, he belonged to the class of students. But, after he was called back to his state, he received his old title as a retired official, although he did not take the actual position. Therefore, he kept the standard of living of a great official. When Yen Yüan died, Yüan's father asked Confucius to sell his carriage in order to get an outer shell for the coffin of Yüan; but Confucius refused to do so. He referred to the fact that, when his own son died, he did not give up the carriage to get an outer shell for him. He said: "It is because that, having belonged to the class of great officials, it is not proper for me to

[1] *Li Ki*, bk. xi, p. 5.

walk on foot." From this instance, we can see how careful Confucius was to maintain his standard of living. Of course, this is a little more social than economic; but it is a very good example of the attention Confucius paid to the standard of living.

3. *Standard of the Class of Students*

In the "Pattern of the Family," there are many details of daily life, and they are essentially common to all classes. We may select some details in order to represent the standard of the class of students. This class is very important, because their living is similar to that of common people. Although the common people may not observe those rules as fully as the students, the rules are nevertheless the pattern of the people to whom the following lessons are taught.

When the sons serve their parents, on the first crowing of the cock, they all wash their faces and rinse their mouths, comb their hair, draw over it the covering of silk, fix this with the hair-pin, bind the hair at the roots with the fillet, brush the dust from the hair-tufts hanging over the forehead, and then put on their caps, leaving the ends of the strings hanging down. They then put on their square black robes, knee-covers, and girdles, fixing in the last their tablets. From the left and right of the girdle they hang their articles for use:— on the left side, the duster made of a handkerchief, the knife and whetstone, the small ivory spike for the opening of knots, and the metal speculum for getting fire from the sun; on the right, the archer's thimble for the thumb, and the armlet, the tube for writing instruments, the knife-case, the larger spike, and the borer for getting fire from wood. Finally, they put on their leggings, and adjust their shoe-strings.

This description seems to have too many details, but it gives a very good picture of the young men in ancient times. When the young women serve their parents or parents-in-law, they dress like these young men, with this difference: they wear the square black silk robes, also with girdles; leaving out such articles as the thimble and armlet, the tube and knife-case, they hang the needle-case, thread and floss, all bestowed in the satchel; then they fasten their necklaces which serve as bags for perfume.

When the young men and young women have thus dressed, they go to their parents and parents-in-law, and care for them in every way. They ask whether they want anything, and then respectfully bring it. They bring to their parents gruel, thick or thin, spirit or must, soup of vegetables, beans, wheat, spinach, rice, millet, maize, and glutinous millet,—whatever they wish, in fact; and their parents are also furnished with dates, chestnuts, sugar and honey, to sweeten their dishes; with the ordinary or the large-leaved violets, leaves of elm-trees, fresh or dry, and the most soothing rice-water to lubricate them; and with fat and oil to enrich them. Waiting till the parents have tasted them, the young people may withdraw.

As to the younger boys and girls, they do not take the full dress of young men and young women, but they all use necklaces as ornamental bags of perfume. At daybreak, they begin to pay their respects to their parents—later, however, than their older brothers and sisters. Their duty is to do the small services for their parents.

All the members living in the inner and outer parts of the house, at the first crowing of the cock, should wash their faces and mouths, put on their dresses, gather up their pillows and fine mats, sprinkle and sweep out the apartments, hall, and courtyard, and spread the mats—each doing his proper work. After sunrise, each attends to his special business.

Besides the old parents who are treated especially well, the children also receive favorable treatment. They go earlier to bed, and get up later. Everything is ready according to what they want; there is no fixed time for their meals. Whenever the parents leave something after their eating, although the sons and their wives may finish the remainder, the sweet, soft, and oily things are specially for the children.[1] This example is given to illustrate the principle of "loving the young".

4. *Standard of the Common People*

The most important of all is the standard of living of the common people. Of course, the living of the common people must be simple, and we cannot expect to have many details about it in the Confucian system. Under the system of *tsing tien*, however, they enjoy a very good living, and their standard is thus summed up by Mencius:

> Around the house of five acres, the space beneath the walls is planted with mulberry trees, with which the woman nourishes silkworms, and thus the old are able to have silk to wear. Each family has five brood hens and two brood sows, which are kept to their breeding seasons, and thus the old are able to have flesh to eat. The husbandman cultivates his farm of one hundred acres, and thus his family of eight mouths are secured against hunger.

According to Mencius, the people of fifty years old cannot be kept warm without silk, and those of seventy cannot be satisfied without flesh. If they are not kept warm by silk, or not satisfied by flesh, it is said that they are starved and famished.[2] Therefore, the silk for dress and flesh for food are not the luxuries of the old, but their necessities. From this point of view, we may say that the standard of the common people is by no means low.

[1] *Li Ki*, bk. x, pp. 449-453.

[2] *Classics*, vol. ii, pp. 461-2.

"Nourishing the old" is a special principle of Confucius, and it raises the standard of living. According to the "Royal Regulations," for those of fifty, the grain is fine and different from that used by the younger people. For those of sixty, flesh is kept in store waiting for their order at any time. For those of seventy, there is a second service of savory meat. For those of eighty, there is a constant supply of delicacies. For those of ninety, food and drink are never out of their chamber; wherever they wander to another place, it is required that savory meat and drink should accompany them.[1] There is a strict rule that the old of the common people should not eat their meal without flesh.[2] Therefore, the standard of the common people is kept up by the old, and it can never be lowered.

According to the *tsing tien* system, however, although the persons fifty years old may be clothed with silk, and those of seventy may eat flesh, nothing is said about those who are younger than fifty or seventy years. We may suppose that the young people cannot consume such things in daily life, and that they are especially given to the old, because the productive power of ancient times was very limited.

What we have described of the standard of common people, however, is mixed up with the theoretical points of Confucius. But we want to know the actual condition of the people at that time. There is a valuable statement given by Li K'o,[3] the pupil of Tzŭ-hsia, and the minister of Marquis Wên of Wei (128-165 A. K. or 424-387 B. C.), indicating exactly the economic condition of the

[1] *Li Ki*, bk. iii, p. 240.

[2] *Ibid.*, p. 244, and bk. x, p. 462.

[3] His name is correctly recorded in the *Historical Record* (chs. xxx and cxxix) and in the *History of Han* (ch. xci). But the latter makes a mistake in ch. xxiv, where his name is given as Li Kuei.

farmers. Since Li K'o lived shortly after Confucius, but much earlier than Mencius, his statement probably shows the facts of Confucius' age. He says:

Now, one man, having five mouths in all, cultivates the land of one hundred acres. He reaps annually from each acre one bushel and a half of grain; the total amount is one hundred and fifty bushels. Subtracting fifteen bushels for the taxation of one-tenth, there remain one hundred and thirty-five bushels. For food, each person consumes one bushel and a half monthly; five persons consume ninety bushels for the whole year. There remain forty-five bushels. One bushel is worth thirty coins; the total value is one thousand three hundred fifty coins. Subtracting three hundred coins for the expense of social gathering and religious worship, there remain one thousand fifty coins. For clothing, each person spends three hundred coins on the average; five persons spend one thousand five hundred for the whole year. There is a deficit of four hundred fifty. If they are so unlucky as to have expense for sickness and funeral, or for the extra impositions of government, such expenditure still has not been included in this account.[1]

This statement gives a statistical view of the unhappy condition of farmers, and is the most reliable information which we now have. Since agriculture was the principal occupation of the ancient Chinese, the economic condition of the whole people must have been very bad. Hence Li K'o introduced his famous system of equalizing the price of grain for their relief.[2] Such a bad condition was probably not confined to the state of Li K'o, but prevailed over the whole empire. It is no wonder that Confucius devotes his attention first to the economic life of the people.

[1] *History of Han*, ch. xxiv.

[2] See *infra*.

CHAPTER XVI

Particular Expenditures

Although the standard of living may include all kinds of expenditures, we prefer to discuss some particular expenditures separately, in order to show the characteristics of Confucius' system. These expenditures are: the expenditure for a marriage, the expenditure for a funeral and mourning, the expenditure for ancestor-worship, and the expenditure for social intercourse. The theories of these expenditures are extremely complex; they are not only economic, but also sociological, political, philosophical, ethical and religious. Of course, we are most interested in the economic aspect. But, as we are studying the system of Confucius, we have to consider many other aspects which are peculiar to Confucius and are correlative to economics.

I. MARRIAGE

First, we shall discuss the expenditure for a marriage. Since Confucius makes marriage a necessity of human life, he reduces its expense to the minimum. According to the *Canon of Rites,* there are six rites for marriage. After the family of the girl has accepted the proposal, the first rite is "giving a choice" to her father; the second is "inquiring into the name" of the girl. These two rites are consummated at one time. The third is "giving the lucky result" of divination; the fourth is "giving engagement;" the fifth is first "asking about the date" of the wedding, and then announcing it. All these five rites are performed by a proxy sent by the father of the bridegroom. The sixth rite is "personal receiving," an act of the bridegroom himself.

The rite of "giving engagement" is performed by the use of a bundle of silk and two pieces of the fur of a deer. The bundle of silk contains five rolls; each roll is folded double, and is forty cubits in length.[1] Three rolls are black, and the other two crimson. The two pieces of deer's fur can be used for dress. Besides "giving engagement," the other five rites are all performed by the use of a domestic goose for a present. This token is intended to represent the regularity and faithfulness of the relation of husband and wife. Requiring only five geese, five rolls of silk and two pieces of deer's fur, this ceremony of marriage is inexpensive. Of course, the expense of an American marriage can cut down to even less than this, but, according to Confucius' system, this is the lowest limit.

In the *Canon of Poetry,* there is a poem written by a heroic girl. She has promised to marry a man of Fêng, but his family wants to receive her before the rites of marriage are completed. She refuses to allow them to do so, on the ground that marriage is a most sacred thing and cannot be consummated without the full observance of rites. His family prosecutes her and causes her to be brought to court. But she insists that, if one single thing has not been presented, and one single rite has not been completed, she will not leave her home even if she sacrifices her life. Her poem runs as follows: "Although you have brought me to court, your offerings for the rites of marriage are not sufficient." It says again: "Although you have brought me by prosecution, I will not follow you."[2]

By selecting this poem in his Canon for an example of a

[1] *Li Ki,* bk. xviii, p. 172.

[2] *Classics,* vol. iv, pt. i, pp. 27-8.

marriage that is good, not only morally, but also legally, Confucius shows that he does not approve of allowing people to marry without going through the six rites, on the pretense that they have not the means. Indeed, he regulates the relation of husband and wife very carefully in the beginning, and does not make marriage too easy for the young couple.

Although Confucius does not make marriage too easy, he makes it as simple as possible. He is most fond of music, and employs it for all fortunate occasions; yet he omits music from the ceremonies of marriage. Confucius says:

> The family whose daughter is married, does not extinguish its candles for three nights, thinking of the separation that has taken place. The family that has received the bride, for three days has no music; the bridegroom is thinking that he is about to take the place of his parents.[1]

According to this expression, marriage is not a gay ceremony, but a solemn business through which the son assumes responsibilities of his own and feels that his parents are getting older. It should be quiet and sober. Therefore, the *Record of Rites* says that at the marriage ceremony, music is not employed, and that there is no congratulation on marriage.[2]

Confucius limits the expense of marriage to a minimum, but he cannot help making the feast necessary. Since he separates the two sexes very severely, he must not allow the new couple to keep so quiet as not to give a conspicuous notice to society. In order to mark the new relation between bride and bridegroom, a feast is necessary to notify the public. The *Record of Rites* says: "The bridegroom should make a feast and invite the people of the town and

[1] *Li Ki*, bk. v, p. 322.

[2] *Ibid.*, bk. ix, p. 442.

his friends to attend it, in order to give its due importance to the separate position of man and woman."[1] Of course, this feast must cost something, but its expense cannot be saved because it has social and ethical value.

As the feast must necessarily be given by the bridegroom to his townsmen and his friends, although there is to be no congratulation, the guests cannot simply attend the feast without any social obligation. Hence the congratulation takes place under another name. It is not said to be a congratulation upon the marriage, but only a present for the entertainment of the guests. The language used by the messenger for such a congratulation is given by the "Details of Rites:" "So-and-so has sent me. Having heard that you are having guests, he has sent me with this present."[2] Such a present may consist of four pots of spirits, ten pieces of dried meat, and a dog.[3] Although it may not be too expensive, it will yet cost a family a good deal. As marriage is necessary in the social life, this expenditure is also necessary. In the present day, however, such a congratulation is directly expressed for the happiness of the wedding, and not for the gathering of the guests.

To-day, the Chinese still observe these rites of marriage in their essentials. But they increase the expense greatly. It would be much better to return to the rules of Confucius, and make marriage again simple and economical.

II. FUNERALS

Second, we shall study the expenditure for the rites of a funeral and mourning. This is the most important point in the religion of Confucius, and we cannot help discussing it at some length. We shall take up certain details first, and discuss the theory later.

[1] *Li Ki*, bk. i, p. 78. [2] *Ibid.* [3] *Ibid.*, bk. xv. p. 76.

At the ceremony of "slighter dressing" of the dead, the sheet for a ruler's body is embroidered; for that of a great official, white silk; for that of a student, black silk;—each has one sheet. But there are nineteen suits of clothes for each of them; a suit is made up of a long robe and a shorter one placed over it, and there must be the upper garment together with the lower garment. At the "fuller dressing," each of them has two sheets; but a ruler has one hundred suits of clothes; a great official, fifty; and a student, thirty. For the coffins, the largest or outermost coffin of a ruler is eight inches thick, the next, six inches, and the innermost, four inches. The larger coffin of a great official of the highest grade is eight inches thick; and the inner, six inches; for one of the lowest grade, the dimensions are six inches and four. The coffin of a student is six inches thick. For the outer shell of the coffin, a ruler uses pine; a great official, cypress; a student, various kinds of wood.[1] When Confucius became the magistrate of Chung-tu, he made an ordinance that the coffin of the common people should be four inches thick, and its shell five.[2] This is only an instance to show the expenditure for the funeral.

Now, we come to the contributions for the funeral. As the funeral system is so expensive, there is really a need of contributions, besides the fact that they have ethical and social reasons. According to the *Canon of Rites* and the *Spring and Autumn*, we may divide these contributions into three kinds. First, there are the contributions for the dead. Some are called "shroud," such as the sheets and clothes. Some are called "gift," such as the "spiritual vessels." This gift is not regular, but just according to what the contributor has. If a prince of state gives it to a student, it will be one hundred eighty cubits of silk. When

[1] *Li Ki*, bk. xix, pp. 185-199. [2] *Ibid.*, bk. ii, p. 150.

the contributor knows the dead, his contribution should be of the first kind. Second, there are the contributions for the mourner. This is called "help," and is performed by the use of money and other articles of wealth. When the contributor knows the mourner, his contribution should be of the second kind, in order to form a mutual help and to supply the deficiency. Third, there are the contributions for the dead and the mourner both. These are called "covering." Such things are the bundle of silk, carriage, horse, sheep, *etc.* They are used both for the obsequies of the dead, and for the financial assistance of the mourner. When the contributor knows them both, his contribution should be of the third kind. By these contributions, society is interwoven like a net, and wealth is distributed to and fro like the tide. But they form an expenditure to the contributor. If a poor man cannot contribute anything, it is a custom of the Chinese for him to help his relatives and friends by his labor instead of wealth. Generally a man, for the funeral of his relatives and close friends, contributes both labor and wealth.

The reasons Confucius makes the rites of funeral so expensive are four: (1) ethical, (2) aesthetic, (3) social and (4) economic. Let us first consider the ethical reason. We already know that, under Confucius' teaching, filial piety is one of the chief virtues of his moral code. We have already seen that, when the parents are living, the rites of serving them are very numerous; but how is it when they are dead? When one treats his parents well at the beginning, he must treat them well at the end. If he is careful for their living and careless for their death, it means that he is respectful to those who have knowledge and disrespectful to those who have no knowledge; it denotes a rebellious heart and is the practice of the unfaithful man. Even if we have a rebellious heart toward a servant, we are still ashamed; how can we have such a heart toward our parents? Death is the end of human life; it affords our last chance to render service to our parents.[1] Confucius says: "Man may not have shown his self-devotion to something else, but he must show it at the funeral of his parents."[2] Mencius says: "The nourishment of parents when living is not sufficient to be accounted the great thing. It is only in the performing of their obsequies when dead that we have what can be considered the great thing."[3] According to Confucius, if a man, at the death of his parents, has no devotion, he must be a hard-hearted creature, without any feeling of humanity. Therefore, Confucius establishes his funeral rites to make it necessary for the people to observe them. This is really an advancing step to lead the people to do their duty; since they must serve their parents faithfully even after they are dead, how faithful must they then be when their parents are alive!

Ethical reasons are of fundamental importance in connection with the funeral rites, and yet we cannot explain on ethical grounds why such rites should be as expensive as Confucius prescribes. This is because of aesthetic considerations. Tzŭ-yu says: "Among the rites, some are intended to lessen the display of feeling, while others purposely introduce things to excite it. To give direct vent to the feelings and display them without restraint is the way of barbarism." Therefore, the funeral rites are not simply to express the feeling of sorrow, but also carefully to regulate it in a proper way, for the direction of average people. He continues: "Whenever a man dies, there arises a feeling of disgust at the corpse. . . . On this account, there is the wrapping of it in the shroud, and there are the cur-

[1] *Hsun Tzŭ,* bk. xix.

[2] *Classics,* vol. i, p. 344.

[3] *Ibid.,* vol. ii, p. 322.

tains, plumes and other ornaments of the coffin, to preserve men from that feeling of disgust."[1]

Hsun Tzŭ has given the same reason as that of Tzŭ-yu. If the dead has no decoration, it becomes a bad thing; and if it becomes a bad thing, man will have no sorrow for it. Just losing a parent within a single day, and burying him, nevertheless, without any sorrow, it is similar to the death of a beast. How can it be done in such a way without great shame? Therefore, in the ordering of funeral rites, there are added more decorations at each step of the ceremony, in order to counteract such a tendency.[2]

Beside the ethical and aesthetic reasons, there is the social reason. As Confucius marks the social distinctions for the living, he also marks them for the dead. An emperor is placed in his coffin on the seventh day after his death, and interred in the seventh month. A prince of a state is placed in his coffin on the fifth day, and interred in the fifth month. A great official, a student, and the common people are placed in the coffin on the third day, and interred in the third month.[3] The reasons why the funeral is thus delayed are, (1) that the articles required for the dead may be completed, and (2) that the guests coming to attend the funeral may arrive. But we must understand that during such a period there is great expense.

There is, however, the significance of social distinction. The funeral of an emperor is attended by all the princes under the imperial jurisdiction; that of a prince, by those of the states which have diplomatic relations; and that of a student and the common people, by all their relatives and friends. But the funerals of those who have been punished by criminal law are not allowed to be attended by any

[1] *Li Ki*, bk. ii, p. 177.
[2] Bk. xix.
[3] *Li Ki*, bk. iii, pp. 222-3.

people, except the wives and sons. There are only three suits, and the coffins are only three inches thick. The coffins are not allowed to have any decorations, or to be conveyed away in the day time. They are buried at night, and excluded from the regular ceremony. There is no mourning at all for them; after the burial everything is over. This is a most disgraceful thing. Therefore, the scale of the expenditure for a funeral is a reflection of the life of the dead; and, if the financial condition allows it, a man should not let his parents fall into the class of criminals. When a man is living, he should be glorious, and when he dies, he should be bitterly lamented.[1] This is the social reason for the expensive funeral.

Finally, and most important for our treatment, there is an economic reason,—the satisfaction of human wants. This is explained very clearly by Mencius. He says:

In the most ancient times, there were some who did not inter their parents. When their parents died, they took them up and threw them into some water-channel. Afterwards, when passing by them, they saw foxes and wild-cats devouring them, and flies and gnats biting at them. The perspiration started out upon their foreheads, and they looked away, unable to bear the sight. It was not due to other people that this perspiration flowed. The emotions of their own hearts affected their faces and eyes, and instantly they went home, and came back with baskets and spades and covered the bodies.[2]

This is a description of the development of the funeral in the rudest stage, and it indicates that funeral is necessary to satisfy the psychological wants of man.

Since society is higher in civilization, the human wants for a funeral are more complex; hence Confucius' system

[1] *Classics,* vol. i, p. 349. [2] *Ibid.*, vol. ii, pp. 259-260.

arises. Man does not satisfy his wants by a simple covering of the body of his parent, but in a very handsome way. This is characteristic of human wants. After Mencius had buried his mother, Chung Yü, his pupil, questioned him about the wood of the coffin, which seemed too good. Mencius replied:

Anciently, there was no rule for the size of either the inner or the outer coffin. In middle antiquity [the Hsia and the Yin dynasties], the inner coffin was made seven inches thick, and the outer one the same. This was done by all, from the emperor to the common people, and not simply for the beauty of the appearance, but because they thus satisfied the natural feelings of their hearts. If prevented by statutory regulations from making their coffins in this way, men cannot have the feeling of pleasure. If they have not the money to make them in this way, they cannot have the feeling of pleasure. When they were not prevented, and had the money, all the ancients used this style. Why should I alone not do so? Moreover, is there no satisfaction to the natural feelings of a man, in preventing the earth from getting near to the bodies of his dead? I have heard that the superior man will not, for all the world, be niggardly to his parents.[1]

Again, Mencius says: "To make the people have no dissatisfaction about the nourishment of the living and the funeral of the dead, is the first principle of a good government."[2] In other words, the economic condition of the people is the first object of a good government, and such a condition must be satisfactory. But what we should understand is that the Confucians put the nourishment of the living and the funeral of the dead in the same rank, as the two necessities of economic life.

These four reasons explain why Confucius made the

[1] *Classics*, vol. ii, pp. 221-2. [2] *Ibid.*, p. 131.

funeral rites. But we may raise a question as to whether he was so superstitious as to believe that the dead really have knowledge or power. The answer must be no. On such an important point, we must quote him directly. Confucius says:

In dealing with the dead, if we treat them as if they were entirely dead, that would show a want of affection, and should not be done; or, if we treat them as if they were entirely alive, that would show a want of wisdom, and should not be done. On this account, the vessels of bamboo used in connection with the burial of the dead are not fit for actual use; those of earthenware cannot be used to wash in; those of wood are incapable of being carved; the lutes are strung, but not evenly; the pan pipes are complete, but not in tune; the bells and musical stones are there, but they have no stands. These things are called "spiritual vessels", because the dead are treated as the unknowable spirits.[1]

From this statement, we know that Confucius treats the dead as midway between dead and alive, in order to avoid being either unkind or unwise. There is another statement of his which is very striking. When Tzŭ-kung asks him whether or not the dead have knowledge, he replies:

If I were to say that the dead have knowledge, I am afraid that filial sons and dutiful grandsons would injure their substance in paying the last offices to the departed; and if I were to say that the dead have no knowledge, I am afraid that unfilial sons and undutiful grandsons would leave their parents unburied. If you wish to know whether the dead have knowledge or not, you will know it yourself when you die. There is no need to discuss this point at the present.[2]

[1] *Li Ki*, bk. ii, p. 148.

[2] *Park of Narratives*, bk. xviii. *Cf. Classics*, vol. i, p. 99.

Confucius regulates not only the rites of funeral, but also the periods of mourning, which have great importance for economic life. We shall not go into any details of mourning, except the mourning for parents. The period of mourning for parents in ancient times was one year only. Confucius doubles this period; the actual length of time is twenty-five months, and the nominal title is "three years' mourning." Within this period, the son should not drink wine, not eat meat, not live with his wife. Confucius says: "A superior man, during the whole period of mourning, does not enjoy pleasant food which he may eat, nor derive pleasure from music which he may hear. He also does not feel at ease, if he is comfortably lodged. Therefore, he does not do such things at all."[1] Mencius says: "For the three years' mourning, the garment of coarse cloth with its lower edge even, and the eating of congee, are common to all, from the emperor to the mass of the people."[2] This is a return by the son for the benefits he has received from his parents. Confucius explains: "It is not till a child is three years old that it is allowed to leave the arms of its parents. Hence the three years' mourning is a universal system of the empire."[3]

The rites of funeral and mourning are the creeds of Confucius. When Confucius and his disciples preach the doctrine of filial piety, these rites are used as the means for conversion. But the anti-Confucians attack them as the weakest points. Among all the anti-Confucians, Mo Ti is the chief. He is a pupil of Confucius, but he is not satisfied with the rites of funeral and mourning, so he establishes his new school against his old master. These rites are the fundamental differences between Confucianism and Moism.

[1] *Classics,* vol. i, p. 328.
[2] *Ibid.*, vol. ii, p. 236.
[3] *Ibid.*, vol. i, p. 328.

But why does Mo Ti differ from Confucius at this point? His argument is based entirely upon economic grounds. As we are treating the economic principles of Confucius, we may take up some points from the argument of Mo Ti, in order to enable us to understand Confucianism better.

The economic argument of Mo Ti has two points: first, these rites cannot increase wealth; and second, they cannot increase population. By the expensive funeral, too much wealth is buried, and by the long period of mourning, production is stopped too long. The existing wealth which has been accumulated from the past is thrown away, and the coming wealth which will be produced in the future is prevented for a long time. This is against the law of increasing wealth. During the different periods of mourning for the different relatives, the physical condition is undermined, and the living is also too coarse; hence many persons die on this account. Moreover, the rites of mourning destroy the sexual relations to a great extent. This is against the law of increasing population. Therefore, Mo Ti establishes his funeral laws as follows: In winter time, the winter clothes are used for the dead; in summer, the summer clothes; but there are no more than three suits. The coffin is only three inches thick. The period of mourning is only three months. As soon as the dead is buried, the living must immediately return to the production of wealth.[1]

Mo Ti uses the economic argument as the strongest point to attack Confucius, and yet he is defeated on the economic ground. He cares too much for production, and too little for consumption; hence he sacrifices the end to the means. This is the point for decisive battle between Confucianism and Moism. Chuang Tzŭ has given the best criticism on Moism, in the following:

[1] *Mo Tzŭ*, bk. xxv.

For life, it is hard; for death, it is cruel; its principle is too dry. It makes men grieve and lament. Its practice is difficult to carry out. I am afraid that it cannot be the principle of a sage. It opposes the natural feeling of the world, and the world cannot accept it. Although Mo Tzŭ can bear it alone, how can he do anything against the world? As he is different from the world, he is too far away to be a king.[1]

From this judgment of Chuang Tzŭ, we need not wonder why Mo Ti has lost his influence, and why Confucius has become "The Throneless King." It is simply an economic reason; Confucius satisfied human wants, and Mo Ti did not.

We must not misunderstand and think, however, that the funeral rites of Confucius are too expensive. He uses still the principle that consumption should be according to the means. His social system is based on the scale of virtue; those of greater virtue occupy the higher position and get more wealth; hence they should have better funerals. Moreover, he is the real reformer of the funeral system of his time. During the Chou dynasty, life was luxurious, and the expenditure for funerals was most excessive, even to burying men alive for the service of the dead. It became much better when Confucius regulated the funeral of different classes by a certain standard, beyond which they could not go. According to Confucius, all the things used for the dead should be entirely different from those used by living men. For examples, the carriages of clay and the figures of straw simply represent spiritual ideas but do not have much economic value. Even using a wooden image to bury with the dead Confucius condemns severely,—how can he approve a funeral which is really too expensive?[2]

[1] *Cf. Sacred Books,* vol. xl, p. 219.

[2] *Li Ki,* bk. ii, p. 173.

Therefore, in the *Spring and Autumn,* he records the sepulture of Huan Wang in order to condemn the extravagant burial even of an emperor.[1]

Confucius uses exactly the same principle for three years' mourning; it cannot be made longer for the superior men, but it cannot be made shorter for the inferior men. All the rites of funeral and mourning are based on the golden mean, and they satisfy the human wants.

III. ANCESTOR-WORSHIP

Third, we shall study the expenditure for ancestor-worship. This is also a most important point in the religion of Confucius, and we must study it at its root. According to Confucius, ancestors should be worshiped by all classes, from the emperor to the common people.

This means an increase in expenditure. First, they must build the ancestral temples; and such temples must be better than, or at least equal to, the residential houses. When a superior man is about to engage in building, he should build the temple first, and the residence last. Although the common people cannot have the right to build a temple, they must give up some part of their house for the worship of their ancestor, and it must cost them something. Second, they must have sacrificial dress. Those officials who receive land for salary should make such dress without delay. Even though they were cold, they should not wear the sacrificial dress for protection. Third, they must make the sacrificial vessels. Although the common people who do not receive land as salary cannot have them, the family of officials must make them first, and the vessels for the use of the living afterwards. Even though they were poor, they should not sell the sacrificial vessels.[2] Fourth, they must have the offerings. When the offerings are presented by

[1] Third year of Duke Chuang.

[2] *Li Ki,* bk. i, pp. 103-4.

the emperor, there are the small things, such as the sauerkraut of water plants, and pickles from the produce of dry grounds; the fine things, such as the stands for the bodies of the three victims and the supplies for the eight dishes; and those things produced under the best influences of light and shade, such as strange insects, and the fruits of plants and trees. Whatever the heaven and the earth have produced, if they can be used for offerings, are all exhibited there to show the great abundance of things.[1] Even among the offerings of the common people, we have already seen that they should present the different things according to the four seasons.[2] Therefore, in ancestor-worship, there must be an expenditure added to the cost of living.

Let us now consider why Confucius approves ancestor-worship. This is the fundamental basis of Confucius' religion. He advocates one supreme God, but he has also a companion of God, that is, one's father. Hence his religious system is dualism. God is our common father, without whom we cannot have life; but we have also a specific father, without whom we still cannot have life. If God is our only father, we may be born into any other life and it is not necessary that we be human beings. If the specific father is our only father, we may lose the best elements of nature and have no spiritual life. Hence Confucius recognizes these two fathers; adding a mother to them there is the Confucian doctrine of trinity. If we leave out the common father, we shall be too narrow-minded, too egotistic, unkind to the human race, and against the law of love. If we leave out the specific father, we shall be too loose in the family relation, too altruistic, undutiful to our own father, and against the law of wisdom. As love and

[1] *Li Ki*, bk. xxii, p. 238.

[2] See *supra*, pp. 260-261.

wisdom are the balance of Confucius, he combines the two principles, and establishes his dual religion.

Confucius says:

> By the ceremonies of the sacrifices to Heaven and Earth, we are to serve the Supreme God, and by the ceremonies of the ancestral temple, we are to worship the ancestors. One who understands the ceremonies of the sacrifices to Heaven and Earth, and the meaning of the several sacrifices to ancestors, will find the governing of a kingdom as easy as to look into his palm.[1]

By this statement, he points out that the worship of God and that of ancestor are equally important on different occasions. But he has still another statement to point out that the worship of God and that of ancestor can be held on the same occasion. He says:

> In filial piety there is nothing greater than the reverential awe of one's father. In the reverential awe shown to one's father there is nothing greater than making him the correlate of Heaven. The Duke of Chou was the man who first did this. Formerly the Duke of Chou at the border altar sacrificed to Hou Chi as the correlate of Heaven, and in the Brilliant Hall he honored Wên Wang, and sacrificed to him as the correlate of God.[2]

Indeed, as long as we have not reached the stage of Great Similarity, and have the tie of family, ancestor-worship is quite justifiable.

There arises a question as to whether Confucius believes that the ancestor is really equal to God. The answer must be no. It is simply that the descendant contributes the greatest honor to his ancestor. Because it is only a social

[1] *Classics,* vol. i, p. 404.

[2] *Sacred Books,* vol. iii, pp. 476-7.

honor, Confucius makes the emperor the only one to have the right of sacrificing to God; otherwise, as Confucius recognizes that everyone is the son of God, why should everyone not sacrifice to him, and why should everyone not make his own father equal to God? In the social system of Confucius, the emperor is the chief personality, and in his moral system, filial piety is the chief virtue; hence the father or ancestor of the emperor can enjoy the greatest honor, and the emperor sacrifices to him for the showing of the practice of filial piety to the empire. Moreover, the ancestor who is made the correlate of God must be the most famous one of the dynasty; the number of those ancestors never can be more than two, and the one must be separated from the other when the one is placed as a companion of God. Therefore, we are sure that Confucius does not regard the ancestor as God.

Does Confucius believe in a soul? Yes. It is the soul to which the worship is directed. As soon as the dead is buried, its soul is received home immediately, and it is represented by a tablet. Confucius says: "The physical body goes downwards, but the intelligent spirit is on high." [1] He says again: "The bones and flesh molder below, and, hidden away, become the earth of the fields; but the spirit issues forth, and is displayed on high in a condition of glorious brightness." [2] The *Record of Rites* also says: "The spiritual soul returns to heaven, while the physical body returns to earth." [3]

However, Confucius does not prove the existence of the soul. The *Record of Rites* says: "The flesh of the victim may be presented raw and as a whole, or cut up in pieces, or sodden, or thoroughly cooked; but how can we know

[1] *Li Ki*, bk. vii, p. 369.

[2] *Ibid.*, bk. xxi, p. 220.

[3] *Ibid.*, bk. ix, p. 444.

whether the spirit does enjoy it? It is simply that the sacrificer shows his reverence to the utmost of his power."[1] A similar statement is found in many places of the *Record of Rites*.[2] In fact, the mind of Confucius is not only religious, but also scientific; hence, according to him, the soul is an unknowable spirit.

If the soul is unknowable, why does Confucius make ancestor-worship necessary? It is only on the ethical ground. As we have already said that filial piety is the chief virtue of his moral system, should a son stop observing such an important principle after the death of his parents? Certainly not. It is by ancestor-worship that the nourishment of parents is followed up and filial duty to them perpetuated.[3] Confucius says: "Serving the dead as they were served when alive, and serving the departed as if they were still abiding among us; this is the summit of filial conduct."[4] Therefore, ancestor-worship is exclusively for the sake of virtue, and the worshiper does not seek anything for his own benefit.[5] This is the noblest character of the religion of Confucius.

Since China has adopted Confucianism as the state religion, everyone must conform to the filial duties. According to the *Law Code of the Ts'ing Dynasty*, all the monks and nuns of the churches of Buddhism and Taoism are required to kneel before their parents, to worship their ancestors, and to follow the mourning system. If they do not obey this law, they shall be punished with one hundred blows with the long stick, and shall be driven out of their monastery to stay at home.[6] This shows the peculiar character of the Chinese. Although they allow everyone to have

[1] *Li Ki*, bk. ix, p. 446.
[2] *Ibid.*, bk. ii, pp. 169, 177.
[3] *Ibid.*, bk. xxii, p. 237.
[4] *Classics*, vol. i, p. 403.
[5] *Li Ki*, bk. xxii, p. 237.
[6] Ch. xvii.

perfect freedom of belief, they compel him to perform the social and ethical duties. Therefore, according to the view of the Chinese, ancestor-worship is not a religious rite, in the English sense, but a social and ethical obligation.

In conclusion, for the funeral rites, the mourning system, and ancestor-worship, the Chinese not only observe the teachings of Confucius, but also go a little farther, although changes in many details are necessary.

IV. SOCIAL INTERCOURSE

Fourth, we shall study the expenditure for social intercourse, namely, "the presents of introduction." According to the ceremonies of Confucius, when anyone calls on another for the first time, he must bring a present to express his respect and sympathy. When the feudal princes pay their visit to the emperor, or visit among themselves; when a man first becomes an officer, or first advances to a higher official rank, and then pays his first visit to his ruler, or his superior, or his compeer; when officials call on the foreign princes who have just come to visit their own county; when the boy first meets his teacher; when a woman first sees her parents-in-law, and the princess or queen; and, indeed, when all persons first meet other persons of higher rank or the same rank; it is necessary to take presents. But such presents are not made by superiors to their inferiors.

The things used for presents of introduction are regularly prescribed. They are different according to the social standing of the callers, and have representative significance referring to their personal characters. The present of the emperor is spirits of black millet. He is too high to be a guest of the feudal princes, and yet, when he comes to inspect their state, he uses the spirits in their ancestral temple in order to show the ceremony of his arrival. The present of the feudal princes is their symbols of jade. The present of a high minister is a lamb; and that of a great official, a goose; both are alive. The present of a student is a dead pheasant; but in summer time, the pheasant is dried in order to avoid its smelling. The present of the common people is a duck; that of a boy, ten pieces of dried meat. The present of a woman is entirely different from that of a man; throughout all classes, women use the fruits of the *hovenia dulcis,* and of the hazel tree, dried meat cut fine, and hash with spices, jujube dates, and chestnuts. If in an army out of the towns, having no regular present, a tassel from a horse's breast, an archer's armlet, or an arrow, one may use for the present. Judging from this instance, if one cannot find the regular present in some locality, he may use any seasonable thing.[1]

These presents are only to represent the respect of the guest, and the host cannot make use of them for his own advantage. When the princes visit the emperor or visit each other, the presents of different jades are immediately returned to them. When the inferior calls on the superior, the presents of different animals are not accepted, or they are returned after the calling is over. If men of the same rank call on each other, the presents will be returned to the guest when the host repays his visit, on the same day, or another day. It is only the prince who can accept presents from his officials without return, and yet he may give them a banquet. At all the callings of the same rank, as soon as the formal meeting is over, the guest is invited to dine with the host.[2]

So far as the present of introduction is necessary for the first calling, no matter whether it will be returned or not, it is a necessary expenditure. It makes the life of society

[1] *Li Ki,* bk. i, p. 119. [2] *Canon of Rites,* ch. vii.

harmonious and respectful, but it cannot occur without the use of wealth. As regards the expenditure of social intercourse, there are many kinds of gifts to show friendship according to different occasions. But we need not go into them, because they are not necessary expenses.

In the present day, the custom of bringing presents of introduction for the first visit has been changed to other forms or other names, and has been practically abolished. The only remaining trace of this custom is in the group of pupils. When a student goes to school, he must give something, mostly in the form of money, as the present of introduction to his teacher or teachers at least the first year, or at the beginning of every year. Very recently, since schools of the modern type have been established, this custom is abolished in some schools, while it remains in others. The difference is that when one is considered as a personal pupil to his personal teacher, he brings the present of introduction; but when the institution takes the place of his teacher, he is under no obligation to do so. China as regards this custom is thus in a transitional period.

PART III

PRODUCTION

BOOK V. FACTORS OF PRODUCTION

CHAPTER XVII

Three Factors of Production

For the three factors of the production of wealth, we may select the following passage from the "Great Learning":

> The superior man must be careful about his virtue first. Having virtue, there will be the man. Having the man, there will be the land. Having the land, there will be the wealth. Having the wealth, there will be its use. Virtue is the root, and wealth is only its outcome.[1]

This principle is originally applied to the ruler. If a ruler has virtue, he can rule the man, hold the land, accumulate the wealth, which means here, capital, and have many things for use. But this principle can be applied to everybody, generally. Take the business man, for instance. He must possess some virtue first, either physical, mental or moral—the word virtue is used in its broad sense. If competition were perfectly free, he would get wealth in proportion to the virtue he possessed. If he have no virtue at all, or if he, in some way, fail to show his virtue (such as being able to work, and not working at all), he would be an outcast, and he could not get any wealth by himself. In society, there is no such person. If there is any, he cannot live very long. The loafer, the

[1] *Classics,* vol. i, p. 375.

parasite, and the thief, although they are bad men, still have some particular virtue for getting wealth. Therefore, virtue is the root, and wealth is only its outcome.

Thus, according to the "Great Learning," the factors of production are three. The first is the man who has any virtue; the second is the land, and the third is capital. All the three factors belong to the productive sphere. Then the word "use" appears. With the word "use," consumption begins.

The principle of dividing the productive factors into three is a general economic principle. It can be applied even to a single man in savage life. First, he himself must be a human being. Second, he must live on some kind of land, and use either fishing land or hunting land. Third, he must have some kind of capital to help his fishing or hunting. In primitive life, the capital must be subordinate to the land, because he can live without capital, but he can never live without land. In social life, land is only a part of capital, and man can have many other capital goods without owning land. Therefore, in social life, there are only two factors—man and capital goods. But, in Confucius' time, it was not so. Under the *tsing tien* system, every man accepted a portion of land, otherwise he could have no other capital goods, or very few. Therefore, land was a separate factor, and played the most important part among all capital goods. Moreover, in economic dynamics, the difference between land and artificially made goods becomes prominent, because land is not made and not perishable. The "Great Learning" is correct in treating these three factors separately.

Taking a nation as an economic unit, this principle is still more true. The first element of the wealth of a nation is man, the second is land, and the third is capital. Unoccupied land never can form a nation, unless it belongs to man. Those who have merely perishable capital goods never can form a nation, unless they own some land. There are the stateless people, who have men, land, and capital, but have no nation. But there is no nation that has neither men, nor land, nor capital.

According to the order of the "Great Learning," we shall discuss human beings first, and then nature. In other words, we shall make the man precede the land. It is true that the land is not made by man, even existed before man. But it is equally true, that the land is useful to man simply because man comes into it, otherwise the whole world is only a wilderness. Economics is not a natural science, but a human science. We should care for the man first. Moreover, since human power has been developed, nature is subject to man. All the natural forces are only machines, helping to produce wealth, but the real ruler of the natural world is man. For these reasons, we shall discuss man before discussing land

This order has produced a special economic influence upon the Chinese. Why does China have a large population? Why do the Chinese like to have even more children than their fortune can support? Why do Chinese scholars never think of such a theory as limiting the population? It is because the "Great Learning" states that man is the first factor of production. According to this principle, land and capital both come after man. This principle is familiar to all the Chinese. They have a proverb: "Money is made by man." For their greetings, their first phrase is "increasing sons," and the second is "accumulating capital." When a new year comes, the people write or say, "The man and the capital both are successful." They are very glad to have more members in a family, in a community, or in the whole nation, not only for social pleasure, but also for economic production, because they think that man is the chief productive factor. This is undoubtedly due to the influence of the "Great Learning."

Henry George says: "It is not the increase of food that has caused this increase of men; but the increase of men that has brought about the increase of food. There is more food, simply because there are more men."[1] Such a theory is the common idea of the Chinese. And the "Great Learning," in putting man before land and capital, has exactly the same theory.

In the very beginning of the subject of political economy, the first part of his *General History of Institutes,* Tu Yu (died 1363 A. K. or 812 A. D.) also enumerates the three factors of production. He says:

> The grain is the controller of the life of man; the land is the ground upon which the grain is grown; and the man is the object for which the ruler administers his government. Storing the grain, the national reserve will be abundant; distinguishing the land for agricultural purposes, the food will be sufficient; and making an investigation of the men, the service of the public labor will be equal. When a ruler understands these three things, it is called a good government.

His statement is from the standpoint of a ruler, but the three things are common to all economic life. The word grain is the chief representative of capital, which we shall discuss later; while the words land and man have no need of explanation. Therefore, according to Tu Yu also, the factors of production are three,—namely, capital, land and man. His order is just the reverse of that of the "Great Learning." But they are essentially th same, because he names them in the order of a climax, while the "Great Learning" does the opposite.

[1] *Progress and Poverty,* p. 97.

CHAPTER XVIII

Labor—Population

I. IMPORTANCE OF POPULATION

Since man is the first factor of production, we should first discuss man in the collective sense—that is, the population. The *Analects* tells us, "To anyone bearing the tables of population, Confucius bowed forward to the cross-bar of his carriage."[1] This shows that Confucius attached much importance to the tables of population. Chu Hsi comments:

> The action of Confucius was due to the importance of the number of people. Man is the most intelligent of all the creatures, and the people are regarded as the heaven of the emperor. Therefore, according to the *Official System of Chou*, when the number of people was presented to the emperor, he accepted it kneeling. How should one whose position was lower than that of the emperor not give respect to the number of population?

From the example of Confucius, the Chinese always think that population is the chief element of the national assets.

The *Official System of Chou* has many passages in regard to population. We shall select only a few of them. Among the duties of the vice-president of the department of people are these: he shall investigate the number of males and

[1] *Classics*, vol. i, p. 236.

females who live in the city, the suburb and the country, and pay the different kinds of taxes. He shall distinguish the noble and the common, the old and the young, and the sick people. He shall denote those who are exempted from taxation, and state their rules of worship, of drink and food, of funeral, *etc.* He shall send the statistical laws to each of the local governors, ordering him to record the size of the population of his province and also the number of their horses, cows, sheep, pigs, dogs, hens, carriages, wagons, and vehicles, and to distinguish their various kinds of wealth. The governors are required to report quarterly those numbers to this department in order to form the basis of administration. Every three years there is a "great comparison" of all the population and capital. During the "great comparison" this department shall accept the statistics from all the feudal states and the crown provinces.[1]

There is the bureau of people for registering the size of the population. All the people, from the babe who has teeth up to the man, are recorded in the census. This bureau distinguishes their residence, whether in the city, the suburb, or the country, classifies them according to sex, and adds births and deducts deaths annually. During the "great comparison" of every three years this bureau reports the census to the department of justice. In the tenth month the minister of justice presents the census to the emperor. The emperor accepts it kneeling, and keeps it in the sacred college. The imperial historian, the auditor and the prime minister, respectively, keep duplicates in order to help the administration of the emperor.[2]

According to the *Official System of Chou*, there is a statistical comparison of the distribution of population by sex. In order to facilitate a study of the statistics of population,

[1] Ch. xi. [2] Ch. xxxv.

we may present its statements in the form of a table, as follows:[1]

Province	Male	Female
Yang Chow	2	5
King Chow	1	2
Yü Chow	2	3
Ts'ing Chow	2	3
Yên Chow	2	3
Yung Chow	3	2
Yu Chow	1	3
Ki Chow	5	3
Ping Chow	2	3

However far from the truth these figures may be, the table shows that in the majority of the provinces the number of females was greater than that of males. It is interesting to know that a predominance of females is not merely a modern phenomenon, but was a phenomenon of ancient times. This is probably because hard work and nervous strain have chiefly fallen upon men.

From the *Official System of Chou* we see how careful the emperor was to learn the size of the population. The statistics described not only the population, but also all kinds of capital goods. In a word, the governmental power touched the actual life of the people in every aspect. It was, however, not a despotism, but a democracy, because the local officers who exercised the governmental power were the people themselves. In the Chou dynasty, under feudalism, the political division was small and somewhat independent, and the ruler held by hereditary right, so that the ruling class and the subject knew each other very well, and administration was easy. Since the Ch'in dynasty (331 A. K. or 221

[1] Ch. xxxiii.

B. C.), however, under the absolute monarchy, the central government has directly controlled the whole empire, and the governors have been only temporary officers, so that the mandarin and the people are strangers, and the administration is necessarily inefficient. Therefore China could not get even an accurate census, because the government has kept aloof from the people.[1]

The importance of the study of population is summed up by Hsü Kan (died in 768 A. K. or 217 A. D.) as follows:

> A peaceful government is dependent upon the prosperity of industry, the prosperity of industry upon the equality of public labor, and the equality of public labor upon the accuracy of the census. Therefore, the accuracy of the census is the foundation of the administration of a state. . . . Indeed, the number of population is the source of everything, and everything takes it as a standard. To distribute the land, to impose the taxes, to produce the products, to regulate salaries and wages, to do the public work, to raise the army, to establish the national institutions, to adjust the household economy, to observe the social and moral laws, and to set aside the punishment, all these are the results of a careful study of the number of population.[2]

In short, population is the basis of social, political, and economic adjustments.

II. LAW OF POPULATION

1. *Population and Land*

In connection with the policy of dealing with population, the first thing is the work of settlement. According to the

[1] *Cf. infra.*

[2] *General Research on Literature and Authorities,* written by Ma Tuan-lin, a great authority at the beginning of the Yüan dynasty, published in 1873 (1322 A. D.), ch. xii.

"Royal Regulations" this is in charge of the minister of works. With the various instruments he measures the land for the settlements of the people. He distinguishes the geographical situations, such as the mountains and rivers, the oozy ground and marsh; and he observes also the temperature of the four seasons.[1] In short, the first principle is that the population must be adjusted to the natural environment.

Second, the density of population must agree with the extent of the land. The "Royal Regulations" says:

In settling the people, the land is measured for the formation of cities, and then measured again in smaller portions for the allotments of the people. The land and the population must agree with each other. There is no land left out of use, and none of the people left to wander about idle.[2]

We should not miss, however, the most important point which governs these two principles, namely, governmental control of population. Since the minister of works has charge of the settlement of the people, it is he who distributes the people in accordance with the natural environment and the land, and not the people themselves. Although the government may simply follow what the people want, it takes very active measures. Therefore, the distribution of population is a function of the government.

The government, however, must be in harmony with the real interest of the people, and it should not change their adaptation to the environment. Confucius says:

The sage kings showed their sense of the state of harmony in the following way: they did not make the occupants of the hills remove and live by the streams, nor the occupants of the

[1] *Li Ki*, bk. iii, p. 228. [2] *Ibid.*, p. 230.

islands remove and live in the plains; and thus the people complained of no hardship.[1]

The commentator says that the inhabitants of the hills are interested in the animals; those of the islands in the fishes and salt; and those of the plains in the different kinds of grain. The government should let them live respectively in those localities to which they have been accustomed, and should not change their occupations and make hardships for them. If the people lose their occupation, they will be poor; and if they are poor, they will give way to unbridled license. Therefore, the governmental distribution of population is necessarily harmonious with the people themselves.

The principle that the population must agree with the extent of the land is held by all the scholars. In 702 (151 A. D.), Tsui Shih says that the ancient sages distributed the cultivated land to every man, and the land was proportional to the population. Now, in some provinces the population is dense and the land is insufficient to support it, while in other provinces the population is sparse but the land is uncultivated, although it is fitted for the growing of grain. The old plan of removing the poor people who cannot have their own occupation to those places where the land is plenty should here be followed. This is a policy for the development of the land and the help of the people.[2] This theory of Tsui Shih's represents the common idea of the Chinese.

In the Southern Sung dynasty, the capital was in Hangchow, Chekiang province, and surrounding the capital there was an over-population. Therefore, Yeh Shih (1701-1774 A. K. or 1150-1223 A. D.) proposed to remove the surplus from the over-populated regions to those that were under-populated. He says:

[1] *Li Ki*, bk vii, p. 392.

[2] *General Research*, ch. ii.

The importance of the administration of a state lies in the possession of the people. If the people are many, the land is developed, the taxes are increased, the public laborers are numerous, and the army is strong. . . . Therefore, when there are people, they must be directed to the development of the land. If the land is developed, the taxes are increased. Therefore, when they live at home they can do the public labor, and when they go abroad they can become soldiers. But this is not the case now. They are caused to live in poverty and suffering, because they have no land to establish their own occupation. Those who are dull and unskilful become loungers or dependent servants, and those who are strong and selfish become small dealers or robbers. They can roughly get food for the morning and evening, but cannot make a home. Even during a good year, when food is cheap, the people are afraid that they cannot get even a pint or a peck of it. Generally, those who can pay the taxes and serve the public labor are less than one-third of the whole population. The landowners do not till the land themselves, and the tillers own no land. Therefore, although the population multiplies and prospers, it cannot be of any use to the state. . . . Under such circumstances no land can be developed and no tax be increased. The people simply gather together for the getting of food and clothes by means of robbery and stealth. It makes their habits covetous, licentious, deceitful, luxurious, and without faithful and honest conduct. Such a people, however, how can it be thrown away like spoiled fish or flesh?

His conclusion is that they should be removed to the underpopulated provinces. By this means more land will be developed, more taxes will be collected, and the people can be either soldiers when they are abroad, or public laborers when they are at home. Therefore, the wealth of a nation will naturally grow up without special effort. This he considers a very important part of public policy.[1]

[1] *General Research,* ch. xi.

It should be noticed that both Tsui Shih and Yeh Shih are more in favor of agriculture than of industry. Although the commercial and industrial cities can maintain more population, they think that the condition of the poor is very bad, because they are merely dependents. Hence, they both use the term " own occupation " for the object of their advocacy. In order to make the poor have their own occupation and become independent of the rich, the only thing the state can do is to give them free land. Since the land of the cities where the poor concentrate is not enough, they cannot have any free land unless they are removed to the under-populated places. Therefore, the theory of Tsui Shih and Yeh Shih is to enable the poor to have an occupation which can be called their own. In other words, they want to make the dependent laborers become independent farmers. If they should see the factory system of to-day, they would advocate their plan still more strongly.

The above-mentioned policy of moving the population is based on economic pirnciples, and we have entirely omitted those policies based on military defense. But we should give a few details about the removal of population in ancient times. In 383 A. K. (169 B. C.) Chao Tso (died 398 A. K) says:

I have heard that, in ancient times, the moving of population from a distance to the empty land was like this: In the first place, the temperature of the climate is examined into, the taste of the water tested, the fitness of the soil judged, and the richness of the plants looked into. Then the city is established and the walls built, the streets fixed and the houses separated, the roads of the farms connected and the boundaries of the field divided. Their houses are first built. Each house has one hall, two chambers, and the different doors. Within the house the articles and instruments are laid down. The people may have residence when they come, and have something for use when they work. Therefore the people are encouraged in moving to the new city, and do not mind leaving their old homes. Furthermore, they are given doctors for the cure of their sickness and priests for the exercise of their worship. Between the two sexes, the people have marriage; for birth and death, they help each other; for the funeral, they have a common cemetery. Their plants are flourishing, their animals are growing, and their houses are complete and comfortable. All these make the people feel their place pleasant and dispose them to live there permanently.[1]

From such a description we can see how active the government was when it moved the people. This is a very valuable statement, because it gives some details of the ancient system.

Since the Han dynasty, the policy of moving population has been carried into effect many times. For an example we may select the decree of Ming T'ai Tsu, which was given in 1921 A. K. (1370 A. D.). It runs thus:

The five prefectures, Suchow, Sungkiang, Kiahsing, Huchow and Hangchow,[2] are over-populated. The people cannot have land for cultivation, and usually pursue the secondary occupations without getting sufficient food. In Linhao,[3] my native prefecture, the land is not developed, and there is unopened wealth in the ground. The people of those five prefectures who own no land should be directed to go there for the cultivation of land. The land which they may cultivate shall be given to them for their private property. They shall be supplied with money, food, oxen and seed, and they shall be exempted from taxation for three years. The distribution of land shall be according to the number of men and their

[1] *History of Han,* ch. xlix.

[2] In the provinces of Kiangsu and Chekiang.

[3] The present prefecture of Fungyang, Anhui province.

physical sufficiency, but none shall be allowed to own too much land.[1]

This decree is a general provision for the removal of population.

This question will arise: Why should the government control the distribution of population? Under the theory of free competition, the population would naturally distribute itself nicely. But there are many circumstances under which competition is not free, and especially among poor people. In the first place, they will not care to move, because it is human nature to become attached to the old place. In the second place, they do not know how to move, because they do not know what place is good for them. A number of obstacles, such as the differences of dialects, customs and climates, and especially the poor transportation, all prevent them from moving. In the third place, they cannot move themselves by their empty hands. Therefore, the moving of population by the government is a necessary thing. It is a good policy, first, for the poor themselves, and next, for the nation as a whole. It is good not only for their economic life, but also for their moral and social conditions, and many other things. Moreover, this policy is not compulsory, but voluntary. The government gives only the inducement to encourage their hope, but not force to increase their fear. Therefore, government control of population is a good thing.

In the present day, as the population of China is dense in the east and the south, but sparse in the west and the north, she should move the people from the former to the latter. She should move not only the poor, but also the rich, be-

[1] *Continuation of the General Research on Literature and Authorities*, edited under the imperial direction of Kao Tsung, and published in 2335 (1784 A. D.), ch. ii.

cause the rich have capital. She should move not only the manual laborers, but also the professional men, because those men have more intellectual power. Such a great movement must be carried on by the state, in order to make Manchuria, Mongolia, Chinese Turkestan and Tibet nearly equal to China proper. Building railroads, increasing political districts, establishing public schools, distributing free land, starting factories, and developing every kind of industry—all of these will encourage the immigrants and improve the natives. The state should give a number of immunities and privileges to the immigrants; otherwise they will not migrate. Moreover, she should select the best natives from among those regions to come to the most important cities to study everything, in order to assimilate the Chinese civilization and spread it among their own people. In a word, she should unify the whole empire for the realization of the "great uniformity" of Confucius. There is no reason why there should be a distinction between China proper and the rest of the state. This has become the public opinion in China to-day.

2. *Population and Food*

The relation of population and food is indicated by Confucius himself. He says: "The important things for a government are the people and food."[1] The commentator says that the people are important because they are the root of a state, and that the food is important because it is the life of the people. Therefore, it has become the common saying of the Chinese: "The state regards the people as its root, and the people regard the food as their heaven."

The relation between population and food is familiar to every one, and especially since the doctrine of Malthus was

[1] *Classics,* vol. i, p. 351.

set forth. According to him, if the population increases beyond the proportional increased or acquired produce of the country, the deaths will shortly exceed the births, unless an emigration takes place.[1] Therefore, the increase in population is dependent upon the supply of food. For the misery of the unfortunate population, Mencius gives a similar expression. When he talked to King Hui of Liang, he said that the rulers of Ch'in and Ch'u robbed the people of their time, so that they could not plough and weed their fields. The results were that their parents suffered from cold and hunger, and that their brothers, wives, and children were separated and scattered abroad.[2] Again, when he talked to Duke Mo of Tsau, he said that, in calamitous years and years of famine, the old and weak have been found dying in the ditches and water-channels, and the able-bodied have been scattered about to the four quarters.[3] Therefore, according to Mencius, when there is an insufficiency of food, there are two things for the people—emigration and death. These are the two positive checks to population.

For the adjustment between population and food, Mencius has the great principle of political economy, shown in the conservation of natural resources, the *tsing tien* system, the control of prices, *etc.*; that is, to increase wealth in general and not to increase food in particular. How can he approve a half measure which does not increase the food at all, but simply distributes it in accordance with the condition of the people? The King Hui of Liang said to Mencius that, when the year was bad on the inside of the river, he removed as many of the people as he could to the east of the river, and conveyed grain to the country on the inside; and that when the year was bad on the east of the river, he

[1] *The Principle of Population*, Ashley's edition, pp. 39-40.

[2] *Classics*, vol. ii, pp. 135-6.

[3] *Ibid.*, p. 173.

acted correspondingly. He spoke of such measures with great pride, but Mencius did not give him his approval. The reason is that a ruler should adopt the fundamental principle for the permanent increase of the wealth of the people, and should not resort to the temporary removal of either people or food, as a great measure.[1]

3. *Population and Wealth*

The most important support of the population is not land, nor food, but wealth. If we have more wealth, we may utilize the land either more extensively, or more intensively, or both; and we may produce more food. Therefore, the relation between population and wealth is the fundamental thing. This principle was recognized by Confucius. When he went to Wei, as we have mentioned above,[2] he gave his impression from his carriage by saying, "How numerous are the people!" "Since they are thus numerous," asked Jan Yu, "what more shall be done for them?" "Enrich them," was the reply. By this answer Confucius indicated that wealth is most important for the population. As soon as the population is large, the first thing is the increase of wealth. Although he did not give the details as regards how the enrichment was to be made, such a general statement covers the whole economic field. Indeed, whatever can make the people rich is the thing which should be used for the support of population.

Confucius appreciated a large population, because it is an indication of national prosperity. But he did not think that a large population is good when its wealth is not equally distributed. He said that we should not be troubled lest the people should be few, but should be troubled lest they should

[1] *Classics,* vol. ii, pp. 129-132.

[2] *Cf. supra,* pp. 94-95.

not have equality of wealth. If they have equality of wealth, they will have no poverty, and they will be in a condition of harmony. If they are harmonious, their number will not be few.[1] Therefore, no matter whether the population is large or small, wealth is most important for avoiding poverty and bringing harmony. Since Confucius was not a pure economist, but a general reformer, he spoke of the wealth of the people from the distributive, rather than from the productive, point of view. But his view is quite correct. For if wealth were not equally distributed, the population as a whole would suffer from poverty and lack of harmony, even though its production were great.

The relation between population and wealth is also pointed out by the "Miscellaneous Records." First, a large territory must be sufficient to support a corresponding population. Second, the same number of population must have the same efficiency. "If there is a large territory, and the people be not correspondingly numerous, the superior man regards it as a shame. If another government has the same population as his own, but has a double efficiency, the superior man regards it as a shame."[2] The word superior man refers to either the ruler or the officer. The first defect comes from the fact that he cannot make the wealth sufficient to support a large population in correspondence with the extent of the land, and this causes the people to desert his territory. Therefore, even though the land is plentiful, the population is sparse, because population depends not merely upon the land, but upon the wealth. In the second case, although he possesses the same density of population as does his neighbor, the merit of his neighbor is double his. This means that he has the same number of men, but accomplishes only half the work of his neighbor.

[1] *Cf. infra.*

[2] *Cf. infra*, p. 165.

This points out the difference between the size of the population and the efficiency of production. The mere possession of a large population is of no use, unless it gives a corresponding amount of production. Therefore, if the large territory cannot support a large population, and the large population cannot give a large production, these two cases are both regarded by the superior man as his shame. In short, wealth must be in accordance with the population.

III. MIGRATION OF POPULATION.

1. *Freedom of Movement.*

The fundamental principle underlying the problem of population is the freedom of movement. According to the principles of the *Spring and Autumn*, there is a division of territory, but there is no division of people. This means that the people may either emigrate or immigrate, without a permanent residence. Under such a principle the people have perfect freedom of movement. When the government is good the people immigrate, and when it is bad they emigrate. The number of people is the index of the political condition of the government and the economic condition of the people. Therefore, the merit of the officials is tested by the examination into the size of population.

The chief cause of emigration is economic. So long as the people are satisfied with their economic condition, they will stay even though there might be some other great evils. When Confucius passed by the side of Tai Mountain, and saw a woman who was wailing bitterly by a grave, he sent Tzŭ-lu to question her. She said: "Formerly, my father-in-law was killed here by a tiger. My husband was also killed by another; and now my son has died in the same way." Confucius said: "Why do you not leave the place?" The answer was, "There is no oppressive government here." He then said to his pupils: "Remember this, my little children. Oppressive government is more terrible than tigers." [1] In fact, the worst thing to drive the people away is an oppressive government, especially if it touches the economic life of the people by heavy taxation.

On the other hand, the chief cause for immigration is also economic. According to Chao Tso, people seeking their economic interest anywhere are like water running to a low place, and they do not choose any particular region in the four corners.[2] The mobility of population, then, is like water. If the economic interest of one locality is greater than that of another, the people will emigrate from the latter to the former, when there is no obstacle. Therefore, both emigration and immigration depend upon economic principles.

2. *Encouragement of Immigration in General*

Since Confucius regards immigration as a sign of good government, he advocates the encouragement of it. Confucius says·

> If a ruler love propriety, the people will not dare not to be reverent. If he love righteousness, the people will not dare not to submit to his example. If he love good faith, the people will not dare not to be sincere. Now, when these things obtain, the people from all quarters will come to him, bearing their children on their backs.[3]

He thus shows that the immigration of the people is the result of a good ruler. When the Duke of Yeh asked Confucius about government, Confucius said, "Good government obtains when those who are near are made happy, and those who are far off are attracted to come." [4] By this

[1] *Li Ki,* bk ii, pp. 190-191.

[2] *History of Han,* ch. xxiv.

[3] *Classics,* vol. i, p. 265.

[4] *Ibid.,* p. 269.

statement he makes the immigratoin of the remote people one of the two objects of good government. Again, he says: "If remoter people are not submissive, all the influences of civil culture and virtue are to be cultivated in order to attract them to come; and when they have come, they must be made contented and tranquil." [1] Therefore, to attract the immigrants to come in is the doctrine of Confucius. This means to win the heart of the people, and to conquer them by culture and virtue.

Mencius has made a similar statement. When he talked to King Hsüan of Ch'i, he said:

> Now, if your Majesty will institute a government whose action shall be benevolent, this will cause all the officers in the world to wish to stand in your Majesty's court, and all the farmers to wish to plough in your Majesty's fields, and all the merchants, both traveling and stationary, to wish to store their goods in your Majesty's market-places, and all traveling strangers to wish to make their tours on your Majesty's roads, and all throughout the world who feel aggrieved by their rulers to wish to come and complain to your Majesty.[2]

In fact, this is the condition of a royal government. It makes the state the center of the immigration of the whole world, and conquers the whole world by the institutions of benevolent government instead of military force. This is the real meaning of the word "king" or "royal" in the Confucian sense. It is universalism in contrast to imperialism.[3]

For the encouragement of immigration, exemptions are given to the immigrants. For example, we may quote this

[1] *Classics,* vol. i, pp. 308-9.

[2] *Classics,* vol. ii, pp. 146-7. The benevolent government means the *tsing tien* system; *cf. infra,* pp. 501-6.

[3] *Cf. infra.*

passage from the "Royal Regulations:" "When the people of the noble families move to the feudal states, they are discharged from service for three months. When the people move from the feudal states to the noble families, they are not required to take service for a round year."[1] For the explanation of the text, K'ung Ying-ta says:

> In the feudal states, the land is larger, and the public labor requiring the people to do service is less; hence the people desire it. Therefore, they are exempted from service only for three months. . . . In the estates of the noble families, the land is smaller, and the public labor is more. In order to make the people like it, they are exempted from service for a round year.

From this passage we may get two points. First, it shows the freedom of movement. The people may move either from the noble estates to the feudal states, or *vice versa*, as they please. Second, it shows the real encouragement of immigration, because the immigrants get some material gain from such an exemption.

The Confucian theory is exactly the opposite of actual conditions in American and European countries. While the restriction and the exclusion of immigrants in the United States is based mainly on the economic struggle—that is, the laborers want to get more money—the theory of Confucius is based on politics, ethics and religion. Indeed, his theory tends to make a universal empire, a universal religion, a universal conception, a universal law, a universal custom, a universal route, a universal language, a universal calendar, *etc.* These ideas can be summed up in a single word—universalism. Confucius says: "When there is the teaching, there shall be no distinction between the races, nor be-

[1] *Li Ki,* bk. iii, p. 243.

tween the sexes, nor between the classes."[1] From such a point of view it is necessary to encourage immigration in order to realize universalism.

Under the influence of Confucius, China did realize universalism to a great extent, although it was imperfect. Unfortunately, or fortunately, the Opium War brought about by the English broke the Chinese peace and marked a most important epoch in Chinese history. In the past, China was a universal empire, and in the present, she is only one of the nations of the world. Since the Opium War, China has been forced to make unjust treaties, and such terms as "extraterritoriality," "sphere of influence," "shall China be partitioned," "open door," have been introduced. When foreigners come to China, they, although not every one of them, threaten the national sovereignty, deprive the individual of liberty, violate the law of the land, and do anything they please.[2] The Chinese, indeed, sincerely welcome well-behaved foreigners, but there can be none who like such men. The ideal of Confucian universalism is too advanced; it does not fit the world which is still full of injustice. Hence, China is forced back to the lower stage of a national military state. We hope, however, that after China shall be strong enough to maintain peace against any external interference, she will by herself open the door of every part to any foreigner under the Chinese jurisdiction, in order to realize Confucian universalism and to make a world state by means of the national state.

[1] *Cf. Classics,* vol. i, p. 305.

[2] A single instance must stand as a type of multitudinous insults and oppressions which the Chinese have to endure in consequence of the presence of foreigners, protected by extra-territorial rights. At the entrance of the Shanghai Public Garden on the Bund, there is a notice written in Chinese saying: "Dogs and Chinamen are not allowed to come in," posted by order of the Municipal Council, which is composed entirely of the representatives of foreign residents.

3. *Encouragement of Immigration of Artisans and Merchants*

Although immigration in general has a great effect upon the economic life of a nation, its influence is far beyond the economic field. Hence, we now come to immigration in particular—namely, the immigration of artisans and traveling merchants. When Duke Ai asked Confucius about government, he gave him the nine standard rules. Among these, the seventh is to induce all classes of artisans to come in, and the eighth is concerned with the indulgent treatment of foreigners. The former mentions the word artisans expressly, while the latter means foreign merchants especially, although it includes all foreigners in general.

The happy effects of these two rules and the details of practising them are given by Confucius as follows:

> By inducing all classes of artisans to come in, wealth is made sufficient. By indulgent treatment of foreigners, the people of all quarters will come. . . . By daily examinations and monthly trials, and by making their rations in accordance with their labors: this is the way to encourage all the classes of artisans. To escort them on their departure and meet them on their coming; to commend the good among them, and show compassion to the incompetent: this is the way to treat foreigners indulgently.

In short, the government should make the state a center of industry and commerce. In order to accomplish this aim it must encourage immigration.

It is very important to know that, although Confucius is in favor of agriculture, he leaves it out of the nine standard rules, and mentions only industry and commerce. In order to bring out this point we must give the nine standard rules fully. They are as follows: (1) the cultivation of the personality of the ruler, (2) the honoring of men of virtue and talents, (3) affection toward relatives, (4) respect toward the great ministers, (5) kind and considerate treatment of the whole body of officials, (6) dealing with the mass of the people as children, (7) inducing all classes of artisans to come in, (8) indulgent treatment of foreigners, and (9) the kindly cherishing of the princes of the feudal states. This is a complete program of government. It begins with the personal character of the ruler himself; for such a purpose his familiar friends must be men of virtue and talents. Then he must be affectionate to the relatives of his family, and must be good to all the officials and the people. These six rules are all applied within the limit of his own state. Now, for international relations, they are governed by the last three rules. Excepting the last rule as a diplomatic principle, the other two are economic doctrines. It is interesting to see that Confucius always regards economic life not as a national phenomenon, but an international one. Therefore, he does not give any economic principle until he reaches the seventh and eighth rules. It is exactly for this same reason that the "Great Learning" does not touch any economic problem until under the last chapter, namely, the equalizing of the whole world.[1]

Now, we come back to our point. So far as the nine rules are concerned, none of them are economic principles except the seventh and the eighth. But these two rules refer to industry and commerce only, and agriculture is left out entirely. There may be several reasons for this. First, agriculture may be included in industry and commerce, because the one is the primary industry and the other two are secondary. Second, for international competition, industry and commerce may be preferred to agriculture.

[1] *Cf. supra,* pp. 139-142.

Third, since there is a great immigration of "all classes of artisans" and "the people of all quarters," industry and commerce, rather than agriculture, are needed to support such a large population. Confucius may have had all these three points in mind as reasons for referring to industry and commerce only and leaving agriculture out.

There is still another point. For the effect of the indulgent treatment of foreigners, Confucius mentions only that "the people of all quarters will come;" but for that of inducing all classes of artisans to come in, he points out very clearly that "the wealth is made sufficient." Therefore, if a state wants to make wealth sufficient, it must resort to industry. Industry alone can create new wealth, while commerce simply creates new value upon the existing wealth. From this point of view, we may say that Confucius knows the importance of industrial capital. All those points mentioned above are the economic principles of Confucius.[1]

Although the policy of "inducing all classes of artisans to come in" has not been realized in China, it has been carried out very successfully in England and the United States. During the reigns of Edward III and of Elizabeth, the immigration of Flemish workmen gave a great impetus to English industry. It has also contributed to the progress of the United States since 2371 A. K. or 1820 A. D. Had the immigrants not come, the United States would not have been so prosperous as at present. Unfortunately, since China stood as an isolated country for a long period, this policy did not have any marked effect upon her, because the workmanship of the surrounding countries was much lower than that of China. To-day, by the change of methods, China really demands a great number of skilled workmen. But the political interference of foreign countries is a

[1] *Classics*, vol. i, pp. 408-411.

temporary bar to block this demand. We are sure, however, that such a bar cannot last very long, and that the principle of "inducing all classes of artisans to come in" will have a great triumph in the future.

4. *Absence of Race Question*

According to the principles of the *Spring and Autumn*, a nation is called either civilized or uncivilized, not on account of blood, or of geography, but on account of true civilization—rites and justice. There is no race or state which can permanently assume the title of civilized nation unless its actions be just. This is the principle of Confucius; hence, the Chinese have no race question at all.

The absence of race questions in China is due, however, not only to the teachings of Confucius, but also to geographical causes. As China is located in the greatest continent, together with great mountains and rivers, she has produced one great people, and has had no opportunity for a race question. Every one can see from Chinese history that China has accepted any religion and any race from any part of the world. The so-called barbarians were made not only common citizens, but also prominent officials, either civil or military, and feudal princes. Although we have no full knowledge about the earliest history, from the Chou dynasty to the present day, China has had no race prejudice against any other nationality.

The best example of this was given by the Tang dynasty. In 1181 A. K. (630 A. D.), after the Turkish nation was destroyed, besides those who ran to the West, the number who surrendered to the Tang dynasty was about one hundred thousand. Tang T'ai Tsung ordered his courtiers to debate on the treatment of the Turks. Some one wanted to drive them back to their old place. But Wun Yen-po said:

An emperor to the myriad of things is like the covering of heaven and the containing of earth without any exclusion. Now, the Turks come to us because they are powerless. Why should we refuse them? Confucius said that when there is the teaching, there should be no distinction between the races. If we relieve them from death, give them economic occupations, and teach them rites and justice, after several years they will be entirely our citizens. Then we can select their chiefs to come to the capital and to become the imperial guards. Thus they will fear our power and love our virtue. What will be the danger in the future?

T'ai Tsung finally used this policy. He divided their territory into several provinces, and appointed their leaders as the governors. When the Turkish chiefs came to court, they were all appointed as military commanders, and occupied offices in the court. Above the fifth official rank, they amounted to more than one hundred persons, nearly half of the number of the Chinese courtiers. Hence, the Turks living in the capital were about ten thousand families.[1] This shows how broad-minded the Chinese people are. Even when the Turks were conquered, they gave them immediately equality of political rights. Indeed, they put the barbarian races upon the same footing with their own, and assimilated them.

We may ask a question: Why did, and does, the race problem arise in the western world? It seems that it is due to geographical smallness. Since Europe is not a real continent, but only a peninsula of Asia, there are many geographical subdivisions and many small islands and peninsulas. In such an environment, European sectional feeling has been fostered. In ancient times, the Greeks and the Romans, except Alexander and Caesar, knew only the city-

[1] *General Political History,* published in 1635 (1084 A. D.) by Ssŭ-ma Kuang, ch. cxciii.

state. Even in the *Republic* of Plato, his idea is only a city-state, and everything depends upon war. In modern times, the European race feeling is still worse. This seems to be the product of the geographical situation.

Now, we may turn to the United States of America. The United States was founded in the new world by virtuous men, and the Americans are more broad-minded than the Europeans. When the nation grew a little older, however, the old good-faith became less, and the Chinese Exclusion Act began (2433 A. K. or 1882 A. D.). It seems that race prejudice does not come from the American continent itself—such a great new world should not produce such a narrow idea—but from the European peninsula, and especially from the new immigrants. The Exclusion Act is an extremely bad example to the world, and is a serious blemish on the glorious American history. From this point of view, the Americans are inferior to the Chinese.

IV. CONDITIONS WITH REFERENCE TO POPULATION IN CHINA

The reasons for China's large population may be examined from two viewpoints—the relation of husband and wife and the relation of father and son. In other words, we may explain it by the customs of marriage and the doctrine of filial piety.

1. *Marriage*

(a) *Importance of Marriage*

The religion of Confucius is very different from Buddhism and Catholicism. It offers no objection to marriage. Confucius regards marriage not only as human happiness, but as human duty. Mencius says: "That male and female should dwell together is the greatest of human relations." [1] The aged widower and the aged widow are classified as

[1] *Classics,* vol. ii, p. 346.

the most unfortunate people. If marriage is too late, it is regarded as unhappiness. When Mencius describes the social life of the reign of T'ai Wang (died in 680 B. K. or 1231 B. C.), the grandfather of Wên Wang, he says: "At that time, in the inside there were no dissatisfied women, and in the outside there were no lonesome men." This means that all married at the proper time. Such a theory has a great influence on the Chinese population. In China there are practically no unmarried people, except when under special circumstances they are forced to leave their families and become Buddhists. In fact, there are very few people who voluntarily remain in single life. Hence, the Chinese population is the largest in the world.

(b) *Day of Marriage*

Although Confucius thinks that marriage is necessary, he does not make the day of marriage early. A man takes the first ceremony of marriage—that is, the capping—at twenty years, and has a wife at thirty. A woman takes the first ceremony—that is, binding up the hair with the hair-pin—at fifteen, and marries at twenty. If she has not been engaged, she will assume the hair-pin at twenty, and under some circumstances she may marry at twenty-three.[1] This general rule is given in the *Record of Rites* and many other books. It makes the day of marriage so late not as a check to the growth of population, but as a provision for physical development and personal responsibility. The *Great Commentary of the Canon of History* says that the woman may marry at twenty years, because at that time she can understand all the family duties and domestic science, otherwise she could neither serve her parents-in-law, help her husband, nor breed her children.

During the Han dynasty (491 A. K. or 61 B. C.), Wang

[1] *Li Ki*, bk. x, pp. 478-9.

Chi proposed his theory of marriage to the emperor. He thought that marriage is the primary form of social relationship and determines the length of life. If the day of marriage is too early, the pair may have children when they do not understand their parental duties. Therefore, the moral influence is weak, and the people frequently die prematurely. Moreover, if the expenditure on marriage has no limit, poor people, either men or women, cannot marry. Therefore, they do not want to raise children.[1] This theory, although it was not carried out by law, is a general thought of the Chinese.

There are two points in this discussion. One is to improve the physical condition of the people by the postponement of marriage, in order to increase the average length of life. The other is to encourage the marriage of the poor, in order to increase the population. They are not checks, but aids, to population. In China, as ceremony is very important and social relation is very close, marriage is very expensive on both the male and the female side, even among the poorest people. Therefore, the Chinese always try to reduce its expense by reforms of custom, in order to make marriage easy. In short, the people generally think that men or women are happier married than alone, and that wealth will be increased as the number of men increases. Generally speaking, the Chinese marry earlier than Confucius prescribes.[2]

[1] *History of Han,* ch. lxxii.

[2] In Confucius' time, Wu and Yüeh were the two rival states. When Wu conquered Yüeh (58 A. K. or 494 B. C.), she did not take it for her own possession. After peace was made, the king of Yüeh established this policy: The young men should not take the old women, nor the old men the young women. When a girl at seventeen, or a man at twenty, had not married, their parents were held guilty. When a woman was about to give birth to a child, the king should be informed beforehand; then she was cared for by the public physician. If the

(c) *Exogamy*

There are two important customs which have brought about the large population of China—the one is exogamy and the other polygyny. In *Tso's Commentary* the principle of the first institution is given as follows: "When husband and wife are of the same clan, their children do not prosper and multiply."[1] This is a biological principle discovered eighty-six years before Confucius. But this principle had been in practice, by law, since the time of the Duke of Chou (about 564 B. K. or 1115 B. C.). The *Record of Rites* says: "According to the rule of Chou, there is no intermarriage among the same clan, even after a hundred generations."[2] This means that there is no intermarriage of the male lines of the common remotest ancestor. This rule has been observed by all the Chinese. From this principle, on the one hand, the Chinese have enlarged their own race; on the other, they have assimilated all other races. About three thousand years ago different races commingled in China, as the Americans do now.

According to the principles of the *Spring and Autumn*, a man should not marry the relatives of his mother. The reason here is the same as that a man should not marry the daughter of the same clan. This principle is also applied to the lines of the sisters of his father. In the *Law Code of the Ts'ing Dynasty* this principle is applied to a very great

child was a boy, two pots of wine and a dog were given; if a girl, the same amount of wine and a pig. If the mother gave birth to three children, the king supplied a nurse; to two children, he supplied food. He took different kinds of food with him while traveling, in order to feed children. These were his policies for the increasing of population for military purposes. Twenty-one years later, he succeeded in conquering Wu and took it for his own.—*Narratives of Nations*, bk. xx.

[1] *Classics*, vol. v, pt. i, p. 187.

[2] *Li Ki*, bk. xiv, p. 63.

extent.[1] Such exogamy has two great reasons: On the ethical side, it promotes the moral sense and prevents the people from falling in love with their relatives. On the biological side, it gives physical betterment to the couple themselves and multiplies their offspring. This is the second point which has a great effect upon the question of population.

(d) *Polygyny*

For the explanation of the Chinese population, the practice of polygyny must also be referred to. It was an old custom, and it was not abolished, but reformed, by Confucius. According to his regulation, the emperor may have twelve females; the prince, nine; the great official, three; the student, two; the common people, only one. Some authorities say that the emperor and the prince both may have only nine females. Therefore we may take the marriage of the prince as the maximum example. When the prince marries a queen from a foreign nation, she takes her younger sister and niece along with her; then two other nations respectively send one companion to her, together with the companion's younger sister and niece, the whole party being nine females.

The reason the emperor and the prince may have nine females is that they represent the sovereignty of the state and their succession is very important. If they have no son from these nine females, however, they have no reason to take any more. Their marriage is finished at this one time; no second marriage is allowed. They must marry girls outside of their own state. All these regulations make them more respectful and prevent them from loving other women. The younger sisters and nieces, although they may be too young, must accompany the queen at the time of marriage,

[1] Ch. x.

but later return to their own states and remain there until the age of twenty. Why does the queen or the companion take her younger sister and niece along? It is that there may be no jealousy; when one of them has a son, the three will have the same pleasure. Why does she not take two younger sisters instead of the niece? It is because the physical condition of the niece may differ from that of her sister. Why does the prince take girls from three different states? It is for the diversification of the races, lest the girls of the same state have the same blood and give no son at all. In short, all these details make the emperor and the prince sure to have more sons—a political necessity.

The reason the great official may have three females is in honor of the wise and able man, and because of the importance of continuing his lineage. Below the class of great official, the student may have two females. For the common people there is monogamy; hence they are called "single man and single woman."

Although Confucius did not abolish polygyny, he did reform it. At that time the emperor regularly had one hundred and twenty-one females; the prince must have had more than nine; the great official more than three; the student more than two; and the common people more than one. But he reduced the number to a certain limit and did not allow the emperor and the prince to marry a second time. By these means he markedly checked the prevailing custom. During his age, all the great officials, not only the emperor and the princes, held their office by hereditary right; hence, the succession of their family was an important thing. Moreover, Confucius himself thought that the perpetuation of family is a great duty of man. Therefore, he did not, and could not, abolish polygyny entirely.

Confucius' reason for not abolishing polygyny—that is, that a family may perpetuate its lineage—applies especially to the feudal stage. But we must understand that Confucius is in favor of monogamy. Although the emperor, the prince, the great official, and the student may have more than one female, each of them has only one wife. The other females are concubines, simply for the producing of sons, and they cannot be called wives. Since a son is very important for the paternal family, and one wife may fail to give birth to a son, the concubine is recognized by Confucius. But Confucius himself did not have any concubine, although he had the right to have two. In the *Canon of Changes*, he says: "When two women live together, their minds do not move in the same direction." Again he says: "When two women live together, their minds do not agree with each other." [1] From his own practice and from these two passages, we may be sure that he is in favor of monogamy. Indeed, polygyny is for the Disorderly Stage, and monogamy for the Advancing Peace Stage.

As a matter of fact, the Chinese do not follow the regulations of Confucius. They may have as many concubines as their condition allows, although there must be a natural limit. This is an evil custom, indeed, but it still has some merit. From the moral and social point of view, since a man may have concubines openly, he will not resort to prostitution or illegitimate intercourse. From the economic point of view, it may relieve some poor girls from deep poverty. But most important of all is that the practice of polygyny has increased the population to a great extent. This is the reason why we discuss it here. The Chinese, however, are likely to change polygyny into monogamy before very long.

[1] *Yi King,* pp. 243, 253.

2. *Doctrine of Filial Piety*

(a) *Perpetuation of the Family*

In the world there is no nation that has perpetuated its people as a particular race so long as has China. It is the contribution of Confucius, because he preaches the doctrine of filial piety. According to this doctrine the perpetuation of the family is the chief duty of man. Confucius says: "Since the parents have given birth to a son, it is the perpetuation of the human race, and there is nothing greater than this."[1] Hence, a son must continue the line of his parents. Mencius says: "There are three things which are unfilial; but to have no posterity is the greatest of them."[2] The other two unfilial things are, according to Chao Ch'i (died 752 A. K. or 201 A. D.), the commentator, first, by a flattering assent to encourage parents in unrighteousness; and second, not to succor their poverty and old age by engaging in official service. To be without posterity is a fault greater than these, because it is an offense against the whole line of ancestors and terminates the sacrifices to them.

In short, by the statement of Confucius, to give birth to a son is the greatest contribution of the parents to society as a whole; and by that of Mencius, to have no posterity is the greatest offense of a son against all his ancestors. Therefore, the perpetuation of the family is the chief duty of both father and son.

Since we have already discussed the doctrine of filial piety (and the custom of ancestor-worship) from the religious and ethical point of view, we shall now look at it only from its influence on the Chinese population. Under the influence of Confucius, every one wants to marry in order to have sons. The parents can never be satisfied until they finish

[1] *Sacred Books*, vol. iii, p. 479.

[2] *Classics*, vol. ii, p. 313.

for their children the proceeding of marriage, which they regard as an obligation. Among very poor families, it is even the social duty of their friends to help them to marry.

If one has no son, he may take a concubine in the hope of having posterity, and his wife almost always agrees to it. If he has no prospect of having a son, he may adopt a son, either from his own clan or from another. Sometimes even, when he dies prematurely, not having married at all, his family adopts a son for him, in order to continue his lineage

(b) *Return to the Parents*

While the perpetuation of the family is the strongest motive impelling the Chinese to have sons, another stimulus is the expected return to the parents. Since we have already discussed this principle, there is no need of any further explanation. We now simply point out that it has a great influence upon the Chinese population As we have seen, China makes the support of parents a positive law. The parents usually derive their support from their sons. Although the sons are not necessarily dutiful enough to support their parents, the custom has behind it a very strong public opinion; hence, the return to the parents is a general expectation. Therefore, when one has no son, he regards it as the greatest of misfortunes. First, he is afraid that his lineage will be extinguished. Second, he has no hope of being supported in his old age. Third, even when he has no need of support, he needs a son as an object of pleasure, a performer of social and religious duties, *etc* In fact, desire for sons among the Chinese is stronger than among any other people.

The return to the parents may be divided into two categories. One is the material return. Since the support of parents is an obligation of the sons, the parents claim the duties from their sons as creditors from debtors. Hence, the bringing-up of children may be regarded as a provision for the later part of life. Indeed, it is equivalent to an insurance policy, providing a sickness benefit, unemployment benefit, old-age benefit, funeral benefit, *etc.*

The other is the immaterial return, and it may be divided into three things. First, the son may return honor to his parents during their life. Ts'êng Tzŭ says: "He whom the superior man pronounces filial is he whom all the people of his state praise, saying with admiration, 'Happy are the parents who have such a son as this!'—that indeed is what can be called being filial."[1] Second, he may return honor to them after their death. Confucius says that to make our name famous in future ages, and thereby glorify our parents, is the end of filial piety.[2] The "Pattern of the Family" says:

> Although his parents be dead, when a son is inclined to do what is good, he should think that he will thereby transmit the good name of his parents, and carry his wish into effect. When he is inclined to do what is not good, he should think that he will thereby bring disgrace on the name of his parents, and in no wise carry his wish into effect.[3]

Since Confucius regards the name as a very important thing, the parents have expectations from the glory of their sons. In China, whatever official title a son may get may be transmitted to his parents either during their life or after their death, and also to his grandparents and great-grandparents. Third, the son may return homage to his parents in the form of ancestor-worship. Thus we can see how the principle of the returns to parents helps to bring about China's great population.

[1] *Li Ki,* bk. xxi, pp. 226-7.

[2] See *supra,* p. 112.

[3] *Li Ki,* bk. x, p. 457.

V. HISTORICAL STUDY OF POPULATION

The word population is expressed in the Chinese language by two words, " door " and " mouth." " Door " means a family, and " mouth " a person. But we do not like to translate the word "door " into the word family, because China had the "door tax," which made the people conceal their families, and the word "door " cannot represent the word family. For the same reason, the people concealed their number in order to escape the " mouth tax," and so the word " mouth " cannot represent the word person. We shall use these original words, "door " and " mouth," to stand as a picture of the historical Chinese population, and give our population statistics in those terms. Although it is too far from the real figures, it is the only way by which we can get any idea about the history of Chinese population Therefore, we shall give the most important figures, whether the largest or the smallest, of the most important periods, in the form of a table. From the table we can judge something not only about the real population, but also about the economic, social and political conditions.

Population of China at Different Periods

Era of Confucius	Era of Reigning Dynasties	Number of Doors	Number of Mouths	Era of Christ
1654 B. K. (about)	Hsia Yü	......	13,553,923	2205 B. C.
564 " (about)	Chou Ch'êng Wang	......	13,714,923	1115 "
132 "	13th year of Chou Chuang Wang	......	11,941,923	683 "
219 A. K.	36th year of Chou Hsien Wang	......	30,000,000 (about)	333 "
352 "	7th year of Han Kao Ti	......	5,000,000 (about)	200 "
553 "	2d year of Han P'ing Ti	12,233,062	59,594,978	2 A. D.
608 "	The last year of Han Kuang-wu	4,279,634	21,007,820	57 "
707 "	Han Huan Ti	16,070,906	50,066,856	156 "
814 " (about)	Three Kingdoms	1,473,423	7,672,891	263 "
831 "	Tsin Wu Ti	2,459,804	16,163,863	280 "
1044 " (about)	Southern and Northern Dynasties	6,000,000 (about)	40,000,000 (about)	493 "
1131 " (about)	Southern and Northern Dynasties	4,090,000	11,009,604	580 "
1157 "	2d year of Sui Yang Ti	8,907,536	46,019,956	606 "
1178 " (about)	1st year of Tang T'ai Tsung	3,000,000 (less)	......	627 "
1305 "	Tang Hsüan Tsung	9,619,254	52,909,309	754 "
1311 "	Tang Su Tsung	1,933,134	16,990,386	760 "
1396 "	5th year of Tang Wu Tsung	4,955,151	......	845 "
1527 "	Last year of Sung T'ai Tsu	3,090,504	......	976 "
1653 "	2d year of Sung Hui Tsung	20,019,050	43,820,769	1102 "
1711 "	Sung Kao Tsung	11,375,733	19,229,008	1160 "
1744 "	Sung Kuang Tsung	12,302,873	27,845,085	1193 "
1774 "	Sung Ning Tsung	12,670,801	28,320,085	1223 "
1758 "	Kin Chang Tsung	7,684,438	45,816,079	1207 "
1758 " (about)	Sung and Kin	20,355,239	74,136,164	1207 "
1841 "	Yüan Shih Tsu	13,196,206	58,834,711	1290 "
1932 "	14th year of Ming T'ai Tsu	10,654,362	59,873,305	1381 "
1954 "	1st year of Ming Ch'êng Tsu	11,415,829	66,598,337	1403 "
2172 "	1st year of Ming Hsi Tsung	9,825,426	51,655,459	1621 "
2212 "	18th year of Ts'ing Shih Tsu	......	21,068,609	1661 "
2262 "	50th year of Ts'ing Shêng Tsu	......	24,621,334	1711 "
2300 "	14th year of Ts'ing Kao Tsung	......	177,495,039	1749 "
2334 "	48th year of Ts'ing Kao Tsung	......	284,033,755	1783 "
2393 "	22d year of Ts'ing Hsüan Tsung	......	413,020,000	1842 "

The above table shows the size of the population of China proper throughout all the ages, and is based mostly upon the *Three General Researches.*[1] Their materials came from history, and those of history came from the official reports. All the figures of this table are quoted from the *Three General Researches* except those for the years 219 A. K. and 352 A. K., which are estimates. At the end of the Yüan dynasty, about 1918 A. K., although it is an important period, we cannot make an estimate, because there is no basis. All the dates of this table are also quoted from the *Three General Researches*; but in a few cases dates are uncertain, and we have inserted the word " about " to indicate that the dates may not be exact. All the figures and dates of this table are based on a very careful study.

1. *Inaccuracy of this Table*

The statements of this table are very far from accurate. (1) In the reigns of Hsia Yü, of Chou Ch'êng Wang and of Chou Chuang Wang, there are no real records in regard to the population, but only the estimates of Huang-fu Mi (766-833 A. K. or 215-282 A. D.), a great authority.

(2) The most trustworthy figures are those of the Han dynasty.

(3) Among the Three Kingdoms, about 814, the Wei kingdom and the Shu kingdom both had only 943,423 doors and 5,372,891 mouths. After Tsin Wu Ti succeeded to the Wei kingdom, which included the Shu kingdom, he conquered the Wu kingdom in 831 and took 530,000 doors and 2,300,000 mouths by his conquest. The total number of these two sets of figures in 831 was 1,473,423 doors and 7,672,891

[1] They are (1) the *General Research on Literature and Authorities,* chs. x-xi; (2) the *Continuation of the General Research on Literature and Authorities,* chs. xii-xiii; and (3) the *General Research on Literature and Authorities of the Present Dynasty,* ch. iii.

mouths. Why should Tsin Wu Ti in the same year (831) have 2,459,804 doors and 16,163,863 mouths? Although from 814 to 831 the number of the first would increase, it could hardly have doubled in the short space of seventeen years. It seems that the historian's mistake arose from taking the number of the population toward the close of Wu Ti's reign (about 840) and putting it in the year when he had just reunited the whole empire (831).

(4) The Tang dynasty began in 1169, and had lasted 137 years in 1305. At that time the people enjoyed a long golden age, and the population must have increased. Tu Yu says: "It should at least have thirteen or fourteen millions of doors." But, according to this table, in 1305 it had only 9,619,254 doors.

(5) In the Former Han dynasty, the average number of mouths for ten doors was more than 48; in the Latter Han dynasty it was 52 mouths, and in the Tang dynasty, 58 mouths But in the Sung dynasty it was only 21 mouths. There is no reason why one family should have only two persons For instance, in 1774, the 12,670,801 doors of the Sung dynasty had only 28,320,085 mouths. But in 1758, the 7,684,438 doors of the Kin dynasty had 45,816,079 mouths. There is no reason why the Sung dynasty, which had doors nearly double those of the Kin dynasty, should have about half as many mouths as the latter. According to this table, each door of Kin had more than six mouths. If we should take a rate as low as five mouths to each door, Sung should have 63,354,005 mouths. Adding the mouths of Kin on this reasonable estimate, China should have had at least 109,170,084 mouths in 1758.

(6) The census of the Ming dynasty is still worse. We select the figures only about its beginning and its end In 1932 the revolutionary war had only recently ended, and in 1954 the civil war was just finished. If the population

at those periods had grown as large as this table shows, why should it become smaller in the later peaceful time? In fact, China was never able to get a census that was even approximately accurate until 2300.

2. *Causes of the Inaccuracy*

Why did China not have an accurate census? There is a sound reason for it. Because China had a monarchical government it did not touch the people closely, and because the people did not directly enjoy political interest very much they tried to escape from the taxes. Since the "door tax" and the "mouth tax" depended entirely upon the number of the population, the people had to conceal their number in order to evade the taxes; hence, none understood the real population. In the Han dynasty the two taxes were very light, so that the numbers of the population were more trustworthy. After that time, the two taxes were higher, but the number of the population was lower. Why did the government, however, not exercise its force in order to get the full amount of taxes? It is because the government was under the Confucian influence. The Confucian doctrines, such as "Love the people," "light tax," and "benevolent government," were familiar to all the rulers. Hence, the Chinese government generally never dared to exercise a despotic force directly upon the people. If the people wanted to conceal anything, the government could not find it out, because it did not control the actual life of the people. Moreover, the mandarin would have some deep ideas. For example, when Ma Jên-wang[1] made his census he finished it in less than twenty days. Some one was surprised, and questioned him. He said: "If the numbers of population were taken inclusively without remainder, it will induce the

[1] He was made minister of the Liao dynasty in 1664 (1113 A. D.).

trouble of a heavy tax in the future. Generally, taking six or seven out of ten is quite enough." But we must not make such a mistake as to think that the Confucians do not care to have an accurate census Indeed, the Confucians regard the population as the most important thing and value highly an accurate census. A light tax is one thing, but an accurate census is another. Yet, on account of the door tax and the mouth tax, China could not get a good census.

3. *Significance of this Table*

Although this table is inaccurate, it is still valuable If one could completely understand these figures he would be able to master the whole Chinese history. The really hereditary monarchical empire was founded by Hsia Yu. At that time the population was more than thirteen millions The beginning of the Chou dynasty was a golden age As China in about 564 B. K. had more than thirteen millions of population, she should possess much more two hundred years later, because this peaceful period lasted for about three hundred years. We may think that this period fostered the most wonderful civilization of the period of Spring and Autumn (171 B. K.-71 A. K.) and that of Warring States (149-331 A. K.).

As a destroyer of population, war is the worst influence. According to this table, in the beginning of the Han dynasty the population lost five-sixths; in the beginning of the Latter Han dynasty, about two-thirds; in the Three Kingdoms, about six-sevenths; in the latter part of the Southern and Northern Dynasties, about three-fourths; in the beginning of the Tang dynasty, about two-thirds; in the reign of Tang Su Tsung, within the period of only five years, it lost over two-thirds: in the beginning of the Sung dynasty, about two-fifths; in the beginning of the Southern Sung dynasty, more than half; in the beginning of the Yüan dynasty, measured by the number of the "doors," it lost over one-third; in the beginning of the present dynasty it lost about three-fifths. From this point of view, the revolutionary war was a great calamity. It not only destroyed the population, but retarded civilization.

In Chinese history, when her civilization advanced to a high level, it was dragged down by warfare When, after a long time, it rose again, it fell again. It is no wonder that the Chinese progressed so slowly. But, through modern inventions, such as the railroad, telegraph, telephone, *etc.*, which will enable her to change absolute monarchy into a really constitutional monarchy, China may avoid such internal wars as have troubled her in the past, and will permit her civilization continuously to progress. Moreover, as China can never be conquered by any external power, she will be able to change a constitutional monarchy into a real republic, and she might form a world-state with the leading nations, and might realize the Great Similarity of Confucius. Then the whole population of the world will enjoy the Stage of Extreme Peace without any war.

It should be noticed that the magnitude of the figures in this table does not necessarily reflect upon the reigning rulers. Generally, the ruler of the beginning of a dynasty was an able or good man, and that of its decay a weak or bad man. But at the beginning of a dynasty the population would be small, and about the time of its decay it would be large; for in the former case it would suffer from the hard times of the past, and in the latter case it would enjoy the good fortune of the past. This table indicates only the facts of history and does not show exactly what the governments were during the given years. As a rule, however, a large population would be produced under a good government, but such a result would of course follow only after a considerable period.

The most wonderful increase of population was during the Sui dynasty. In the first year of Sui Wên Ti's reign (1132 A. K.), he had only 9,009,604 mouths. In his ninth year (1140 A. K.), he took 2,000,000 mouths from the Southern Chen dynasty. The total number was 11,009,604 mouths. But in 1157 A. K., when only twenty-five years had passed, his son had 46,019,956 mouths. The population increased over fourfold within twenty-five years. It seems that the figures for population increased not on account of the birth-rate only, but mainly on account of the system of taxation. After the great statesman of Sui, named Kao Kung, established a system of taxation in favor of the free citizens by making the taxes light, the people did not like to be the dependents of the higher class for the purpose of evading taxes; hence the number of citizens who paid taxes increased rapidly. Indeed, the Sui dynasty was the richest one in Chinese financial history.

According to this table, before 2300 the population never numbered over one hundred millions. Why should the population figures of the present dynasty be much larger than those of all the past dynasties? It is because the present dynasty has neither "door tax" nor "mouth tax." In 2212 A. K. the number was 21,068,609, and in 2262, 24,-621,334. Throughout fifty peaceful years the population increased only 3,552,725. But in 2300 A. K. the number was 177,495,039. It increased more than seven times in the thirty-eight years. Why should the figures increase so rapidly as this? It was because Shêng Tsu had abolished these two taxes in 2263. His decree is as follows:

> The empire has been peaceful for a long time, so that the population increases numerously. If I increase the amount of taxes according to the present number of population, it is not right; for, although the population becomes larger, the acre-

age of land does not become wider.[1] . . . To-day the public treasury is very rich. Although I have frequently given the exemption, which amounted to ten millions, for several years, the national expenditure has never any trouble of insufficiency. Therefore, I should take the number of people from the present tax-roll as a fixed number to be taxed, and the increased population of the future shall be exempted from any additional tax. What I want is merely the report of the true numbers.

Then the legislature established the law that the amount of poll tax is permanently fixed according to the number of the tax-roll in the year 2262, and that the new increased number, which is called " the increasing population of the prosperous age," shall never be taxed.

This marks a new epoch in Chinese economic history. The population began to show its approximate number in 2300 A. K. Through thirty-four years, to 2334 A. K., the population increased more than half. Through fifty-nine years, to 2393 A. K., it increased less than half. During the T'ai-p'ing rebellion (2401-2417 A. K.) it may have lost a hundred and fifty millions. Although the census of the present dynasty is still not very accurate, it is near the truth. In a few years, when China shall have a regular parliament, accurate statistics of population should be available.

[1] This suggests the Malthusian doctrine.

CHAPTER XIX

Nature and Capital

I. NATURE

1. *The Five Elements*

Since land is only one part of nature, we should first consider all the elements of nature. For this reason we may take up the five elements as presenting an exhaustive classification of natural forces. Although the five elements are the basis of Chinese philosophy, we are concerned here with their economic aspects only.

The "Great Model" puts the five elements in the first of the nine categories. The first element is water; the second, fire; the third, wood; the fourth, metal; the fifth, earth. The five elements in the Chinese language are called "the five movements," because they move and revolve throughout heaven and earth without ceasing. In 6 A K. (546 B. C.), Tzŭ-han, prime minister of Sung, says: "Heaven has produced the five elements which supply men's requirements, and the people use them all. Not one of them can be dispensed with."[1] The Chinese regard all the five elements as the natural forces upon which human life depends.

After having given the names of the five elements, the "Great Model" describes their nature. "The nature of water is to soak and descend; of fire, to blaze and ascend; of wood, to be crooked and to be straight; of metal, to obey and to change; while the virtue of earth is seen in seed-

[1] *Classics,* vol. v, pt. ii, p. 534.

sowing and ingathering." Then it gives the tastes of the five elements: "That which soaks and descends becomes salt; that which blazes and ascends becomes bitter; that which is crooked and straight becomes sour; that which obeys and changes becomes acrid; and from seed-sowing and ingathering comes sweetness."[1] The five elements have their several sounds, colors and airs, as well as tastes; but the text speaks only of their tastes, because they are of greater importance to the people than the others, and they can be the representatives of the others. Leaving out all philosophical points, we may say that the five elements are the basis of production and consumption.

The *Great Commentary of the Canon of History* says: "Water and fire are the things by which the people eat and drink; metal and wood are the things by which the people labor; earth is the thing upon which the life of everything depends. All these give their utilities to man." Therefore, the five elements are originally free goods, because they are produced by nature.

Adding the grain to the five elements, the Chinese call them "the six treasuries." Such a term first appears in the "Tribute of Yü." It says that the six treasuries are greatly regulated.[2] Because the grain is the food of the people, they regard it as equally important with the five elements. According to *Tso's Commentary*, water, fire, metal, wood, earth, and grain are called the six treasuries. They are called treasuries because they are the sources of wealth which depend upon nature. The rectification of the people's virtue, the conveniences of life, and the securing abundant means of sustenance, are called "the three businesses." The six treasuries and the three businesses are called "the nine services."[3] The distinction between the

[1] *Classics,* vol. iii, pt. ii, pp. 325-6. [2] *Ibid.*, pt. i, p. 141.

[3] *Classics,* vol. v, pt. i, p. 250.

six treasuries and the three businesses is that the former are produced by natural power. But the six treasuries, although they depend upon nature, are to be regulated by human power. Therefore, all these are called nine services.

The manner of regulating the six treasuries may be illustrated by a few examples. In ancient times there were many officers controlling these six things. During the reign of Shun, the chief duty of the prime minister was to regulate water and earth. Even after "the great floods" had been repressed (1725 B. K. or 2276 B. C.), the regulation of water remained important to man. Irrigation, navigation, and carrying off the floods are examples of regulating water. Anciently, the regulations of fire were numerous. According to the *Official System of Chou*, there is a bureau of fire. In procuring fire by boring wood, certain woods were assigned to be employed in the four seasons, in order to prevent the seasonal diseases. In spring the fire was taken from the elm and willow; in summer, from the date and almond trees; in the last month of summer, from the mulberry and the wild mulberry trees; in autumn, from the oak and the *yu*; in winter, from the *huai* and the *tan*. In the third month the people were ordered to use fire for pottery and foundery, and in the ninth month they were forbidden to use fire for this purpose. In the hunting of the second month fire was used for the burning of the old grass; after that time the people should be fined if they set fire to the field without permission.[1] Metals and woods were similarly regulated by rules in regard to the management of mines and forests. As to the regulating of the earth and of the grains, we shall speak later.

[1] *Official System of Chou*, ch. xxx.

2. *Control over Nature*

The acme of human power is to control nature. If man can control nature, he is equal to the Supreme Power. But how can man have such power? It is by the most complete sincerity. Indeed, it is the result of the most careful and thorough study of the truth. This is told by the "Doctrine of the Mean." It says:

> It is only he who is possessed of the most complete sincerity that can exist in the world, who can give its full development to his nature. Able to give its full development to his own nature, he can do the same to the nature of other men. Able to give its full development to the nature of other men, he can give their full development to the natures of animals and things. Able to give their full development to the natures of creatures and things, he can assist the transforming and nourishing powers of Heaven and Earth. Able to assist the transforming and nourishing powers of Heaven and Earth, he may with Heaven and Earth form a triumvirate.[1]

The doctrine of controlling nature is very clearly given by Hsun Tzŭ. The seventeenth book of his work is entitled "Essay on Heaven". He uses the word heaven most often in the sense of nature, but we may preserve the word heaven. He says:

> Strongly clinging to the primary industry and saving expenditure, heaven cannot make you poor; when the subsistence is complete, and working at a due time, heaven cannot make you sick. . . . If the primary industry is neglected, and the expenditure is extravagant, heaven cannot make you rich; if the subsistence is insufficient, and the working time is contrary to the natural law, heaven cannot make you healthy.

[1] *Classics,* vol. i, p. 416.

This shows that the accumulation of capital and the preservation of labor are both dependent upon man, and not upon heaven.

According to the theory of Hsun Tzŭ, man is the one who can form a triumvirate with Heaven and Earth. What we call "divine" is simply "the natural deed." A sage does not care to know the Heaven, the supernatural power. When a man has "the natural feelings" and "the natural senses," the most important thing for the control of them is "the natural king," the mind To use the mind for the control of those things outside of the human race is "the natural support," and "the law of natural selection." Therefore, when the natural king is supreme, man "can employ the heaven and earth as the officers and exploit all things as the slaves." This is a materialistic and scientific doctrine in regard to the relation of man and nature. The chief power is the human mind, the natural king.

Now, he makes a comparison between those who can control nature and those who cannot, as follows:

To honor nature and to expect something from it, is not as good as to accumulate things and to shape them. To follow nature and to praise it, is not as good as to control what nature has given and to employ them. To expect the time and wait for it, is not so good as to seize it and to use it. To increase the things according to themselves, is not so good as to transform them by the exercise of human power. To wish the thing and to get the thing as it is, is not so good as to deal with the thing and not to lose any utility of it. To expect the thing grown by nature, is not so good as to have the thing manufactured by man. Therefore, to set aside the power of man and to depend on the power of nature is to lose the nature of everything.

Hence, according to Hsun Tzŭ, man is not the dependent of nature, but its controller.

3. *Conservation of Natural Resources*

The conservation of natural resources takes three forms. The first is the conservation of the living creatures. In ancient times there were four huntings in each quarter of the year. But Confucius lays down a rule that no hunting should be held in summer, because at that season the creatures are growing. The " Royal Regulations " says: " To hunt without observing the rules for hunting is deemed cruelty to the creatures of Heaven." The rules of hunting and fishing are these: The emperor should not surround the hunting-ground, but should leave one opening for the game; and the princes should not take a whole herd by surprise. When the wolf sacrifices its prey, between the ninth and the tenth month, the hunting commences. Until the insects have all withdrawn into their burrows, the tenth month, fire should not be used for hunting. When the otter sacrifices its fish, the tenth month, the foresters begin to enter the meres and dams for fishing. When the dove changes into a hawk, the eighth month, the large and small nets begin to be set for the catching of birds. They should not take fawns, nor eggs. They should not kill pregnant animals, nor those which have not attained to their full growth. They should not throw down nests. These are the rules set forth in the " Royal Regulations." [1]

From the ethical point of view these rules are designed to foster kindness and sympathy, but from the economic point of view they are for the conservation of natural resources. Both points are the objects of these rules. For the practicing of them we may take Confucius as an example. The *Analects* tells that he angled, but did not use a net; and shot, but not at birds perching.[2] This is the

[1] *Li Ki,* bk. iii, pp. 220-221. The note of Prof. Legge makes a mistake, because it says that hunting is forbidden in autumn.

[2] *Classics,* vol. i, p. 203.

principle of humanity. On the other hand, Mencius points out the economic principle, as follows: "If close nets are not allowed to enter the pools and ponds, the fishes and turtles will be more than can be secured."[1] The meshes of a net were anciently required to be four inches in size, and the people might not eat fish under a foot long. Therefore, the conservation of the living creatures is preservation of food for the people.

The second is the conservation of the forests. Mencius says: "If the axes and hatchets enter the hills and forests only at the proper time, the wood will be more than can be used."[2] But what is the proper time? We may find this in the "Royal Regulations." It says, when the plants and trees drop their leaves, the tenth month, the people enter the hills and forests with the axes.[3] According to the *Official System of Chou*, there is a forester to take charge of the rules of forests. For instance, in midwinter the trees on the south of the hill are cut down, and in midsummer those on the north. When the people are admitted to cut down the trees, they are regulated by the number of days. Although we do not know the length of the time period, we may be sure that this rule preserved the trees. In spring and autumn the people should not enter forbidden places to cut down trees, although they may cut the wild trees. If the people steal trees during the forbidden time, they should be fined.[4] These rules are for the conservation of the forests.

The third is the conservation of the mines. The "Doctrine of the Mean" says that the precious treasuries are

[1] *Classics,* vol. ii, p. 130.

[2] *Ibid.*

[3] *Li Ki,* bk. iii, p. 221.

[4] *Official System of Chou,* ch. xvi.

found on the mountains,[1] but it does not touch the conservation of them. The "Royal Regulations" says that the famous mountains and great meres are not conferred on any feudal lords either within or without the imperial state.[2] This rule has two points. On the distributive side it is against monopoly, which will be discussed later. On the productive side it is for the conservation of natural resources. Since all the famous mountains and the great meres are under the control of the central government, no one can exhaust the natural wealth. According to the *Official System of Chou*, all the lands which produce gold, jade, tin, and precious stones are controlled by the miner, an official. He makes severe prohibitions, and orders the people of their neighborhood to guard them. If any mine is opened at a proper time, he draws a map of it, and gives it to those who dig the mine. Around those lands he looks after the prohibitions and orders.[3] These are the rules for the conservation of the mines.

The fundamental principle underlying the conservation of natural resources is the law of diminishing returns. Although this law is not expressed, it is clearly implied.

4. *Influence of Natural Environment*

While nature is a factor of production and is controlled by man, it has in turn a great influence, modifying man. The "Royal Regulations" says:

> In all the settlements, the physical capacities of the people are sure to be according to the sky and earthly influences, as cold or hot, dry or moist. Where the wide valleys and the large rivers are different in shape, people born in them have differ-

[1] *Classics*, vol. i, p. 421.

[2] *Li Ki*, bk. iii, pp. 211-2.

[3] *Official System of Chou*, ch. xvi.

ent customs. The measure of their temperaments, as hard or soft, light or grave, slow or rapid; the taste of their preferences as to flavors; the fashion of their implements and weapons; and the suitability of their clothes—all are different.[1]

According to this statement the natural environment shapes the man. First, it fixes the physical capacities of the people; second, it fosters their temperaments; third, it produces different customs; fourth, it establishes different economic conditions, either in production or in consumption. The teaching is, further, that these differences should not be disturbed by government—a *laissez-faire* policy, in so far; and there is a recognition that in these differences is the basis of international trade.[2]

For the influence of the natural environment upon the people there is a general principle given by Ching Chiang, a widow of the noble family of Lu. She says:

Anciently, when the sage kings settled the people, they selected the poor land for the settlement of them, and made them work hard for the employment. Hence, they ruled the empire for a long time. For if the people are working hard, they will think. If they think, their good thoughts arise. If they are living in an easy way, they will be licentious. If they are licentious, they forget what is good. If they forget what is good, their bad thoughts arise. Therefore, the people of the rich land have no strong character, because they are licentious; and those of the poor land all direct their mind to righteousness, because they are working hard.[3]

Then she describes the different businesses of the two sexes of different classes, from the emperor to the common people.

[1] *Li Ki*, bk. iii, p. 228.

[2] *Cf. infra*, p. 450.

[3] *Narratives of Nations*, bk. v.

When Confucius has heard her words, he tells his pupils to record them.

The principle given by Ching Chiang is a mixture of economics and ethics. We now come to the pure economic principle In the "Biography of Merchants," Ssŭ-ma Chien gives a commercial geography. He describes the geographical situations of the great cities, their natural resources, their population, their history, their prominent occupations, their customs, *etc.* We cannot enter into all the details, but we may condense his conclusion. According to him, in Southern China land was plenty, the population was sparse, the soil was rich, and food was abundant without the fear of famine. On this account the people were lazy, short-sighted, and had no saving. Therefore, there was none who suffered from hunger, but there was no family which possessed a thousand dollars. In Northern China the land was scarce, the population was dense, the soil was good for agriculture, but the people often suffered from flood and drought. Hence, they had a desire for saving Therefore, they were diligent in different industries, such as agriculture, animal-breeding, silk-worm, commerce and speculation, in different localities. Such a difference between Southern and Northern China was true only in ancient times; it has gradually disappeared since the end of the Han dynasty (about 735 A. K. or 184 A. D.). But the theory of Ssŭ-ma Chien is held true by the general mind His theory is like that of Ching Chiang; both are based on the idea that the people are spoiled if they make their living too easily. The only difference is that Ching Chiang looks at it from both economic and ethical points of view, while Ssŭ-ma Chien regards it from the economic viewpoint only. Indeed, natural environment has a great influence in determining the economic conditions and the characters of men It is only when the human power grows greater that the natural power diminishes

II. LAND

1. *Limited in Quantity*

Since the land is the chief representative of the natural things which help production, we may consider it separately. When we study the land question, the first thing that confronts us is that land is limited in quantity. The "Royal Regulations" says:

A space one mile square contains fields amounting to 900 acres. Ten miles square is equal to 100 spaces one mile square, and contains 90,000 acres. A hundred miles square is equal to 100 spaces ten miles square, and contains 9,000,000 acres. A thousand miles square is equal to 100 spaces one hundred miles square, and contains 900,000,000 acres. . . . All within the four seas, taking the length with the breadth, makes up a space 3,000 miles square, and contains 8,100,000,000 acres.

A space 100 miles square contains ground to the amount of 9,000,000 acres. Hills and mounds, forests and thickets, rivers and marshes, ditches and canals, city walls and suburbs, houses, roads, and lanes take up one-third of it, leaving 6,000,000 acres.[1]

2. *Various in Quality*

The second thing that confronts us is that land is various in quality. This is most clearly set forth in the "Tribute of Yü." After Yü repressed the great floods, he divided the Chinese Empire into nine provinces, and classified the land into nine gradations. For convenience of review we may reduce the statements [2] to the form of a table:

[1] *Li Ki,* bk. iii, pp. 244-6.

[2] *Classics,* vol. iii, pt. i, pp. 94-125.

Grades of Land	Names of Provinces	Present Provinces	Color and Nature of Soil
First	Yung Chow	Shensi and Kansu	Yellow and mellow
Second	Sü Chow	Shantung, Kiangsu and Anhui	Red, clayey and rich
Third	Ts'ing Chow	Shantung	Whitish and rich, salt
Fourth	Yü Chow	Honan	Mellow, rich, dark and thin
Fifth	Ki Chow	Chihli and Shansi	Whitish and mellow
Sixth	Yên Chow	Chihli and Shantung	Blackish and rich
Seventh	Liang Chow	Szechuan and Shensi	Greenish and light
Eighth	King Chow	Hunan and Hupei	Miry
Ninth	Yang Chow	Kiangsu, Anhui, Kiangsi, and Chekiang	Miry

This table shows the differences, in color and nature, of the soil with general reference to the whole province, and classifies the land into nine grades. Such a classification is very general and rough indeed, but it indicates that the comparative study of the quality of land had begun at a very early time.

The *Official System of Chou* also classifies the land into nine grades, but it differs from the "Tribute of Yü." While the latter judges the land collectively from the general view of the whole province, it judges the land specifically from the quality of the land itself. According to the *Official System of Chou*,[1] the quality of land is measured by its power of supporting population. It gives expressly only the middle class of land, by saying that a prescribed amount (one hundred acres) of the superior land can support a family of seven persons; of the ordinary land, one of six persons; and the same amount of the inferior land, one of five persons. These are the three kinds of land in the middle class. Such a statement, according to the com-

[1] Ch. xi.

mentary of Chêng Hsüan, implies that there are nine gradations of land, and that only the middle class is given as an example. In the highest class, the land can support either eight, or nine, or ten persons. In the lowest class, it can support either two, or three, or four persons. In the grand division, land is divided into three classes, and in its subdivision, it is divided into nine grades. Such a gradation is determined by the number of people which the land can support.

3. *Different in Location*

Difference in lands are due not only to their qualities, but also to their locations. According to the Confucian theory, the capital city of a state should be in its center. Taking the city as the central point, the land of the whole state is divided up into five zones. Outside of the city, it is called "suburb;" outside of the suburb, "country;" outside of the country, "forest;" outside of the forest, "frontier." [1] These five names are merely geographical divisions for the indication of the difference of location. The widths of all the zones are equal, and they vary only according to the extent of the whole state. In fact, the difference of location is measured from the central city. In a simple way, there are only three divisions, namely, the city, the suburb, and the country, which includes the forest and frontier.

4. *Form of Field*

For the division of the land we must study the system of *tsing tien*. This system is so important that we discuss it separately in another chapter. What we consider here is only the form of *tsing tien*.

In ancient China the land was divided up into the form of *tsing*. *Tsing* means well, which written in Chinese is

[1] *The Oldest Chinese Dictionary* (*Erh Ya*), ch. ix.

井. Since the shape of the field was like the word 井, it was called *tsing tien*. *Tien* (田) means field. One *tsing* contained nine squares of land; each square was of one hundred acres and was called one *fu*; the total amount of a *tsing* was nine hundred acres. This system began with the reign of Huang Ti; it was universally established by Yü, and it was completed in details by the Duke of Chou.

In one square of land the one hundred acres contained ten thousand paces. According to the ancient measures, six feet was one pace, and one hundred paces was one acre. Therefore, one acre was six feet wide and six hundred feet long. Hence, the *Canon of Poetry* says, "The grain is well cultivated all over the long acres."[1] Between two acres there was a small ditch. If there were one hundred acres, there were one hundred small ditches. The acre was higher, and the ditch was lower. Since one ploughshare was five inches wide, and two men using two ploughshares were called a pair, the cultivation of a pair was a foot wide and deep, and this was the form of a small ditch. In cultivation, the farmer first used the plough to turn over the grass, and then formed lines, such as the acres and ditches. This was the plan of one square of land, and the small ditch was the basis of the measure of all the water-channels.

For the system of *tsing tien* the water-channels were very important, because they determined the boundaries of the field and carried off the water of floods. Such a system of water-channels was originated by Yü. After he had fixed the natural waterway he devoted his attention to the artificial waterway along the fields.

In the Chou dynasty the *tsing tien* system was at its height, and the water-channels were complete. According to the

[1] *Classics,* vol. iv, pt. ii, p. 378.

"Record of Industry,"[1] the bureau of civil engineering is in charge of water-channels, and it gives the following standard measures for the making of different waterways: Within the *fu*, a field of one hundred acres, the small ditch running between two acres is one foot wide and deep. Hence, one *fu* has one hundred small ditches. Along the head-line of the field, the large ditch running outside of the *fu* is two feet wide and deep. Hence, three *fu* have only one large ditch in common. Outside of the *tsing* which contains nine *fu*, the ditch is four feet wide and deep. Hence, ten *tsing* have only one such ditch in common. Ten miles square make one *ch'êng*, which contains one hundred *tsing*, and outside of the *ch'êng* the larger ditch is eight feet wide and deep. Hence, ten *ch'êng* have only one larger ditch. One hundred miles square make one *tung*, which contains ten thousand *tsing*, and outside of the *tung* the largest ditch is sixteen feet wide and deep. The length of the largest ditch is uncertain, and its water flows to the natural stream directly. In a *tung*, the *tsing tien* system is complete, and it has five grades of water-channels: (1) the one-foot ditch, (2) the two-foot ditch, (3) the four-foot ditch, (4) the eight-foot ditch, and (5) the sixteen-foot ditch. This is the general rule, but it must be modified according to the geographical situation.

Along all the water-channels, except the one-foot ditch, there were different roads. Along the two-foot ditch the road was large enough for the ox and horse; along the four-foot ditch it was large enough for the wagon; along the eight-foot ditch, for one chariot; along the sixteen-foot ditch, for two chariots; and along the natural stream or artificial canal, for three chariots.[2] These waterways and roads were the general rules for the formation of *tsing tien*.

[1] It was a separate book written during the Chou dynasty. But it is now contained in the end of the *Official System of Chou*, ch. xlii.

[2] *Official System of Chou*, ch. xv.

According to the *Canon of Poetry*, there were two kinds of acres: one kind was called "southern acres," and the other "eastern acres." In the southern acres, the acres and the small ditches all ran east and west, and in the eastern acres they all ran north and south. Because looking from the north the southern acres were arranged in the south, they were called southern acres. Because looking from the west the eastern acres were arranged in the east, they were called eastern acres. The acres were southern or eastern in accordance with the river. Since the Chinese rivers mostly run from the west to the east, the greater part of the land became eastern acres. For, if the river was in the latitudinal line, the largest ditch should be in the longitudinal line; then the next smaller ditch was latitudinal and the four-foot ditch longitudinal; then the two-foot ditch was latitudinal and the smallest ditch longitudinal; hence, the acres were arranged in the east. The southern acres were arranged *vice versa*. The Chinese rivers sometimes run either toward the south or toward the north, so there were also the southern acres. Both the southern and the eastern acres were according to the natural situation of the land.

III. CAPITAL

1. *Capital and Wealth*

The word capital in Chinese is *pen*. Its original sense means the root of a tree; hence, it means the principal part or the basis of anything. The word *pen* used in the sense of capital first appears in *Kuan Tzŭ*, and it has been popularly used to the present day. But the word used in this sense is not to be found in the writings of Confucius. Instead, he uses the word *tzŭ*. The *Canon of Poetry* says: "Ruin and disorder are destroying the *tzŭ* [the capital], and do not show any kindness to our multitudes." [1] The

[1] *Cf. Classics*, vol. iv, pt. ii, p. 502. See also *ibid.*, p. 520.

Park of Narratives says that this sentence expresses grief that disorder is caused by luxury and extravagance, without saving.[1] Chen Huan says that the "accumulated wealth" is called *tzŭ*.[2] Therefore, the word *tzŭ* in Chinese is exactly the word capital in English. In the *Canon of Changes* there is a book on "Traveling," which refers especially to the traveling merchant, although it includes travelers generally. It describes the good condition of a traveling merchant as follows: "The traveler occupies the proper place, carries with him his *tzŭ*, and secures the trusty servants." [3] This statement includes the three factors of production; the word *tzŭ* means capital, while the proper place and the trusty servants refer to land and labor respectively. Indeed, the word *tzŭ* is used by Confucius as capital, because *tzŭ* means accumulation or storage. Hence, the Chinese combine the word *tzŭ* either with the word *tsai* (wealth), or with the word *pen*, for the term capital. The Japanese adopt the latter expression.

The word wealth in the Chinese language is sometimes the same as the word capital. Such a case has been already shown in the "Great Learning." [4] Sometimes the word wealth combining with the word commodity forms the term capital. For instance, Mencius says: "The fields and wilds not being developed, and the commodities and wealth not being accumulated, these are not the chief danger of a state." [5] The two words "commodities and wealth" stand as the English word capital, while "fields and wilds" stand for land. This is the style of Chinese expression.

Since the word wealth is sometimes identified with the

[1] Bk. vii.

[2] In his *Explanation of Mao's Commentary of the Canon of Poetry*, published in 2398 (1847 A. D.).

[3] *Yi King*, p. 188.

[4] See *supra*, p. 293.

[5] *Classics*, vol. ii, p. 291.

word capital, we may find out what is meant by wealth. Hsü Shên's *Dictionary*[1] says: "Wealth is what man regards as valuable." Chêng Hsüan says that wealth includes all money and grain. Money and grain, as we shall see, are the chief representatives of capital goods; hence, Chêng Hsüan takes them for the explanation of the word wealth. Even in the present day the Chinese still use the two words "money and grain" to cover the whole economic field. Although they are not so dignified as the term "food and commodities," they are synonyms. But the best definition of the word wealth is given by Hsiang An-shih (died in 1759 A. K. or 1208 A. D.). He says: "The word wealth is the collective name of all the things in which the people find their utilities." In short, wealth is the general term covering all production and consumption goods, while capital is the particular term covering only production goods and those consumption goods which are used for productive purposes. Hence, the Chinese use such terms as "funds," "principal money," "accumulated wealth" and "mother wealth" for the word capital.

To understand the meaning of wealth we may look at the problem from the standpoint of different classes. According to the "Details of Rites," each class has special representatives of its wealth.

When one asks about the wealth of the ruler of a state, the reply should be given by telling the extent of his territory, and the productions of its hills and lakes. To a question about the wealth of the great official, it should be said: "He has the lands allotted to him, and is supported by the taxes of his people. He needs not to borrow vessels or dresses for his sacrificial occasions." To a question about the wealth of the

[1] It was begun in 651, and presented to the emperor in 672 (100-121 A. D.).

student, the reply should be by giving the number of his carriages; and to one about the wealth of a common man, by telling the number of the animals that he keeps.[1]

According to this passage, the wealth of any class is a collective name for all material things. It does not confine the term wealth to any particular thing. If the people understand this, they never make the mistake of thinking that money is the only wealth, because it does not mention money at all. Indeed, wealth includes both production and consumption goods.

2. *Grain as Capital*

While grain is a consumption good, the Confucians regard it also as a very important capital good; hence, there is the principle of accumulating grain. The "Royal Regulations" says:

> If in a state there is not an accumulation of saving sufficient for nine years, its condition is called one of insufficiency; if there is not enough for six years, one of urgency. If there is not a saving sufficient for three years, the state cannot continue. The husbandry of three years is held to give an overplus of food sufficient for one year; that of nine years, an overplus sufficient for three years. Going through thirty years in this way, though there might be bad years, drought and inundations, the people would have no lack, nor be reduced to eating merely vegetables.[2]

In short, every family must save grain at such a rate that every three years should yield a surplus sufficient for one year. This is the general rule of saving, and grain is only the example, as it was the most important thing in ancient times.

[1] *Li Ki*, bk. i, pp. 115-6.

[2] *Ibid.*, bk. iii, p. 222.

According to the "Royal Regulations," a state as a whole must have an accumulation sufficient for at least nine years. But the accumulation is of nothing but food. Therefore, food is not only a consumption good for the present, but also a capital good for the future. Since food is not a permanent article, it needs a successive renewal for the change of the old. But it serves as a capital good just the same. In fact, in ancient China grain was the chief among all the capital goods, since land was in a separate category; and the accumulation of grain was a national surplus.

In the Han dynasty the theory of accumulating grain was put into full effect. The chief representatives of this theory were Chia Yi and Chao Tso. Chia Yi pointed out to his emperor that if wealth is produced in limited amounts but is consumed without any limit, the capital must in time be exhausted. Now, the people run away from agriculture and turn to industry and commerce. Hence, the consumers are very many, and luxurious habits spread day after day. These two facts are the great injury and the great destroyer of the empire. Those who produce wealth are few, but those who waste it are many: how can the wealth and property of the empire fail to fall short? Indeed, on accumulating and storing up for the future the fate of the empire depends. If grain is plenty and wealth is superabundant, what can we not accomplish? In an attack, we can take what we want; in a defense, we can have a safeguard; in a battle, we can win the victory. In calling the enemy and absorbing the foreigners, who will not come at our invitation? Now, if we drive our people back to the farm for the attachment to primary industry, we shall make every one of the empire eat the produce of his own labor, and the people of little skill and the journeymen turn to the fields. Then the storage and accumulation will be sufficient and the people will enjoy their life. This policy is for the wealth and safety of the empire. Han Wên Ti was influenced by the words of Chia Yi, and he opened " the borrowing field " for his personal cultivation in order to set a good example to his people (374 A. K. or 178 B. C.).

In 384 (168 B. C.) Chao Tso also said to Han Wên Ti that, when the sage kings were in the government, their people did not suffer from cold and hunger. This came about, not because they could feed and clothe them by their own cultivation and weaving, but because they opened the sources of capital for them. Therefore, although Yao and Yü had the flood of nine years, and T'ang had the drought of seven years, the empire did not suffer from famine or pestilence. This was because saving and accumulation were abundant and preparation was completed beforehand. Therefore, the wise ruler encourages the people to take up agricultural occupation, lightens their taxes, and extends the accumulations for the filling of granaries and the preparation against flood and drought. The immediate policy of Chao Tso was to call upon the people for the sending of grain to the granaries in the northern boundary, where the Chinese guarded against the Huns. The people should receive titles from the government, and the gradation of the title should be according to the amount of grain which they sent. After Han Wên Ti had put his policy into effect, he proposed again to order the people to send their grain inland, and Wên Ti followed his advice again. Therefore, during the reigns of Wên Ti and Ching Ti (373-411, or 179-141 B. C.) China was very rich, both the government and the people.[1] It was the contribution of Chia Yi and Chao Tso, and their theory was drawn from Confucius.

[1] *History of Han,* ch. xxiv.

3. *Saving*

Since capital is the result of saving, we now come to the principle of saving. Confucius speaks of saving, not only for the private family, but also for the state. In ruling a state of a thousand chariots, one of the five things is saving in expenditure.[1] In the *Canon of Changes* there is a book called "*Chieh*," which means abstinence, control, restraint, economy, saving, *etc.* It includes three phases—law, ethics and economics. In the beginning of this book it is stated that abstinence is the basis of progress and attainment. But the reader is reminded that if the abstinence is very severe and difficult, it cannot be right.[2] This shows that the principle of saving in the teaching of Confucius is not cruel parsimony but reasonable abstinence.

The chief point of this book is this: "Basing on the principle of abstinence for the making of regulations, it will not injure the wealth, nor hurt the people."[3] This is an abstract economic principle. It refers to either public or private economy. As soon as wealth is injured people are hurt, even in the case of a private person. Therefore, if you wish not to injure the wealth, there must be some sort of regulations, such as financial legislation in a government, or as control of expenditure in a private person, according to the principle of abstinence. Hence, abstinence is the basis for the preservation of wealth and the benefit of the people.

When Confucius speaks of the filial piety of the feudal princes, he says: "Making the saving, and carefully observant of the regulations, they are full without overflowing. . . . To be full without overflowing is the way long to preserve riches."[4] Again, when he speaks of the filial piety

[1] See *supra*, p. 79.

[2] *Yi King*, p. 197.

[3] *Ibid.*, p. 262.

[4] *Sacred Books*, vol. iii, p. 468.

of the common people, he mentions saving in expenditure.[1] Therefore, every class, from the emperor to the common people, must observe the principle of saving.

The importance of saving is thus told by Hsun Tzŭ:

> In the living of a man, he keeps fowls, dogs and pigs, and he keeps also oxen and sheep; but in his eating, he does not dare to have wine and meat. He has plenty of money and stores of grain, but in his dressing he does not dare to have silk. He has the deposit of the most valuable things, but in his going he does not dare to have carriage and horse. What is the reason? It is not because he does not want them, but because he has a long thought and cares for the future, lest nothing will succeed hereafter. Therefore, he saves expenditure, controls wants, and accumulates wealth for the succession. How good it is that he has a long thought and cares for the future in regard to himself! The short-sighted people who are careless for their living do not know even this. They consume food extravagantly, and do not care for the future. Then they exhaust quickly all the means. This is the reason they cannot escape from cold and hunger, and become beggars or victims dying in the ditches.[2]

Indeed, the opening of the sources of income and the saving of expenditure are the only ways for the increase of wealth. They are both familiar to all the Chinese, but the latter only is the way of increasing capital.

[1] See *supra*, p. 157.

[2] Bk. iv.